Structurally Adjusted Africa

Structurally Adjusted Africa

Poverty, Debt and Basic Needs

Edited by
DAVID SIMON, WIM VAN SPENGEN,
CHRIS DIXON AND ANDERS NÄRMAN

Pluto Press
LONDON • BOULDER, COLORADO

First Published 1995 by Pluto Press
345 Archway Road
London N6 5AA
and 5500 Central Avenue,
Boulder, CO 80301, USA

99   98   97   96   95

5   4   3   2   1

The editors and publishers gratefully acknowledge financial support from the
following institutions:

   Department of Human and Economic Geography, University of
     Gothenburg
   Developing Areas Research Group (DARG) of the Institute of British
     Geographers
   Royal Dutch Geographical Society (KNAG)
   Developing Countries Section of the KNAG (KNAG-AOL)
   Peace and Development Research Institute, Gothenburg University
     (PADRIGU)

British Library Cataloguing in Publication Data
A catalogue record for this book is available from the British Library

ISBN 0 7453 0972 0 (hardback)

Library of Congress Cataloging in Publication Data
A catalog record is available from the Library of Congress

Designed and produced for Pluto Press by
Chase Production Services, Chipping Norton, OX7 5QR
Typeset from editors' disk by Stanford DTP Services
Printed in Finland by WSOY

Contents

Part Two – Structural Adjustment and Urban Basic Needs

List of Tables

List of Figures

Acronyms

AAPS	African Association of Political Science
AfDB	African Development Bank
AIDS	Acquired Immune Deficiency Syndrome
ADB	Asian Development Bank
ASEAN	Association of South East Asian Nations
CBOs	community-based organisations
CCM	Chama cha Mapinduzi
CFA	Central African franc
cif	cost/insurance/freight
CILSS	Comité Permanent Inter Etats de Lutte contre la Sécheresse dans le Sahel
CIS	Commodity import support
COMECON	Commission for Mutual Economic Co-operation
DANIDA	Danish International Development Agency
DARG	Developing Areas Research Group
DCs	developed countries
EOI	export-oriented industrialisation
ERPs	economic recovery programmes
ESAF	enhanced structural adjustment facility
ESAP	economic and social adjustment programme
ESCAP	Economic and Social Commission for Asia and the Pacific
EU	European Union
FAO	Food and Agriculture Organisation
FDI	foreign direct investment
GATT	General Agreement on Tariffs and Trade
GDP	gross domestic product
GNP	gross national product
HDI	Human Development Index
IBRD/IDA	International Bank for Reconstruction and Development/International Development Association (both parts of the World Bank)
IDB	Inter-American Development Bank
IFIs	international financial institutions
ILO	International Labour Organization
IMF	International Monetary Fund

INRA	Institut National de Recherche Agronomique
IRAM	Institut de Recherche et d'Application des Méthodes de Développement
ISI	import-substituting industrialisation
KIPOC	Korongoro Integrated Pastoralist Organisation and Conservation
KNAG–AOL	Developing Countries Section, Royal Dutch Geographical Society
NADG	Nordic Association of Development Geographers
NAFCO	National Agricultural and Food Corporation
NEI	Netherlands Economic Institute
NESP	national economic survival programme
NGOs	non-governmental organisations
NICs	newly industrialising countries
NIEO	New International Economic Order
NMC	National Milling Corporation
NSI	National Sugar Institute
OAU	Organization of African Unity
ODA	official development assistance
OECD	Organization for Economic Co-operation and Development
OGL	open general licence
PADRIGU	Peace and Development Research Institute, University of Gothenburg
PAMSCAD	Programme of Actions to Mitigate the Social Costs of Adjustment
PNDC	Provisional National Defence Council
RIDEPs	regional integrated development plans/programmes
SA	structural adjustment
SAF	structural adjustment facility
SALs	structural adjustment loans
SAPs	structural adjustment programmes
SCOPO	Standing Committee on Parastatal Organisations
SDC/Sudeco	Sugar Development Corporation
SDR	Special Drawing Rights
SIAS	Scandinavian Institute of African Studies
SIDA	Swedish International Development Authority
SPA	Special Program of Assistance
SSA	sub-Saharan Africa
SVS	Swedish Volunteer Service
TNCs	transnational corporations
TPC	Tanganyika Planting Corporation
UNB	Université Nationale du Bénin
UNCED	United Nations Conference on Environment and Development

UNDP	United Nations Development Programme
UNECA	United Nations Economic Commission for Africa
UNESCO	United Nations Educational, Scientific and Cultural Organization
UNRISD	United Nations Research Institute for Social Development
UPE	universal primary education
USAID	United States Agency for International Development
WIDER	World Institute for Development Economics Research

Contributors

Chris Dixon, Professor of Geography at London Guildhall University, has worked extensively on development issues in the Pacific Asia region. Recent publications include *Rural Development* (1991), *South East Asia in the World Economy* (1993) and (with D. Drakakis-Smith) *Economic and Social Change in Pacific Asia* (1993).

Leo de Haan is an Associate Professor of Human Geography of Developing Countries in the Faculty of Geographical Sciences at the University of Amsterdam. He currently heads a number of research projects in West Africa. His main research themes are rural development, land management and environmental degradation, and food security. His recent publications include *La Region des Savanes au Togo: L'Etat, Les Paysans et l'Integration Régionale* (1993). Leo de Haan, Andries Klaasse Bos and Clemens Lutz are co-operating in the interdisciplinary research programme on livelihood and the environment of the University of Amsterdam.

Mogens Holm, a sociologist, is currently based at the Centre for Development Research, Copenhagen and recently completed his PhD at Royal Holloway, University of London. Until 1988 he was Senior Lecturer in Sociology at the University of Copenhagen. Then he became a Visiting Professor in the Department of Urban and Rural Planning at the ARDHI Institute, Dar es Salaam and commenced his doctoral research programme, on which his chapter in the present work is based, in 1990.

Andries Klaasse Bos is a Senior Lecturer in Development Economics in the Faculty of Economics and Econometrics of the University of Amsterdam. His main research interests and expertise are agricultural and food policy issues in Africa.

Vesa-Matti Loiske is a human geographer at the Environment and Development Studies Unit, School of Geography at Stockholm University, Sweden. His research, which is part of the research programme 'Man–Land Interrelations in semi-arid Tanzania', is oriented towards the socio-economic aspects of land management and land degradation processes at the local level in sub-humid parts of central Tanzania.

Clemens Lutz is a Research Assistant in the Faculty of Economics and Econometrics of the University of Amsterdam. He has specialised in research on development economics through a long-term research project with the National University of Benin (West Africa). Based on field work, he is now in the final stages of finishing his doctoral dissertation on the functioning of the maize marketing system in Benin.

Milline Mbonile is Lecturer in Geography at the University of Dar es Salaam, Tanzania. In 1993 he obtained his PhD from the University of Liverpool for a thesis on part of which his chapter below is based.

Claude Mung'ong'o is a sociologist at the Institute of Resource Assessment at the University of Dar es Salaam, Tanzania. His research, which forms a part of the research programme 'Man–Land Interrelations in semi-arid Tanzania', is oriented towards the socio-economic aspects of land management and land degradation processes at the local and regional level in semi-arid central Tanzania.

Anders Närman lectures in Development Studies at the University of Gothenburg. He is also responsible for a graduate course in International Development Studies at the University of Oslo. In addition, he has conducted numerous consultancies for the Swedish International Development Authority, Swedish Volunteer Service, HEP/UNESCO and DSE.

David Simon is Reader in Development Geography and Director of the Centre for Developing Areas Research (CEDAR) at Royal Holloway, University of London. He is the author of numerous publications and consultancy reports on development issues with reference to Africa, especially Southern Africa. His books include *Cities, Capital and Development: African Cities in the World Economy* (1992) and (as editor) *Third World Regional Development: A Reappraisal* (1990).

Jan Sterkenburg is a staff member of the Faculty of Geographical Sciences, University of Utrecht, seconded to the Operations Review Unit of the Directorate General for International Co-operation of the Netherlands Ministry of Foreign Affairs. Recent publications include *An Evaluation Study of the Sector Programme for Rural Development* (1992), *Sector Aid and Structural Adjustment: The Case of Sugar in Tanzania* (1992) and *Evaluation of the Netherlands Development Programme with Tanzania, 1970–1992* (1994).

Dan Tevera is a Lecturer in the Department of Geography at the University of Zimbabwe. He specialises in the geography of development and has working experience in a number of African countries, including Botswana where he spent a year in 1992/3 as a sabbatical fellow in the Department of Environmental Science. He is co-editor (with L. Zinyama and S. Cumming) of *Harare: The Growth and*

Problems of the City (1993). He attended the Amsterdam Conference as a SIDA-sponsored visitor to Sweden.

Arie van der Wiel is a staff member of the Operations Review Unit of the Directorate General for International Co-operation of the Netherlands Ministry of Foreign Affairs. Recent evaluation studies conducted are *Aid and Trade* (1990), *Food Aid and Development* (1991), *Sector Aid and Structural Adjustment: The Case of Sugar in Tanzania* (1992) and *Evaluation of the Netherlands Development Programme with Tanzania, 1970–1992* (1994).

Wim van Spengen took his MA degree in development geography from the Free University of Amsterdam in 1973 and his doctorate from the University of Amsterdam in 1992. He has undertaken research in Zambia, Tanzania, India and Nepal, mainly pertaining to the structural–historical characteristics of under-development in the areas concerned. Currently he is a member of staff in the Department of Geography at the University of Amsterdam.

Indra Wahab graduated from the University of Amsterdam in 1969 and received his doctorate from the Free University of Brussels in 1982. His main fields of research are international trade in commodities and economic development in Southeast Asia (especially Malaysia and Indonesia). At the moment he is Associate Professor of Development Economics in the Faculty of Economics and Econometrics at the University of Amsterdam.

The Sponsoring Organisations

The Developing Areas Research Group (DARG) is one of the largest specialist study groups of the Institute of British Geographers. It has a long tradition of activities to promote research on and awareness of development issues. These undertakings include organising national and international conferences on a wide variety of topical research themes; an excellent publication record, including most recently the *Atlas of World Development* (1994); offering annual competitive awards for both undergraduate and postgraduate research in relevant fields; and promoting links with counterpart organisations in other countries.

The Developing Countries Section of the Royal Dutch Geographical Society (KNAG-AOL) brings together Dutch geographers with special interests in developing countries. It has organised conferences and published research over many years. The Section operates as an important agency co-ordinating academic research on developing countries and liaises actively with other segments of the Dutch education community. Some of its members are also actively engaged in development consultancy for the Dutch government and other agencies.

The Royal Dutch Geographical Society (KNAG) is the professional organisation for academic geographers and others with geographical interests in the Netherlands. It has a long tradition of promoting the subject in various ways, both nationally and internationally, and in 1996 is hosting the quadrennial conference of the International Geographical Union (IGU).

The Nordic Association of Development Geographers (NADG) was founded in the mid-1970s as a co-ordinating body for geographers in Sweden, Denmark, Norway and Finland specialising in development issues and problems. Its activities have been centred on a series of seminars and conferences.

The Peace and Development Research Institute, Gothenburg University (PADRIGU) undertakes research and offers various undergraduate and postgraduate courses in Development Studies and International Relations.

The Department of Human and Economic Geography, University of Gothenburg, has expertise in a wide range of subdisciplines, including a special section on Development Geography.

Preface

The origins of this book lie in a series of formal and informal contacts among development geographers in western Europe. Following successful bilateral conferences in recent years between the Developing Areas Research Group (DARG) of the Institute of British Geographers and the Afdeling Ontwikkelingslanden (Developing Countries Section) of the Royal Dutch Geographical Society (KNAG-AOL), and between DARG and the Nordic Association of Development Geographers (NADG), it was decided to expand our horizons by organising a trilateral conference on a theme of mutual interest. This conference, hosted by Wim van Spengen and his colleagues at the University of Amsterdam from 29 to 31 March 1993, focused on 'Structural Adjustment, Global Change and the Conflict over Resources at Different Geographical Scales'. It brought together some 35 participants from the Netherlands, Britain, Denmark, Norway and Sweden, including several Africans based or studying for higher degrees at the universities involved.

Given the quality of the papers presented and the lively discussions which ensued, we decided to seek publication of an edited collection. Inevitably not all the original contributions could be included, and the unenviable task of selection was made far easier for us in that, by coincidence rather than design, the majority dealt with sub-Saharan Africa. Moreover, these papers complemented one another well in terms of geographical scale, economic sector and mode of analysis, providing – as we hope readers will agree – a fresh and stimulating approach to the subject. We thank the small number of those who presented papers that dealt exclusively with experiences outside Africa, or did not fit the overall theme, for their understanding. Non-inclusion of their pieces here in no way reflects the quality of their work. The editorial team comprises the organisers of the DARG (David Simon, Chris Dixon), NADG (Anders Närman) and KNAG-AOL (Wim van Spengen) delegations. The tasks of managing editor and production of the final manuscript fell to me, David Simon, so a disproportionate share of any blame attaching to this volume should be placed at my door.

That this book has seen the light of day at all reflects the enthusiasm and perseverance of many people. First, editing a volume with a group of contributors – for most of whom English is not their first language – spread across five European countries and two in Africa, presents a formidable challenge, even in this age of computers and faxes. Second, the economics of publishing are currently stacked against collected volumes on Africa. On the one hand, financial constraints in Europe and North America have forced educational libraries to cut back severely on their acquisitions – traditionally the backbone of viability for academic books. On the other hand, the market in Africa for books published abroad remains in a state of collapse as a result of the continued decline in foreign exchange rates and the impact of structural adjustment on public expenditure.

Given the subject of this book, the irony was not lost on us. We were therefore determined to get this book published, and to do so in a manner which makes it accessible to the very African countries and societies whose experiences of structural adjustment and economic recovery programmes we document. This has been made possible by generous subventions from DARG, KNAG, KNAG-AOL, the Department of Human and Economic Geography, University of Gothenburg, and the Peace and Development Research Institute, University of Gothenburg (PADRIGU), to underwrite the production costs for books sold in Africa. This generosity is gratefully acknowledged, together with the enthusiasm of Roger van Zwanenberg at Pluto Press for taking on this venture.

David Simon
July 1994

CHAPTER 1

Introduction: The Nature of Structural Adjustment

Chris Dixon, David Simon and Anders Närman

Twenty years ago one of the key issues within the development debate was the demand for a New International Economic Order (NIEO). Existing structures were based on inequality and the countries of the south tried to bargain for a more equal voice in international institutions and a fairer distribution of global resources. At least in principle, many bilateral donors seemed to be rather sympathetic towards the rights claimed by Third World nations. At that time, development strategies were sharply divided between those predicated upon socialist principles derived largely from the models of the Soviet Union, China and eastern Europe, and overtly capitalist programmes based on the philosophy of economic growth, capital accumulation and modernisation.

The situation today, as it has evolved since the late 1980s and into the mid-1990s, is dramatically different. We are now said to be part of 'one world' in which global economic structures, based on the principles of a 'free' market, are not to be questioned. This state of affairs is now taken for granted and, instead of calls for a NIEO, we hear a chorus of consent demanding that the poor countries of Latin America, Asia and Africa adjust their economies to these overriding trends. Leading actors in this shift of emphasis are the so-called Bretton Woods institutions, primarily the World Bank (International Bank for Reconstruction and Development (IBRD) and International Development Association (IDA)) and the International Monetary Fund (IMF). One of the principal bones of contention in the present development debate is whether the new policies have come into existence due to some kind of emerging realism, or whether they are a result of a cynical self-centred approach favouring the economic supremacy of the industrialised nations of the world.

The ideological origins of structural adjustment programmes (SAPs) can be traced back to the free-market and free-trade ethos derived from Adam Smith and David Ricardo. According to this line of thought, the present economic crisis in Third World countries can be overcome only if they restructure their economies to become active players in a common strategy for world prosperity based on competition in the international export market. One of the principal objectives of SAPs is to achieve just this, based on a particular reading of the nature and causes of the malaise affecting most Third World countries. In the following section we expand upon this theme, sketching the main components of economic crisis and tracing the immediate origins of SAPs. An appreciation of these policies and their political and economic antecedents is essential for an understanding of sub-Saharan Africa's (SSA's) recent experience in the context of adjustment, which forms the subject of this book. Not only have per capita incomes (at least in measured forms) fallen to the point where SSA is now the poorest continental region in the world, but more countries in SSA than anywhere else have sought to adopt or have been pressurised into implementing SAPs and subsequent economic recovery plans (ERPs).

The Origins of Structural Adjustment

The international economy entered a new and perhaps critical phase during the 1970s. This was characterised by general economic instability and a rapid succession of global economic shocks, starting in 1971 with the unilateral suspension of the Bretton Woods arrangement by the US. This was followed by the dramatic oil price increases of 1973 and 1979, the transition from fixed to flexible exchange rates and a sharp rise in international interest rates. These events had a deep impact on the less developed, non-oil-producing economies of the Third World. The effects reverberated through the 1980s and into the 1990s.

The aftershocks have manifested themselves in a variety of ways, most notably in a global tendency towards recession and unemployment, rising debt levels, low and declining primary commodity prices, balance-of-payments deficits and increasing protectionism. However, these effects have been extremely uneven in both timing and intensity. Indeed, perhaps the most significant characteristics of the post-1970 period have been the increasing uncertainty and unevenness of development. It is worth noting, however, that, in contrast to the general picture, a small number of developing countries, especially the newly industrialising countries (NICs) in Pacific Asia, have enjoyed a positive net resource flow from industrialised countries.

In general, individual Third World economies reacted to the external shocks by implementing a variety of short-term, often *ad hoc* domestic stabilisation measures (Lee, 1987). In many instances these involved the IMF, World Bank and the various regional agencies such as the African Development Bank (AfDB), Asian Development Bank (ADB) and Inter-American Development Bank (IDB). However, the severity and protracted nature of the problems that beset many economies had, by 1979, convinced the World Bank that longer-term programmes of economic adjustment were necessary. This logic was initially applied to the most heavily indebted countries, Brazil and Mexico.

In 1980 the World Bank officially approved what became known as 'structural adjustment lending'. This was, 'lending designed to support major changes in policies and institutions of developing countries that would reduce their current account deficits to more manageable proportions in the medium term while maintaining the maximum feasible development effort' (World Bank, 1981, p. 69).

The World Bank approach was mirrored by and increasingly synchronised with those of the IMF, AfDB, ADB, IDB and many bilateral lenders. For all of these donors, structural adjustment loans (SALs) were closely tied to medium-term adjustment programmes with conditions which stipulated policy and institutional changes. Thus, during the early 1980s there was a rapid increase in 'policy-related' lending to less developed countries.

Initially the agencies were at pains to present the adjustment of a country's economy as simply taking into consideration attendant economic circumstances and market conditions. However, the broad principles of structural adjustment

are closely identified with the ideological belief in the superiority of the market over economic planning. At their root is an almost mystical faith in the private sector which, operating under freer domestic and external market conditions, will provide the motive power for a resumption of growth and development. (Cleary, 1989, p. 45)

Thus, at the core of structural adjustment is a disillusionment with the efficiency of state intervention. This is of course closely allied to the so-called 'conservative revolution' in the major OECD countries. However, the political and economic situation in the less developed countries is radically different from that which heralded major policy reorientations in the OECD group. In consequence, there is likely to be a mismatch in terms of values and objectives of OECD-based theory and the views of developing country governments (Stevens and Killick, 1989, p. 27).

In essence, as Slater (1993) has emphasised, the policies advocated by the international and regional development agencies comprised a revival of economic liberalism. The key elements of this neo-liberalism are market-oriented development strategies, a minimal role for the state, free trade, financial discipline, comparative advantage and prosperity through economic growth.

The economies of Pacific Asia have been widely cited as examples of the success of such market-oriented, outward-looking liberal development strategies (World Bank, 1993a; OECD, 1992), despite widely accepted evidence that the NICs of Pacific Asia were the product of state- rather than market-led development (see, for example, White, 1988; Dixon and Drakakis-Smith, 1993; Henderson, 1993).

The international agencies have indulged in a considerable measure of 'double-think' with respect to the role of the state in the development of the Pacific Asian economies, thus perpetuating the myth of their long-term *laissez-faire* development, while attributing the economic problems they experienced during the early 1980s to state involvement in the market, and their subsequent rapid economic recovery to successful liberalisation (World Bank, 1993a). Thus the Pacific Asian economies are presented as both examples of successful long-term liberal development *and* successful short-term structural adjustment, the latter responsible for reducing the distortions that we had been told were not there. The agencies thus present a distorted and confused image of the Pacific Asian economies which is used to persuade the rest of the developing world that liberalisation is an essential requisite for rapid economic growth.

While there have been degrees of liberalisation in the Pacific Asian economies since the early 1980s, the international agency view is profoundly ahistorical. In terms of the generation of rapid and sustained rates of economic growth in the Pacific Asian economies during the 1960s and 1970s, state-led development was appropriate to national, regional and international economic and political situations. Similarly, the elements of liberalisation that have occurred during the 1980s and 1990s must be seen as responses to changed circumstances. Certain elements of state-led development had outlived their usefulness, in many cases because of their very success. Liberalisation was thus a factor in their continuation of high rates of economic growth and structural change, but not a cause thereof.

The confusion (perhaps deliberately engineered) over the Pacific Asian economies (Dixon and Drakakis-Smith, 1993) also highlights the confusion over the terminology of structural adjustment. Particularly during the early 1980s, the term 'structural adjustment' was frequently treated as synonymous with 'development' and 'structural transformation' (Streeten, 1987). More recently any liberalisation measures, whatever their origin, have tended to be lumped under the structural adjustment label.

The Policy Prescriptions

Despite the wide range of multilateral and bilateral agreements that have been involved in SAPs and the varied circumstances of each country, there has been a remarkable similarity in the policies imposed. Until recently, the prescriptions were so uniformly applied that critics referred to them as little more than a blueprint. For the reasons explained above, these policies have been developed around the central principle of the superiority of the market over the state, and predicated on what became the conventional wisdom of the early 1980s:

> that after or accompanying a decline in aggregate demand steps must be taken to reduce the overall capital–output ratio. This was to be achieved through improved efficiency by rationalising government policy whereby distortions were reduced or removed leading to resource allocation into sectors enjoying comparative advantage and improving capacity utilisation by alleviating supply constraints. A reduction in the overall capital–output ratio would mitigate the adverse impact of the lower volume of investment on economic growth. In addition, the improved efficiency of the economy would make manufactured exports more competitive, thereby increasing export earnings to alleviate the

initial problems caused by the adverse movement in the external environment. (ADB, 1990, p. 11)

This was essentially the rationale of the SAPs, which have become the 'new orthodoxy' of development (Yagci *et al.*, 1985; Lal, 1984). A critical assumption was that 'efficiently produced' manufactured goods would find a ready market. In this respect the NICs were presented as role models for less sophisticated economies in general, regardless of the significance of the non-manufacturing sectors, or particular national, regional and global circumstances.

SAPs have been succinctly described as containing 'three basic components. ... These are getting prices right, letting markets work and reforming public institutions' (Wardham, 1989, p. 210). More fully, 'The process of structural adjustment refers to changes in the organisation, composition, and orientation of an economy which are necessary if an economy is to remain (or become more) competitive in the world economy' (Koppel, 1990, p. 5).

In practice, the SAPs have contained four key elements:

- the mobilisation of domestic resources;
- policy reforms to increase efficiency;
- the generation of foreign exchange earnings from non-traditional sources; and
- the establishment of a non–inflationary role for the state.

These represented a major reorientation in orthodox development thinking as policies, not aggregate demand (as in the 1960s), or the allocation of investment to projects (as in the 1970s) had become the 'cutting edge' (ADB, 1990, p. 13). This key assumption was drawn from neo-classical economic theory: 'as government reduces the scope and intensity of its intervention the private sector, operating the renewed and strengthened market processes, will quickly appear to (re-) take the initiative the government's withdrawal makes possible' (Koppel, 1990, p. 6).

In essence, the 'frontiers of the state were to be rolled back', 'distortions to the market' eliminated and restrictions on the free flow of trade and capital substantially reduced: overall national economies were to become more fully integrated into the international capitalist system. Sometimes the specific policies prescribed have been distinguished in terms of their sequencing. Initially, so-called *stabilisation* measures were to be implemented to halt the slide. These include a public sector wage freeze, reduced price subsidies and currency devaluation. Once the situation had been brought under control, longer-term *adjustment* policies, including broad export promotion, economic liberalisation and the privatisation of state or parastatal assets could be implemented to restructure the economy.

During the 1980s a large proportion of developing countries accepted the need for reforms along the lines suggested by the international agencies. Between 1979 and 1987 the World Bank approved 52 structural adjustment loans and 70 sectoral adjustment loans. In addition to the agency-based programmes, a number of countries implemented a variety of 'home-grown' adjustment and liberalisation programmes. Many of these were closely tied to multilateral and bilateral loans. Within the broad parameters outlined above, the content of individual programmes has been extremely varied. Indeed, they have now become increasingly country specific (ADB, 1990, p. 34), albeit as a result of trenchant criticisms and the shortcomings of earlier 'blueprint' or blanket policies. In addition, programmes advocated by the agencies have been tempered by the recognition of the need at least to acknowledge the existence of distributional issues, poverty and the environment (ADB, 1990, p. 23). These variations have added to the difficulty of evaluating the impact of structural adjustment policies.

Evaluation of Structural Adjustment Programmes

Despite their 'blueprint' element, evaluation of the impact of adjustment programmes is greatly complicated by the large range of policies associated with the term and the variety of distinctive, often overlapping, programmes to which individual countries have been subject. Evaluations carried out in particular countries can reach totally contradictory conclusions, depending on the research concept being used and the theoretical perspective adopted. If economic growth and modernisation are deemed the key development objectives, then SAPs and ERPs may be able to generate a positive outcome, as the World Bank is wont to claim for Ghana, its current African showpiece (Kanbur, 1993; World Bank, 1993b). Viewed from an alternative perspective, however, any macro-economic success thus claimed could be totally unjustifiable in terms of the immediate suffering caused to the most disadvantaged members of society on the basis of some assumed future 'trickle down' of benefits.

In more general terms, the differing perspectives are well illustrated by the ongoing controversy between the IMF and World Bank on the one hand, and the UN Economic Commission for Africa (UNECA) on the other, over how to interpret SAPs. The debate has particular relevance given the African focus of this book. The UNECA has repeatedly criticised SAPs on account of their social costs, uneven burden and lack of demonstrable economic benefits, proposing instead a less globally integrationist, more autonomous development strategy based on selective spatial closure and greater intra-African interdependence as well as changes in fiscal and monetary policy (UNECA, 1989; Nyang'oro and Shaw, 1992). Inevitably, too, economic agendas have their political counterparts and progenitors. Thus, western donors have recently added political conditionalities – measures to promote apparent democratisation and 'good governance' – to the economic conditionalities of structural adjustment. The UNECA proposals are in turn derived from a very different politico-economic vision. These issues are taken up by David Simon and Anders Närman in Chapters 2 and 3 respectively.

Although the majority of sub-Saharan African (SSA) countries are currently undergoing some form of economic adjustment or reform programme, they have found themselves in this situation through very different circumstances. In some cases, like Burkina Faso, it took a coup to topple a president (Thomas Sankara) who was strongly opposed to the IMF/World Bank programme, before it was accepted by the government and implemented. In Ghana, on the other hand, a total change of heart by President Jerry Rawlings was sufficient to introduce a wide-ranging programme, regarded as a model by international financial institutions. In Zambia, imposition of the original SAP was followed by street riots in the capital, Lusaka, and contributed to the ousting of President Kenneth Kaunda in the country's first multiparty elections in 1992. Following a long period of self-reliant *ujamaa* policies, Tanzania has now carried out a series of SAPs. For Zimbabwe, one of the more recent SAP recruits, a major debate has now erupted as to whether the structural adjustment programme is a home-grown package or just the same kind of external directive prescribed for most other African countries. However important politically, this difference is immaterial in terms of the actual impact of such policies, as Dan Tevera shows in Chapter 5. Ahead of the transition to majority rule, South Africa began implementing its own version of SAP policies.

The debate over the impact of structural adjustment is further clouded by what is examined, at what level and at what stage of the adjustment process:

- Which sector? The impact has been generally adverse on rural sectors, with the exception of certain commercial agricultural, mining and processing activities. In general, export-oriented manufacturing has benefited while previously protected and subsidised domestically-oriented sectors have been adversely affected. The formal employment sector has in almost all cases contracted while the informal sector has expanded. The latter is now being seen by some advocates as a benefit of structural adjustment.
- Which groups of people? The rural poor, urban poor and various public employees have generally experienced declining incomes, although agricultural producer price increases have encouraged many peasants to produce for the market above their subsistence requirements.
- Which indicators – growth of GDP, income distribution or overall welfare and level of human development?
- What stage? In the early stages, changes such as exchange rate reforms are implemented but those that 'bite' into powerful political influences and institutions must come later. Here again, the distinction between stabilisation and adjustment becomes salient.

These issues will be explored in greater detail and in varying contexts throughout this book. Most existing published studies, while drawing attention to the role of such factors as political will, administrative capacities and levels of human resource development, have been dominated by considerations of macro-

economic policy and associated indicators (Koppel, 1990, p. 5). These have concentrated on the degree to which the policies have been implemented *per se* and
the achievement of macro-economic targets. With few exceptions, the reports
of the IMF and IBRD have been highly critical of national governments. Indeed,
in this respect, the vast majority of studies of the Pacific Asian economies have
followed the pattern of the reviews conducted by the ADB, World Bank and
IMF. This stands in marked contrast to the situation in SSA, where the majority
of evaluations not undertaken by official international and national agencies have
concentrated on issues and constraints other than the macro-indicators. Even at
the macro-level, however, considerable difficulties are encountered in separating
the impact of structural adjustment from other national and global changes. This
is the problem of establishing the 'counterfactual situation', i.e. what the position
would have been in the absence of a specific policy or group of interventions.

Further, in evaluating the differential impact of structural adjustment little
attention is devoted to the situation prior to its implementation. Far too often,
all changes that have taken place since are regarded as being products of the reforms.
Thus the continued deterioration of conditions in much of SSA is seen by critics
of structural adjustment as a direct result of these programmes, while its advocates
see the deterioration as being a result of either unsuccessful implementation or
of the necessity for the corrective measures to 'hurt' in the short run (World
Bank, 1992). In contrast, within Pacific Asia renewed economic dynamism has
been interpreted as being a direct result of rapid 'successful' structural adjustment.

Conclusion

Most comparative evaluations of the success of SAPs have largely ignored the
differences between individual programmes and, more significantly, the radically
different economic and political conditions under which the policies have been
implemented. Hence it is unsurprising that for the SSA economies examined in
detail in Chapters 5–9 of this book the international agencies have been, in general,
extremely critical of the 'limited', 'partial' or 'slow' implementation of structural
adjustment. In addition, even those countries which have most fully implemented
agency policies, at the cost of considerable economic and political disruption
and declining living standards for large sections of their populations, have been
told that either the programmes have not been far reaching enough or this is
part of a necessary protracted transition towards economic stability and long-
term economic growth.

These pronouncements contrast markedly with the reporting of the 'success'
cases – Chile, Thailand and Ghana (World Bank, 1990, 1993b). These countries,
one in each of the major continental regions, are cited as examples of full and
rapid implementation of SAPs which has resulted in economic stability and periods
of sustained rapid economic growth. In all cases the agencies maintain that it is
the adoption of the 'correct' economic policies which has been critical. Thus

these examples are held up to the rest of the Third World as 'models' to be emulated. According to the IMF and IBRD, Chile, Thailand and Ghana implemented structural adjustment successfully and have been rewarded with economic stability, high international credit ratings, an influx of foreign direct investment (FDI), transnational corporation (TNC) activity and a period of rapid economic growth. However, these three radically different countries contrast in almost every respect and with typical conditions in SSA.

Chile has an exceptional natural resource endowment, and its development, in association with limited processing, has been the basis of the country's recent economic growth. The development of export-oriented manufacturing has been of only limited importance in Chile's recent period of economic growth and structural change (Gwynne, 1993). In contrast, Thailand's recent accelerated economic growth has rested on the rapid development of a manufacturing export sector. In this respect Thailand is much closer to the guiding principles of structural adjustment outlined above, although Bangkok's industrialisation long predates SAPs.

Ghana has a less impressive natural resource and export-oriented agricultural base than Chile, and a far more modest industrial sector. Ghana's reputation in World Bank eyes rests on the apparent arresting of long-term and extreme economic decline and mismanagement, bringing inflation under control and reducing considerably the state's interventionist stance. Deregulation, liberalisation, the removal of price subsidies and associated stimuli to private enterprise, foreign investment and export promotion have combined with these changes to produce a positive annual GNP growth rate of 2 per cent in recent years under the ERP (Kanbur, 1993). Interestingly, there has been a significant *increase* in government expenditure as a fraction of GNP, financed especially by dramatic improvements in the effectiveness of revenue collection. Although the continuing existence of some poverty – especially in rural areas – is acknowledged, notwithstanding a special Programme of Actions to Mitigate the Social Costs of Adjustment (PAMSCAD), 'this should not detract from the weight of evidence in favor of the view that on average poverty in Ghana declined over the ERP period' (Kanbur, 1993, p. 2). While the proverbial corner may have been turned, many Ghanaians are struggling to make ends meet in the face of these rapid 'adjustments', even contesting the success claimed by the World Bank and the government. They point, for example, to a widespread decline in urban living standards and a rise in urban poverty. As argued above, the precise questions asked and evidence collected are clearly crucial in determining the outcome of evaluations of SAPs and ERPs.

Nevertheless, the implication from the World Bank's perspective is all too clear: if Chile, Thailand and Ghana can do it why can't other countries? Where rapid economic growth is not being achieved, the major international agencies tend to view the countries concerned as 'basket cases'. In such countries, the objective of structural adjustment is to make the economy as stable as possible, and minimise both the 'welfare drain' on the international economy and the risk of external commitments not being met. In this task the new international order and the role of the UN/US as the policer of political stability cannot be ignored. As will be discussed in Chapter 2, this also relates to the imposition of political conditionalities by aid donors.

Outline of the Book

The central aim of this volume is to develop our understanding of the interaction between contemporary processes of inequality, indebtedness and adjustment in the world system, and conditions on the ground as they affect particular regions, countries and communities in SSA, currently the poorest continental region in the world. The particular focus of the book is the political and social economy of structural adjustment and associated programmes of change at different spatial scales. Whereas the position of the main Latin American debtor countries, which catapulted the 'debt crisis' into global popular consciousness in 1981/2, has since stabilised and in some respects even improved, SSA has plunged consistently further into the red over the last decade.

The book has been organised into four parts to maximise its internal coherence and facilitate its use by readers in search of specific material. It is designed to integrate different scales and levels of analysis, from the continental to the local, highlighting the politico-economic, social and cultural interconnections which are all too often ignored. The collection of case studies on Tanzania is an important feature, reflecting the variety and strength of research by members of the groups from which the authors are drawn and providing a comprehensive picture of how SAPs interact with other developments in affecting different communities, localities and sectors within one country. The Tanzanian experiences are also important because of the signal position of that country in the iconography of post-colonial struggles, given its efforts to pursue a form of African socialist development based on prioritising equity and local needs rather than seeking functional integration into the world market. The ultimate failure of that experiment forced the government to revert to the market-oriented policies imbedded in successive SAPs since 1981.

The first part addresses the broad nature and impact of SAPs across SSA. In Chapter 2, David Simon sets the context with an overview of debt, democracy and development in SSA. While this region's debt burden is comparatively modest, it is the heaviest of any region relative to the size and fragility of the national economies. In addition, the situation has deteriorated steadily since 1980, despite the implementation of structural adjustment and ERPs. Overall, SSA is becoming increasingly peripheral to the global economy. Simon also provides a cogent critique of the apparent concern for democratisation which has become an important element of donor conditionality. Based on western concepts of representative democracy, these notions are inherently limited and rarely correspond to the demands of oppressed peoples. While clearly controversial on account of the politics of conditionality, the liberalisation advocated by donors may neverthe-less open up areas for new grassroots political action and loosen the grip of the dominant and unrepresentative political cultures in SSA.

Anders Närman continues the theme of deepening crisis in SSA in Chapter 3, emphasising the significance of the manner in which the region was 'plugged' into the global economy in unequal relationships of dependence. From the per-spective of the international economy and its regulators, any form of self-reliance by individual countries is anathema and Third World countries cannot be allowed to escape from dependency. This discussion leads into an exposition of the social costs of structural adjustment with particular reference to education and employment.

Chapter 4 moves the focus down one level, to the sub-continental region, with an examination of the issue of food security in West Africa by Leo de Haan, Andries Klaasse Bos and Clemens Lutz. They conclude that SAPs are inhibiting regional integration, which is a prerequisite for the improvement of the regional food security situation. Structural adjustment has made West African economies more inward looking, preoccupied with restructuring their national economies rather than considering links with their neighbours.

Part II comprises two chapters on the urban impacts of structural adjustment, with particular reference to people's ability to meet their basic needs. In Chapter 5 Dan Tevera focuses on how 'home-grown' SAPs have affected the ability of Zimbabwe's urban poor to provide for their basic needs and the 'coping strategies' that they have employed to deal with the crisis of survival and social reproduc-tion. Since the implementation of the SAP in 1990 the Zimbabwean economy has shown no signs of improvement, only signs of deepening crisis. Urban households are now trapped between the inability of employers to raise wage levels and increases in rents, transport costs and food, in a situation of shrinking social services.

Continuing this theme in Chapter 6, Mogens Holm reviews the impact of SAPs on urban development and living standards in Tanzanian intermediate towns. The programmes have recentralised the Tanzanian administration, leading to changes in local investment patterns and the functions of intermediate towns as links between rural production and urban markets. The intermediate centres have come under increasing pressure as they have become major foci for in-migration. Overall, structural adjustment has resulted in a concentration of development in major centres at one end of the spectrum and in villages at the other, thus contributing to infrastructural decay at the very time when pressure on facilities has been unprecedented. These perspectives are underpinned by a large interview survey of migrants in Makambako (Iringa region) and Babati (Arusha region).

Part III provides three complementary perspectives on the impact of SAPs in different rural contexts in Tanzania, where reform programmes have been in place since the implementation of the National Economic Survival Programme in 1981. In Chapter 7, Jan Sterkenburg and Arie van der Wiel examine the impact of SAPs on the sugar sector. Between 1986 and 1992 liberalisation policies resulted in the ex-factory price of sugar rising tenfold, production expanding and the profitability of the sugar companies rising significantly. In addition, there was an expansion of employment in the factories and on the estates and increased income for outgrowers. However, these benefits for certain elements in the sugar sector have to be balanced against the other well-documented adverse impacts on employment, welfare and living standards for the population as a whole.

In contrast to this macro-study, in Chapter 8 Milline Mbonile presents a detailed review of the impact of structural adjustment at the local level. This study reveals a remarkable range of positive and negative results. For example, while price rises increased income for some households, expanded crop production and diversified land use, there was also substantial deforestation. Such experiences warn against the temptation to make simplistic generalisations. Chapter 9 continues at a similar geographical scale, with a contribution by Claude Mung'ong'o and Vesa-Matti Loiske of four comparative local studies of peasant responses to SAPs. These showed that all the communities have experienced increased difficulties in local resource management since the implementation of structural adjustment. Communal resource systems have given way to neo-liberal, individualised resource use. These changes have resulted in increased social stratification, poverty, sharecropping, land sales, land degradation and breakdown of communal control and regulation. Groups that were already weak before structural adjustment have been further impoverished and marginalised.

One of the problems with focusing exclusively on a single continental region is the inherent danger of generalising on the basis of such research findings and experiences. It is both salutory and important, therefore, to relate the SSA experience to that of other Third World regions. This is the purpose of Part IV, which contains two explicitly comparative chapters. In Chapter 10 Indra Wahab reviews the degree to which structural adjustment has reduced government budget deficits and expenditure in a sample of countries drawn from all developing continents, which are then compared with evidence from a small sample of industrialised countries. The available data possibly underestimate substantially the fall in government expenditure. However, there are indications that, despite declining expenditure, government budget deficits have increased, thus implying that the decreases in state revenues have exceeded the falls in expenditure. This is a direct result of the reductions in taxation on international trade resulting from the implementation of SAPs.

Given how markedly different the context for the implementation of SAPs is in Pacific Asia, Chris Dixon explores the possible lessons for SSA which can be drawn from the experience of that region in Chapter 11. In Thailand, for example, the programmes agreed with the IBRD and IMF were incomplete when they were abandoned during 1985 and 1986. Only once there had been substantial economic recovery were structural adjustment measures implemented. More generally, the exceptional nature of Pacific Asia's long-term development pattern is stressed. Contrary to common belief, the role of the state has been crucial in most of the dynamic economies of the region. In addition, the increased presence of TNCs and influx of investment combined to undermine the economic and, more significantly, the political strength of the highly protected import-substituting manufacturing sector. A long-term view is therefore essential to an understanding of the differences between SSA and Pacific Asia.

Finally, in Chapter 12 Wim van Spengen provides a brief synthesis, drawing together some of the principal strands of analysis from the preceding chapters and highlighting areas of agreement and difference by way of conclusions. A number of major issues emerge from the book:

1. Despite superficial similarities, structural adjustment policies have become increasingly varied in content and more so in actual implementation, even within sub-Saharan Africa.
2. The context in which structural adjustment policies have been implemented has been far from uniform.
3. Studies have almost invariably concentrated on either the macro-economic indicators or on the adverse impact of programmes on particular groups. Few studies have hitherto looked at those sectors or groups which have gained, or taken a holistic view of the impact of programmes, and this is one of the features of this book.
4. Analysts have experienced considerable difficulty in separating the impact of structural adjustment from other concomitant factors such as drought, political disruption and general economic problems.
5. The implementation of structural adjustment was facilitated to a significant extent by the collapse of eastern Europe.
6. The relationship between structural adjustment and the future of democracy and associated institutions has become increasingly intertwined as a result of power differentials and the imposition of overtly political conditionalities. Nevertheless, it is apparent that much research remains to be done on the whole question of both the immediate and long-term impact of SAPs on Third World economies, societies and political structures.

References

Asian Development Bank (1990) *Annual Report 1990*. Manila.

Cleary, S. (1989) 'Structural adjustment in Africa'. *Trócaire Development Review*, pp. 41–59.

Dixon, C. and Drakakis-Smith, D. (1993) 'The Pacific Asian region'. In C. Dixon and D. Drakakis-Smith (eds) *Economic and Social Development in Pacific Asia*. Routledge, London, pp. 1–21.

Gwynne, R. (1993) *Chile to 1994: More Growth Under Democracy*. Economist Intelligence Unit Special Report no. 2085, London.

Henderson, J. (1993) 'The role of the state in the economic transformation of East Asia'. In C. Dixon and D. Drakakis-Smith (eds) *Economic and Social Development in Pacific Asia*. Routledge, London, pp. 85–114.

Kanbur, R. (1993) The economic reform program and the poor in Ghana. Paper presented to the Conference on Sustainable Environmental and Resource Futures for sub-Saharan Africa, Accra, 22–6 March.

Koppel, B. (ed.) (1990) *Structural Adjustment and Policy Reform: Impacts on Small and Medium Enterprises in the Asian Economies*. Asian Productivity Organisation, Tokyo.

Lal, D. (1984) *The Real Effects of Stabilisation and Structural Adjustment Policies*. World Bank Staff Working Paper no. 636, Washington, DC.

Lee, J. (1987) *Domestic Adjustment to External Shocks in Asia*. Asian Development Bank, Economic Staff Papers no. 39, Manila.

Nyang'oro, J. E. and Shaw, T. (eds) (1992) *Beyond Structural Adjustment in Africa: The Political Economy of Sustainable and Democratic Development*. Praeger, New York.

Organization for Economic Co-operation and Development (1992) *Development Co-operation: 1992 Report*. Paris.

Slater, D. (1993) The geopolitical imagination and the enframing of development. Paper presented at the Trilateral Conference on Global Change, University of Amsterdam.

Stevens, C. and Killick, T. (1989) 'Structural adjustment and Lomé IV'. *Trócaire Development Review*, pp. 25–40.

Streeten, P. (1987) 'Structural adjustment: a survey of issues and option'. *World Development*, 15, pp. 1469–82.

United Nations Economic Commission for Africa (1989) *African Alternative Framework to Structural Adjustment Programmes for Socio-economic Recovery and Transformation*. UNEAC, Addis Ababa.

Wardham, E. A. (1989) 'Structural adjustment in Indonesia: exports and the "high cost economy"'. *Indonesia Quarterly*, XVII, pp. 207–17.

White, G. (1988) Developmental states in East Asia: an introduction. In G. White (ed.) *The Developmental State in East Asia*. Macmillan, London, pp. 1–29.

World Bank (1981) *Annual Report*. Washington, DC.

World Bank (1990) *World Development Report 1990*. Oxford University Press, New York.

World Bank (1992) *Sustainable Rapid Development*. Washington, DC.

World Bank (1993a) *The East Asian Miracle Economies*. Washington, DC.

World Bank (1993b) *Ghana 2000 and Beyond: Setting the Stage for Accelerated Growth and Poverty Reduction*. Washington, DC.

Yagci, F., Kamin, S. and Rosenbaum, V. (1985) *Structural Adjustment Lending: An Evaluation of Program Design*. World Bank Staff Working Paper no. 735, Washington, DC.

PART ONE

Crisis and Change in Sub-Saharan Africa

CHAPTER 2

Debt, Democracy and Development: Sub-Saharan Africa in the 1990s[1]

David Simon

Introduction

It is still generally axiomatic to associate the debt crisis with Latin America, since that is where the long-term problems first erupted into 'crisis' in 1982, and where many of the instruments devised to try to deal with the situation, e.g. debt–equity swaps, have been most widely implemented. It is true that the principal Latin American debtor countries, Mexico and Brazil, remain top of the global table in terms of the current dollar value of their external debts, although the total they owe has actually declined somewhat over the last decade. As will be shown below, their plight, and that of Latin America as a whole, has lessened on certain key variables although deteriorating modestly on others. The economic and social costs of structural adjustment faced by these countries, and especially by their poor, are also well known. In this sense, the level of competition for resources within and between communities, regions and even countries has undoubtedly risen.

At the same time, although the dominant image of sub-Saharan Africa (SSA) abroad is that of being a 'basket case', a continent wracked by famine, poverty, war and destitution on an almost unprecedented scale, the growing severity of its debt crisis is less well known. Few people realise, for example, that:

- the situation has deteriorated consistently and dramatically since 1980;
- SSA's *relative* debt burden is now the heaviest of any Third World region, despite its *total* debt amounting to only 10–11 per cent of total Third World debt;
- this situation has persisted despite the almost continent-wide implementation of structural adjustment and economic recovery programmes over the last twelve years; and
- SSA is the world's poorest region by an increasingly wide margin.

1. Preliminary versions of this chapter were presented at the Conference of Socialist Economists, Polytechnic of Central London, 10–12 July 1992, and at the School of Geography, University of Hull, 4 February 1993. Colin Stoneman, Chris Dixon and Wim van Spengen also provided helpful comments.

Central to any analysis of the continent's current situation and future prospects is the disproportionate concentration of low-income countries among the 45 states in SSA. Indeed, no fewer than 16 of the world's 20 poorest countries in 1990, ranked by the World Bank in terms of GNP per capita, were in SSA. The implications of crisis and poverty for conflict over economic, environmental, political and social resources are clearly profound (e.g. O'Connor, 1991; Onimode, 1988; Overseas Development Institute/Save the Children Fund, 1988; South Commission, 1990). As explained below, this chapter explores these issues and prospects for alternative, more balanced and democratic forms of development in the context of the evolving post-Cold War global order.

The debt crisis erupted into global consciousness in dramatic fashion with the announcement by Brazil and Mexico in 1982 that they were unable to maintain debt service payments. Inevitably, however, the roots of crisis stretch back considerably further. The causes, course and consequences of this near-systemic collapse have been much debated, with differing shares of the 'blame' being laid at the door of the debtor states, the international banks, First World governments and the logic of the global capitalist system (cf. Corbridge, 1993; George, 1988; Krueger, 1987; Schatan, 1987). However, unlike Husain and Underwood (1991) and Mistry (1991), none of these studies draws attention to what we might call the 'silent crisis': the fact that aggregate and relative indebtedness in SSA have been rising quietly but dramatically. The IMF's near-hegemonic official discourse and the simplistic 'solutions' of structural adjustment and stabilisation arising out of it put both the blame and the burden of compliance squarely on debtor countries. Moreover, the ultimate objective of such policies with respect to SSA is to (re-) stabilise and entrench the existing international division of labour predicated on 'free trade' and supposed comparative advantage, rather than to permit the coexistence of different or more autonomous development paths. Although somewhat more subtle and nuanced, the World Bank's approach is little different in essence (World Bank, 1981, 1989).

This should come as no surprise, being entirely consistent with the *raison d'être* of the two Bretton Woods institutions. That 'free' trade is little more than a myth, and that the existing, highly-inequitable global relations of production and exchange reduce or eliminate the potential advantages of increased or more 'efficient' exports of primary commodities by most countries of the South, have been well known for at least 30 years. As most recently and clearly documented by Barratt Brown and Tiffin (1992), these arguments apply *a fortiori* to Africa (and thus SSA), the continent still most heavily dependent on such exports. What is arguably therefore surprising – and depressing – is that the free trade thesis should again have emerged as the dominant and official international development discourse, especially in view of continued protectionism in the North and a sustained misrepresentation of the experience of and policies pursued by the newly industrialising countries (NICs). Ultimately, this reflects the power of free trade advocates, especially since the dissolution of various socialisms as alternative development models, rather than the power of the thesis itself.

The basic features of structural adjustment and stabilisation programmes will not be detailed here, as they have been dealt with in Chapter 1 and have not varied much between countries, especially in SSA, a fact which is particularly problematic in view of the considerable diversity of countries and conditions in SSA (Hoogvelt *et al.*, 1992). In addition to the IMF and World Bank's own evaluations, the range of detailed country studies by other analysts of the impact of structural adjustment policies is also growing (Cornia *et al.*, 1992; Mahjoub, 1990a; Mosley, Harrigan and Toye, 1991; Okogu, 1992; Onimode, 1988, 1989; Stewart *et al.*, 1992; Woodward, 1992). Although these policies have usually been undertaken at the behest of the IMF/World Bank as the precondition for aid, a few countries, such as Burkina Faso, Zimbabwe and recently also South Africa, have imposed similar sets of measures upon themselves. Unsurprisingly, assessments of the effects of structural adjustment also differ radically and even reach opposite conclusions.

Analysing a range of economic performance and policy variables, Conway and Greene (1993) argue that African countries performed more poorly in response to external shocks and internal adjustments over the 1976–86 period than developing countries elsewhere. Although this is attributable partly to economic structure and lack of resilience, they also discern a significant difference between those countries within the CFA franc zone and those outside it, which they explain as reflecting the benefits of monetary and fiscal discipline and security accorded to the Francophone group.

Conversely, Logan and Mengisteab (1993) found no significant difference in economic performance between those African countries (both within and outside the CFA zone) which could be characterised as strong and weak reformers during the 1980s. This they attribute to the inappropriateness of the adjustment policies, which have failed to take account of African socio-cultural structures and have merely sought to duplicate western market systems in a very different context and without taking account of the impact on 'traditional' systems. In a similar vein, Mosley and Weeks (1993) find little evidence that there is a sustained economic recovery under way on the continent. Their study suggests, moreover, that such differences in relative performance between countries as have occurred reflect the general coherence of government policies and 'healthy' movements in real exchange rates and public expenditure on development rather than being the result of IMF/World Bank adjustment programmes *per se*.

In her recent comprehensive review of this literature, Jespersen (1992, pp. 13–14) argues that:

All in all, however, the data point to the less satisfactory performance of adjustment policies in sub-Saharan Africa than in other groups of countries (such as the manufacturing-exporting countries) ... Broadly speaking, stabilisation achieved positive but modest results in sub-Saharan Africa in the 1980s. This occurred despite large real exchange rate devaluations, substantial cuts in public expenditure and credit ceilings and the introduction of support prices ... Of course, stabilisation performance varied from country to country ... With few exceptions, stabilisation was accompanied by sharp losses in GDP growth, investment and human capital development. Of the 18 countries which managed to stabilise their economies in the 1980s, only five recorded positive growth in GDP per capita.

This echoes the conclusion of Killick's (1991) survey that:

there is a distinct shortage of countries of which it can be convincingly claimed that adjustment programmes have made a decisive difference, particularly in Africa and Latin America ... Moreover, the question of sustainability of the reforms – their ability to produce consistently better results over a period of years – is particularly critical, and there is an even smaller number of countries of which it can be said that improvements have become self-sustaining.

From these and other studies (e.g. George, 1988, 1992), we also know that it was the poor – especially women, labourers and small farmers – who, along with the environment, suffered most, and that the worst impacts were felt over the first few years; second-stage economic and social recovery programmes have attempted to address the harshest consequences to some extent. Overall, however, poverty and social differentiation have increased dramatically and in many areas the environment has been exploited more intensively (e.g. through loss of fallow periods, inability to afford fertilisers, accelerating felling of woody biomass, bringing unsuitable and progressively more marginal land under cultivation) in the struggle to survive and to boost cash crop exports in order to offset steadily deteriorating terms of trade. On the other hand some structural adjustment programme (SAP) policy instruments, e.g. increased agricultural producer prices and reduced urban bias as a result of the abolition of various explicit and implicit urban subsidies, are likely to have had beneficial impacts on the environment. The overall outcome is likely to vary significantly by location, social group and scale of (dis)aggregation, both within and between countries. While the contributions to Reed (1992) are likely to prove controversial, the book does highlight the complexities involved in seeking to discern the effects of SAPs, economic recovery programmes and economic and social action programmes on the environment.

The point mentioned in passing in the previous paragraph about deteriorating terms of trade warrants some elaboration. For SSA excluding Nigeria the terms of trade declined by no less than 25 per cent between 1980 and 1988 (Husain and Underwood, 1991, p. 67). At the same time, Husain (1993) shows how the terms of trade for some of Africa's principal export commodities, e.g. cocoa from Ghana and copper from Zambia, changed markedly *in opposite directions* over the 1986–90 period. Generalisations therefore need to be qualified.

In this context, Jespersen's (1992, p. 50) conclusion is telling:

While some limited progress was recorded in terms of stabilisation and micro-economic efficiency, and while the adjustment policies adopted should not be seen as the cause of the crises of the 1980s, these policies were not able to offset the negative trends in the international environment and to steer the African economies towards a long-term growth path. In this sense, these policies have shown only limited relevance to long-term development, largely because of the inconsistency between several of the adjustment instruments and long-run social and economic objectives.

In a similar vein:

> it should be reiterated that if the ultimate objective of structural adjustment is really to turn the economies of these countries around, rather than just to assure a degree of debt repayment, then the programmes need to take full cognizance of the damaging role of the debt burden. The present situation is clearly not sustainable, because although some real growth has taken place, all the other indicators are largely unfavourable, with the growing debt stock being the most important impediment to a realisation of the potential benefits of structural adjustment. (Okogu, 1992, p. 55)

Even as respected a commentator as Gerald Helleiner (1992) has argued cogently that the influence of the IMF and World Bank has become excessive in Africa and that continued donor obsession with conditionality has little to do any more with the prospects of debt repayment. In addition, greater differenti-ation between – and sequencing of – adjustment policies is warranted in the African context on account of different and diverse conditions. Moreover, underfund-ing by donors of adjustment programmes raises the risk of programme failure more than the absence of further reforms on account of the severe impediments to the utilisation of even existing capacity represented by foreign exchange shortages. There is undoubtedly a growing consensus on these issues in the recent critical literature (Cornia *et al.*, 1992; Husain and Underwood, 1991; Killick, 1991; Riddell, 1992; Stewart, 1991; Stewart *et al.*, 1992; Woodward, 1992).

Against this background, the objectives of this chapter are:

- to highlight salient dimensions of SSA's growing global peripherality and deepening economic crisis with reference to a wide range of both conventional and unconventional variables;
- to examine the implications of the changing world order and structural adjustment programmes for SSA's struggle to survive and improve its future prospects; and
- to explore the interaction of powerful external economic and political agendas with those from within in order to tease out the scope for genuine democratisation and substantive development over the next few years.

Economic Crisis and Increasing Peripherality

External Trade

Broadly speaking, the structures of SSA's imports and exports remain stagnant and very unfavourable. Table 2.1 shows that machinery, transport equipment and other manufactures accounted for two-thirds of SSA's imports in 1990. Fuel, food and other primary commodities comprised the remaining third. These sectoral percentages are comparable with those for the other continental regions shown, except that food is the highest apart from the Middle East and North Africa. The latter's high food imports are unsurprising, given that region's dominant climate and environment.

However, SSA is one of the world's major producers of agricultural commodities. Of particular concern is that SSA is no longer self-sufficient in food, as production has failed to match the 3 per cent annual population growth rate. Since the early 1980s food imports have risen by roughly 10 per cent per annum, starkly underlining SSA's vulnerability and reversing earlier gains in food production in the late colonial and/or early post-colonial periods.

Table 2.1: Structure of Imports (percentage share) 1990

Region	Food	Fuels	Other Primary Commodities	Machinery & Transport Equipment	Other Manufacturing
Sub-Saharan Africa	16	14	4	30	36
East Asia and Pacific	7	9	10	38	35
South Asia	13	16	10	20	41
Europe	11	17	9	34	34
Middle East and N. Africa	17	6	6	33	37
Latin America and Caribbean	12	13	7	31	35
Low- & Middle-Income Countries	11	11	8	34	36
Low-Income Countries	12	9	8	33	38

Notes:
1. Percentages are of respective regions' imports.
2. Data weighted by size of flows.
3. All SSA classified as low income except:
   (a) lower-middle-income: Zimbabwe, Senegal, Côte d'Ivoire, Cameroon, Congo, Botswana, Angola, Namibia;
   (b) upper-middle-income: South Africa, Gabon.
4. Low-income includes India and China.
Source: World Bank (1992) *World Development Report 1992*.

The sectoral composition of exports (Table 2.2) also shows clearly how dependent SSA remains on primary commodities, the world market prices of which have been depressed since the mid-1970s. An extraordinary 92 per cent of SSA's exports in 1990 comprised fuels, minerals, metals, agricultural, fish and forestry products. This is put into stark perspective by Avramovic's (1991, pp. 51–2) evidence, based on World Bank data, that the export of manufactures from SSA rose 'powerfully' – by 42 per cent in US dollar terms between 1980 and 1987 alone. Eleven countries excluding South Africa exported manufactures worth over US$100 million in 1988. However, this would seem to contradict other World Bank data reproduced in Table 2.3 below.

Table 2.2: Structure of Exports (percentage share) 1990

Region	Fuels, Minerals & Metals	Other Primary Commodities	Machinery & Transport Equipment	Other Manufacturing	Textiles & Clothing
Sub-Saharan Africa	63	29	1	7	1
East Asia and Pacific	13	18	22	47	19
South Asia	6	24	5	65	33
Europe	9	16	27	47	16
Middle East and N. Africa	75	12	1	15	4
Latin America and Caribbean	38	29	11	21	3
Low- & Middle-Income Countries	31	20	15	35	12
Low–Income Countries	27	20	9	45	21

Notes:
1. Percentages are of respective regions' exports.
2. Data weighted by size of flows.
3. All SSA classified as low income except:
  (a) lower–middle–income: Zimbabwe, Senegal, Côte d'Ivoire, Cameroon, Congo, Botswana, Angola, Namibia,
  (b) upper–middle–income: South Africa, Gabon.
4. Low–income includes India and China.
Source: World Bank (1992) *World Development Report 1992*.

According to Table 2.2, even the Middle East and North Africa were marginally less dependent on primary exports; by contrast, the rapidly developing regions of Asia and the Pacific had no more than about 30 per cent of their exports in these sectors. Herein lies one of the principal sources of SSA's difficulties in seeking to escape from its present predicament. Although no real prospect of increased prices exists in the near future, the implementation of IMF/World Bank structural adjustment policies has actually *increased* output of primary commodities such as cotton and copper, thus undermining the earlier efforts of some SSA countries at diversification and weakening them still further. These issues will be returned to below.

Sectoral Growth Rates

In terms of the percentage change in value added, SSA has performed worse than any other region since the onset of the first oil crisis in the early 1970s. This is true of agriculture, SSA's principal economic base, as well as the industrial and service sectors (Table 2.3). Mineral extraction forms the major industrial activity. The transformation of industrial performance from the 1965–73 period, when it grew more rapidly than any other region, was very marked. However, as stated above, these trends do not tally with the other World Bank data cited by Avramovic (1991). Detailed further research would be required to resolve this anomaly, but manipulation of data by the IMF and World Bank is not unknown:

> To evaluate the World Bank's programmes we should proceed in two stages. First, we should use their own figures, their own language, to see whether what they have set out to do has been done. So we use their own figures, to show them that even what they have said they would do, they have not done. Then we go a step further, to say, even if the figures show that they have done what they set out to do, that does not solve our problems. What we show ... is that they have manipulated the figures.
>
> In his letter of resignation, Mr Budhoo of the IMF accused the organization of systematically manipulating figures in Third World countries in order to produce bogus results. That allegation was probed by an international group of experts and was found to be correct. (Onimode, 1990, pp. 55–6)

Returning to Table 2.3 it is evident that, whereas services provided the fastest source of economic growth in other Third World regions, the performance of this sector in SSA declined in each successive period, although its growth rate remained positive.

Table 2.3: Sectoral Growth Rates 1965–89
(Average annual percentage change of value added)

Country group	Agriculture			Industry			Services		
	1965 –73	*1973 –80*	*1980 –89*	*1965 –73*	*1973 –80*	*1980 –89*	*1965 –73*	*1973 –80*	*1980 –89*
Low-income economies	2.9	1.8	4.3	10.7	7.0	8.7	6.3	5.3	*6.1*
Middle-income economies	3.2	3.0	2.7	8.0	4.0	*3.2*	7.6	6.3	*3.1*
Severely indebted middle-income economies	3.1	3.6	2.7	6.8	5.4	*1.0*	7.2	5.4	*1.7*
Sub-Saharan Africa	2.2	–0.3	*1.8*	13.9	4.2	*–0.2*	4.1	3.1	*1.5*
East Asia	3.2	2.5	5.3	12.7	9.2	10.3	10.5	7.3	*7.9*
South Asia	3.1	2.2	2.7	3.9	5.6	7.2	4.0	5.3	*6.1*
Latin America and the Caribbean	3.0	3.7	*2.5*	6.8	5.1	*1.1*	7.3	5.4	*1.7*

Note: Figures in italics in the 1980–9 columns are not for the full decade.
Source: World Bank (1990) *World Development Report 1990*, p. 162.

External Debt Burden

Table 2.4: External Debt Burden 1990 (1980)

Region/Country	Total external debt as percentage of exports of goods and services	Total debt service as percentage of exports	Interest payments as percentage of exports
Sub-Saharan Africa	324.3 (96.8)	19.3 (10.9)	8.9 (5.7)
Low-income countries, *of which*	218.5 (105.1)	20.1 (10.3)	9.3 (5.1)
1 Mozambique	1,573.3	14.4	7.7
2 Tanzania	1,070.7 (317.8)	25.8 (19.6)	10.9 (10.0)
3 Ethiopia	480.3 (136.2)	33.0 (7.6)	8.1 (4.7)
4 Somalia	2,576.2 (252.0)	11.7 (4.9)	5.8 (0.9)
9 Malawi	328.5 (260.8)	22.5 (27.7)	9.1 (16.7)
17 Nigeria	242.7 (32.2)	20.3 (4.2)	12.1 (3.3)
18 Niger	464.2 (132.8)	24.1 (21.7)	8.9 (12.9)
25 Kenya	306.3 (165.1)	33.8 (21.4)	14.8 (11.3)
27 Ghana	353.4 (116.0)	34.9 (13.1)	9.9 (4.4)
34 Lesotho	41.2 (19.5)	2.4 (1.5)	0.8 (0.6)
Lower middle-income countries, *of which*	179.0 (115.2)	20.3 (18.8)	8.4 (9.1)
45 Zimbabwe	155.0 (45.4)	22.6 (3.8)	9.6 (1.5)
46 Senegal	236.8 (162.7)	20.4 (28.7)	8.1 (10.5)
48 Côte d'Ivoire	487.4 (160.7)	38.6 (28.3)	13.3 (13.0)
56 Congo	352.5 (146.7)	20.7 (10.8)	10.5 (6.7)
71 Botswana	22.9 (17.8)	4.4 (1.9)	1.6 (1.1)
Upper middle-income countries, *of which*	132.1 (159.6)	17.9 (31.0)	8.2 (16.6)
93 Gabon	138.4 (62.2)	7.6 (17.7)	5.0 (6.3)
East Asia and Pacific	91.1 (88.8)	14.6 (13.5)	5.8 (7.7)
South Asia	281.5 (162.9)	25.9 (12.2)	13.1 (5.2)
Bangladesh	448.2 (345.6)	25.4 (23.2)	7.7 (6.4)
India	282.4 (136.0)	28.8 (9.3)	15.9 (4.2)
Europe	125.7 (90.6)	16.9 (15.9)	6.8 (7.1)
Middle East and North Africa	180.3 (114.9)	24.4 (16.4)	8.1 (7.4)
Latin America and Caribbean	257.4 (196.8)	25.0 (37.3)	13.3 (19.7)
Mexico	222.0 (259.2)	27.8 (49.5)	16.7 (27.4)
Brazil	326.8 (304.9)	20.8 (63.1)	8.2 (33.8)

Note: Regional and income category averages are weighted by size of flows.
Source: World Bank (1992) *World Development Report 1992*.

SSA now shoulders the heaviest debt burden of any Third World region, in terms of total external debt as a percentage of the exports of goods and services (Table 2.4). Having been one of the least heavily burdened on this variable in 1980, SSA's position deteriorated dramatically during the 1980s (Chirwa, 1991) to the point where its debt was equivalent to three and a quarter times the value of exports. In the poorest countries, especially Mozambique, Somalia and Tanzania, the deterioration has been nothing short of catastrophic. Ethiopia and Niger are also in desperate situations. Although other regions also recorded increases on this variable, the change was from a higher base and more modest. Even Latin America, the fulcrum of the debt crisis, is now less badly off. Mexico's position has actually improved, while Brazil's worsened only marginally.

The other two variables in Table 2.4 provide further evidence of SSA's problems, with the total debt service burden almost doubling. Although most other regions – including Latin America – were still worse off in 1990, the improvement in Latin America's position since 1980 stands in stark contrast to SSA's deterioration.

In dollar terms, of course, as shown in Table 2.4, SSA's total debt is still modest compared with most other regions; however, relative to the size, structure and extremely fragile nature of SSA's economies, the situation is undoubtedly worse. The general malaise can be attributed to a number of interacting causes, especially inappropriate policies, continually depressed world commodity prices on which SSA is more dependent than any other region except the Caribbean, rising protectionism in the north and the impact of structural adjustment policies. However, it is also notable that many parts of the region, including three of the poorest countries (Mozambique, Somalia and Ethiopia) have been wracked by armed conflicts over much of the decade. These have killed or wounded vast numbers of people, displaced millions of others within those countries or across their borders, absorbed a disproportionately high share of government expenditure, brought the destruction of infrastructure and productive assets and precluded agricultural activity over large parts of the countries.

One indicator of the extreme external pessimism at SSA's ability to repay its outstanding official debt is the heavy discounting on the secondary debt market. The debt paper of most countries can be bought for under 10 per cent of its face value, so that huge profits are now commonly realised when even marginally improved economic news boosts the value to, say, 15–20 per cent of its face value. This 'exotic debt' market has recently been booming, in part because it provides new foreign investors with a cheap source of capital through debt–equity swaps (*Africa Confidential*, 18 December 1992).

Net Flows of Official Development Assistance

From Table 2.5 it is evident that SSA has become the largest recipient region of official development assistance (ODA) in the Third World, following large increases in early 1980s. While the data reveal that both bilateral and multilateral donors have responded to the continent's crisis to some extent this, of course, indicates little about the adequacy of that response or the quality of ODA in terms, for example, of the extent of aid tying. Many bilateral donors, especially the US and UK, have been increasing the political as well as economic conditionalities attached to their disbursements. Aid is being more selectively applied between countries, sectors and even specific projects in accordance with donor preferences and preconditions. Furthermore, it is apparent that external funding

Table 2.5: Official Development Assistance (ODA) by Region and Origin* (in current US$million)

Region	1984	%	1988	%	1989	%	1990	%
A. Europe								
1. Net disbursements (all sources), of which	414.7	1	522.6	1	356.7	1	1,496.5°	3
2. from DAC countries	302.0	73	477.1	91	358.7	101	783.5	52
3. by multilateral agencies	74.3	18	86.0	16	39.7	11	41.5	3
B. Africa								
1. Net disbursements (all sources)	11,375.2	37	17,694.0	38	18,286.2	39	25,512.0	43
2. from DAC countries	7,515.9	66	12,532.1	71	12,654.0	69	16,561.9	65
3. by multilateral agencies	2,823.3	25	4,924.6	28	5,528.8	30	6,104.2	24
B1. Africa North of Sahara								
1. Net disbursements (all sources)	2,424.3	8	2,527.2	5	2,445.9	5	7,146.4‡	12
2. from DAC countries	2,156.0	89	2,205.9	87	2,090.8	85	4,142.3	58
3. by multilateral agencies	211.0	9	286.1	11	355.0	15	265.4	4
B2. Africa South of Sahara								
1. Net disbursements (all sources)	8,211.1	27	14,801.6	32	15,304.3	32	17,879.4	30
2. from DAC countries	5,216.1	64	10,123.5	68	10,220.7	67	12,146.3	68
3. by multilateral agencies	2,506.7	31	4,482.4	30	4,983.5	33	5,626.1	31
C. North & Central America								
1. Net disbursements (all sources)	2,248.4	7	3,213.6	7	3,380.4	7	3,991.1	7
2. from DAC countries	1,775.3	79	2,697.3	84	2,865.0	85	3,471.8	87
3. by multilateral agencies	473.2	21	515.9	16	514.5	15	519.6	13
D. South America								
1. Net disbursements (all sources)	1,101.6	4	1,639.4	4	1,885.6	4	2,078.0	3
2. from DAC countries	774.5	70	1,271.6	78	1,518.0	81	1,631.9	79
3. by multilateral agencies	329.6	30	368.1	22	368.3	20	446.2	27
E. Middle East								
1. Net disbursements (all sources)	3,456.2	11	2,441.5	5	2,305.4	5	4,118.2$^\phi$	7
2. from DAC countries	1,537.1	44	1,913.9	78	1,806.9	78	2,200.5	53
3. by multilateral agencies	233.7	7	232.8	10	364.0	16	560.2	14
F. South Asia								
1. Net disbursements (all sources)	4,544.7	15	6,718.9	14	6,309.8	13	6,334.6	11
2. from DAC countries	2,184.2	48	3,991.2	59	3,658.7	58	3,343.3	53
3. by multilateral agencies	2,310.3	51	2,767.5	41	2,693.7	43	3,004.4	47
G. Far East								
1. Net disbursements (all sources)	2,852.4	9	5,520.9	12	6,292.2	13	6,997.9	12
2. from DAC countries	2,205.2	77	4,326.4	78	5,086.1	81	5,595.4	80
3. by multilateral agencies	547.8	19	1,200.0	22	1,208.1	19	1,364.2	19
H. Oceania								
1. Net disbursements (all sources)	971.7	3	1,436.4	3	1,361.6	3	1,348.5	2
2. from DAC countries	912.4	94	1,291.3	90	1,273.6	94	1,214.7	90
3. by multilateral agencies	59.3	6	144.9	10	87.8	6	133.5	10
Total								
1. Net disbursements (all sources)	30,984.9	100	46,370.1	100	47,281.1	100	59,828.2	100
2. from DAC countries	19,693.8	64	33,155.9	72	34,228.1	72	40,225.7	67
3. by multilateral agencies	7,637.0	25	11,326.9	24	11,736.3	25	13,447.1	22

Notes:
* Neither the annual totals nor percentages for all regions add up exactly to the global totals because of various unspecified and unallocated disbursements.
° Turkey received a dramatically increased allocation in 1990.
‡ Egypt received a dramatically increased allocation in 1990.
$^\phi$ Syria received a dramatically increased allocation in 1990 (back to levels of 1987 and earlier).
Source: OECD (1992) *Geographical Distribution of Financial Flows to Developing Countries; Disbursements, Commitments, Economic Indicators, 1987/1990.*

is often less certain and sustained than both promised and required to support structural adjustment and stabilisation programmes – which are acknowledged to be medium- to long-term undertakings (Helleiner, 1992).

Africa as a whole has seen its share of total ODA rise gradually from 37 per cent in 1984 to 43 per cent in 1990. Africa north of the Sahara received a threefold increase in current dollar terms over the period, taking its share of the global total from 8 to 12 per cent. However, this was almost entirely due to Egypt's vastly increased receipts in 1990; until then the region had seen its ODA receipts remain constant in dollar terms and declining in proportional terms. SSA saw its current dollar receipts more than double, with its share of the total rising from 27 to 30 per cent – although it had stood at 32 per cent in 1988 and 1989. By contrast, all other regions apart from the Far East have seen their proportion of ODA stagnate or decline. Europe's small receipts had also been declining until a dramatic increase for Turkey in 1990 inflated the figure.

The Extent of Aid Reliance

The receipts of ODA per capita in SSA averaged just under US$34 per capita, a figure exceeded only in the Middle East and North Africa (Table 2.6). However, the importance of ODA to the economies of SSA is far greater than elsewhere. Particularly among the continent's low-income countries, which are also the poorest in the world in terms of per capita GDP, the extent of aid reliance is striking. Over two-thirds of Mozambique's GNP was provided as ODA in 1990, while the figures for Ethiopia and Somalia both exceeded 45 per cent and in several others they were above 20 per cent. By contrast, even though several lower middle-income African countries received comparable or higher ODA payments, these comprised a far smaller percentage of GNP (Table 2.6). The seriousness of the African situation is underlined by the fact that the global average for low-income countries was a mere 2.8 per cent of GNP and for lower middle-income countries 1.6 per cent.

Private Foreign Investment

Net flows of foreign direct investment (FDI) have been declining consistently in both absolute and relative terms. SSA now receives only about 6 per cent of total western private FDI in the Third World. Bennell's (1990) very useful study of British firms' strategies of FDI in industry shows how Africa has sunk to near irrelevance. From around 4 per cent of UK worldwide net industrial FDI in the mid-1970s, the figure had fallen to just 0.5 per cent in 1986. The decline in net earnings from Africa declined more modestly, from 4.7 to 3.4 per cent over that period,

> but it will undoubtedly continue to fall in the future, given the already dramatic fall in the relative size of British net investments in Africa. For

British industrial capital as a whole, therefore, Africa is now of minor interest. While investment in Africa has collapsed, British industrial FDI in the rest of the world has grown enormously, recording a nearly fourfold increase in annual net investment levels (in current prices) between 1978 and 1986 ... What is clear is that African participation in this process is at best marginal ... In mid-1989 there were just 96 British registered companies out of a total of over 20,000 in the UK with active investments in industrial enterprises in English-speaking Africa. (Bennell, 1990, pp. 159–60)

Table 2.6: Extent of Aid Reliance 1990

		ODA (US$million)	Per capita ($)	ODA as percentage of GNP
Sub-Saharan Africa		16,810	33.9	9.6
Low-income countries, *of which*		29,353	9.6	2.8
1	Mozambique	946	60.2	65.7
2	Tanzania	1,155	47.1	48.2
3	Ethiopia	888	17.4	14.6
4	Somalia	428	54.8	45.9
6	Chad	315	55.5	28.6
9	Malawi	479	56.3	25.7
11	Burundi	265	48.8	24.0
12	Zaïre	823	22.0	10.9
13	Uganda	557	34.1	18.4
16	Mali	474	56.0	19.4
18	Niger	358	46.7	14.2
25	Kenya	1,000	41.4	11.4
27	Ghana	465	31.2	7.4
30	Zambia	438	54.0	14.0
34	Lesotho	138	78.0	24.5
Lower middle-income countries, *of which*		14,369	26.0	1.6
45	Zimbabwe	343	35.0	5.5
46	Senegal	739	99.8	12.7
48	Côte d'Ivoire	689	57.9	6.9
53	Cameroon	483	41.2	4.3
56	Congo	209	92.0	7.3
71	Botswana	148	118.2	5.5
Upper middle-income countries, *of which*		3,517	8.5	0.1
93	Gabon	140	123.0	3.0
East Asia and Pacific		7,771	4.9	0.8
South Asia		6,174	5.4	1.6
Europe		1,420	14.1	0.4
Middle East and North Africa		9,680	37.8	3.4
Latin America and Caribbean		5,380	12.3	0.4

Notes:
1. Data differ somewhat from those published by OECD.
2. Per capita data based on World Bank population estimates.
Source: World Bank (1992) *World Development Report 1992*.

The reasons are numerous, and although the relative importance of particular factors differs between countries and over time, the overall picture is remarkably consistent and bleak. The bottom line is undoubtedly that rates of return on investment (especially in hard currency terms) have generally fallen to the point where the considerable effort and risk involved are no longer justified. Many firms are disinvesting: Bennell found that one-third of British companies had already done so in the decade to 1989 (Bennell, 1990, p. 169). This trend reflects firms' perceptions of overall economic conditions as well as the disincentive provided by both direct and indirect forms of government intervention and the impediments to competition. Specific problems often cited include discrimination in favour of local firms, the owners of which are politically well connected; excessive bureaucratic red tape; restrictions on access to foreign exchange for the import of capital equipment, spares or essential inputs; delays and restrictions on the repatriation of profits (sometimes because of foreign exchange shortages); and widespread corruption, now increasing even in erstwhile favoured investment loci such as Kenya. Certainly, rates of return in regions of the Third World with which SSA is increasingly in competition for foreign private and official resources, especially Southeast Asia and the Pacific Rim, have been consistently higher. Indeed, the gap has been widening (Bennell, 1990; Simon, 1992; World Bank, 1992). Moreover, the collapse of state socialism in central and eastern Europe, symbolised by the breakup of COMECON and then the Soviet Union itself, has – at least initially in terms of purchasing the best former state enterprises – provided very attractive openings to western capitalists, absorbing flows which might otherwise have been invested in Third World countries, including Africa to some extent.

Emerging Stock Markets

Further evidence of the scarcity of local and foreign investible surpluses, or the inappropriateness of vehicles for mobilising such resources, is the insignificance of stock markets in the region. A major study by *The Economist* included only two from SSA – Nigeria and Zimbabwe – in the ranks of what it labels emerging stock markets around the world. These two were also the smallest (Economist Publications, 1990). However, a number of other SSA countries, including Botswana, do have modest markets. For example, Kenya has been upgrading its long-moribund stock exchange, finally establishing a trading floor in 1991 as part of the efforts of the Capital Markets Development Authority to vitalise the country's capital markets (Simon, 1992). Newly-independent Namibia also established a small exchange in 1992. Of course, the continent's doyen of stock markets, the Johannesburg Stock Exchange, has a long history and ranks in the world's top twelve in terms of value of shares traded.

Net Resource Transfers

The net balance of resource flows to SSA is difficult to compute accurately and the figures presented in various studies differ according to the specific statistical conversion factors used and the definitions and bookkeeping conventions adhered to. For example, with the writing-off of debt, former loans are often converted into grants, and this is reflected as a positive resource transfer in donor calculations, despite the fact that no new resources have changed hands. Most sources suggest that the overall balance has remained positive since at least the early 1980s. Riddell (1992) puts the figure at US$9 billion in 1984 and within the range US$13–17 billion per annum thereafter. Recent World Bank data support this, and show a figure of $15 billion for 1991 (*The Economist*, 1993, pp. 69–70).

However, SSA's resource balance with the IMF has been negative since 1986, and that with the World Bank, while still positive, is lower than in the past (Avramovic, 1991; Hoogvelt *et al.*, 1992; Killick, 1991; Riddell, 1992). Net outflows from SSA to the IMF averaged US$0.7 billion per annum over the period 1986–90, despite the introduction of concessionary facilities such as the structural adjustment facility (SAF) and enhanced SAF (ESAF). The World Bank has disbursed rapid loans under special facilities, e.g. the Special Program of Assistance (SPA), to ensure that severely indebted countries in Africa will not experience a net resource transfer to the Bank. While this has provided an overall net annual transfer of US$1–1.2 billion to SSA since the mid-1980s, some of the major debtor countries made net payments to the Bank in several of these years (Avramovic, 1991, pp. 44–6).

The picture with respect to individual bilateral donor countries is more varied although, as already shown, the proportion of ODA directed to SSA has increased over recent years. Private resource flows have tended to be negative, with continuing capital flight from many African countries coupled with declining net FDI and large debt repayments to creditor banks in the North. However, it must be pointed out that one of the distinguishing features of SSA's debt is the high proportion of official debt relative to private commercial debt. Whereas negotiations with the Club of London (creditor banks) are more important for Latin America, for example, SSA's fate is more bound up with the Club of Paris (official creditors).

The Location of Headquarters of Transnational Corporations and International Organisations

This variable provides another perspective on SSA's peripherality (Table 2.7). While forecasts or suggestions of the demise of the state as one of the primary institutions regulating human activities are clearly premature, there is evidence that the importance of transnational corporations (TNCs), non-governmental organisations (NGOs) and intergovernmental organisations has been increasing (e.g. Morss, 1991). Analysis of the locus of decision-making in these organisa-

Table 2.7: African Cities with the greatest number of Secretariats of International Organisations

City	Principal Secretariats				Secondary Secretariats				Grand Total
	A	B	C	Total	A	B	C	Total	
Nairobi	0	30	69	99	0	2	4	6	105
Dakar	0	25	33	58	0	5	1	6	64
Addis Ababa	0	10	38	48	0	1	3	4	52
Tunis	0	17	21	38	0	1	2	3	41
Abidjan	0	13	24	37	1	0	2	3	40
Cairo	4	18	14	36	1	1	0	2	38
Lagos	1	14	13	28	1	1	1	3	31
Accra	0	13	14	27	0	0	1	1	28
Ouagadougou	0	5	19	24	0	1	1	2	26
Harare	0	4	10	14	1	0	7	8	22
Yaoundé	0	8	10	18	0	3	0	3	21
Some comparisons:									
Asia									
Bangkok	5	12	77	94	1	1	3	5	99
Manila	2	26	50	78	2	4	7	13	91
Kuala Lumpur	2	19	30	51	1	1	0	2	53
New Delhi	5	11	22	38	2	3	1	6	44
Jakarta	1	6	29	36	0	3	3	6	42
Seoul	1	7	9	17	2	1	2	5	22
Latin America and Caribbean									
Buenos Aires	3	42	24	69	12	7	6	14	83
Mexico City	3	31	40	74	2	1	5	8	82
Santiago	0	18	51	69	2	1	5	8	77
Caracas	0	25	412	66	2	3	5	10	76
Bogotà	1	18	10	29	2	1	3	6	35
São Paulo	1	11	8	20	2	0	0	2	22
Europe									
Brussels	90	299	592	981	13	43	45	101	1,082
Paris	155	257	368	780	33	49	43	125	905
London	130	137	233	500	9	11	20	40	540
Rome	18	19	388	425	6	6	9	21	446
Geneva	73	44	244	361	15	7	27	49	410
North America									
New York	17	26	188	231	10	7	34	51	282
Washington, DC	18	19	120	157	8	6	17	31	188
Montreal	12	6	19	37	3	2	5	10	47
Ottawa	5	4	15	24	1	0	1	2	26

Notes:
1. International organisations include all non-profit bodies, whether governmental or non-governmental.
Secretariats located in differently-named suburbs/districts are not always included.
2. A: International organisations with global or intercontinental membership (i.e. *Yearbook* categories A–C).
 B: Regionally-defined membership organisations, representing at least three countries in a particular continent or sub-continent region (i.e. *Yearbook* category D).
 C: Other (including funds, foundations, religious orders etc. (i.e. *Yearbook* categories E, F, R).
Source: Union of International Associations (1990) *Yearbook of International Organizations 1990/91*, Vol. 2, Table 10.

tions can therefore provide an insight into the geography of power of non-state actors. TNC headquarters are still overwhelmingly located in the core countries of the world economy, with Japanese firms having risen dramatically in global importance over the last 15 years or so. Nevertheless, a process of corporate counterpenetration has begun, with firms based in the south investing and expanding their operations internationally. As of 1989, only 34 of the world's 500 largest companies were headquartered in the south, and only three of these were in SSA (Simon, 1992, pp. 49–51).

A similar picture emerges with respect to the headquarters of international organisations. Whereas the total number of primary and secondary secretariats of such bodies in major capitals of SSA compares reasonably well with other Third World regions, the continent performs poorly in both absolute and relative terms for global (as opposed to regional or continental) membership organisations. For obvious reasons it is these organisations which are arguably the most important and powerful (Simon, 1992, pp. 55–6, 83–5). Hence, SSA's poverty and marginality are underlined by its unattractiveness to decision-makers in non-state institutions. This situation is unlikely to change in the short to medium term.

Broader Human Development

Despite its shortcomings (Kelley, 1991; McGillivray and White, 1993), the UNDP's recently devised Human Development Index (HDI) provides a simple guide to how countries perform in social and developmental as well as purely economic terms as measured by GNP per capita alone (UNDP, 1992, 1993). The HDI is a composite index comprising three variables, namely life expectancy at birth (as a proxy for the quality of life and availability of public services), average educational attainment (as a proxy for the life chances and opportunities open to people), and adjusted real GDP per capita (as a proxy for economic development). The original formula has already been modified slightly following debate and evaluation (McGillivray and White, 1993; UNDP, 1993). The range of possible values on the HDI is from 0 to 1, with 0–0.49 representing low levels of human development, 0.5–0.79 medium human development and 0.8–1 representing high levels of human development.

Significantly, none of SSA's states attained a high HDI score in 1990, and only five (Mauritius, Seychelles, South Africa, Gabon and Botswana) were in the medium range, although Mauritius was the top country in the medium HDI category. The remaining 41 all had low levels of human development. Altogether, 17 SSA countries had lower ranks on GNP per capita than on the HDI, 27 had higher ranks and one had equal rank (UNDP, 1992, 1993). Table 2.8 presents a selection of these country data to illustrate the above point. In aggregate terms, therefore, taking social and developmental indicators into account actually worsened the ranking of 60 per cent of SSA countries compared with their purely economic rank. The situation is undoubtedly grim.

This section has sought to document important dimensions of SSA's current predicament by means of a variety of conventional and novel indicators. Although there is some evidence of progress, the overall picture to emerge gives cause for grave concern. In the light of this survey, the analysis in the remainder of this chapter focuses on the global position, role and development prospects of SSA.

Table 2.8: Human Development Index and GNP per capita (Selected SSA Countries)

HDI rank		Real GDP per capita (PPP$)† 1990	Adjusted Real GDP per capita	Human Development Index 1990	GNP per capita rank minus HDI rank*
Medium human development					
56	Mauritius	5,750	4,890	0.794	12
63	Seychelles	4,191	4,191	0.761	−24
85	South Africa	4,865	4,841	0.673	−28
104	Botswana	3,419	3,419	0.552	−35
109	Gabon	4,147	4,147	0.503	−65
Low human development					
114	Cape Verde	1,769	1,769	0.479	2
117	Swaziland	2,384	2,384	0.458	−18
120	Lesotho	1,743	1,743	0.431	3
121	Zimbabwe	1,484	1,484	0.398	−4
126	Congo	2,362	2,362	0.372	−26
127	Kenya	1,058	1,058	0.369	17
130	Zambia	744	744	0.314	4
131	Ghana	1,016	1,016	0.311	9
136	Côte d'Ivoire	1,324	1,324	0.286	−23
138	Tanzania Rep.	572	572	0.270	34
140	Zaïre	367	367	0.262	18
142	Nigeria	1,215	1,215	0.246	11
145	Togo	734	734	0.218	−10
153	Malawi	640	640	0.168	9
156	Central African Rep.	768	768	0.159	−17
157	Mozambique	1,072	1,072	0.154	16
160	Angola	840	840	0.143	−34
164	Guinea–Bissau	841	841	0.090	1
166	Somalia	836	836	0.087	5
168	Mali	572	572	0.082	−14
169	Niger	645	645	0.080	−19
170	Burkina Faso	618	618	0.074	−21
172	Sierra Leone	1,086	1,086	0.065	−17
173	Guinea	501	501	0.045	−41

Notes:
†PPP$ = Purchasing Power Parity $.
* A positive figure shows that the HDI rank is higher than the GNP rank, a negative the opposite.
Source: UNDP (1993) *Human Development Report 1993*.

Critical Geopolitics and the Changing World Order

Under this rubric we need to consider three sets of issues. The first can be dealt with very briefly in order to avoid repeating material covered above.

The Legacy of Structural Adjustment and Economic Recovery Programmes

These have proved economically and politically costly to regimes implementing them, despite some modest improvements in economic stability and economic efficiency, on account of their regressive impact, especially on the urban and rural poor and women. Environmental pressures have also been exacerbated.

The programmes have proved difficult to sustain for both economic and political reasons. A number of governments broke off negotiations with the IMF prior to the conclusion of an agreement. Many others have fallen behind, thus jeopardising the release of further tranches of structural adjustment lending. Resentment at the burden has weakened or contributed to the demise of several regimes when the political cost became too high, especially where democratisation has occurred to some extent (Gibbon *et al.*, 1992). The marked contrast in the treatment received by Kenya and Uganda from donors is relevant here, illustrating well the selectivity of donor aid referred to earlier. Whereas Kenya suffered a moratorium on aid disbursements pending evidence of compliance with economic and political conditionalities, the Ugandan government was allowed to pursue its own agenda to a far larger extent, ostensibly in view of the need to avoid destabilising the country in the wake of its troubled recent history (Dowden, 1993).

The Anatomy of the Post-Cold War 'New World Order'

The demise of (state) socialism in both the Second and Third Worlds since 1988 has left advanced capitalism unchallenged as the dominant mode of production and development model. This has also accelerated and broadened the process begun under structural adjustment conditionalities, of rolling back the state almost everywhere by reducing its direct and indirect economic involvement (Simon, 1995). Especially in SSA, this has meant the virtual end of the developmental state form, irrespective of the state ideology previously followed. However, as Dixon points out in Chapter 11, the same is not true of Pacific Asia.

The new official western discourse of 'good governance' and imposition of progressively greater political conditionality in addition to economic conditionality for the disbursement of ODA, has tended to focus attention on external agendas and pressures for 'democracy'. The particular manifestations of it being demanded amount to little more than a replication of western liberal democratic institutions and procedures, and have thus rightly been criticised as both too limited and at least partly inappropriate. This point will be developed in the next section. Nevertheless, it is important to acknowledge the long and often dangerous struggles for human rights and democratisation within African states. Foreign donor governments have often sought to assist them by using the leverage which foreign assistance gives them. However, the objective has not always been achieved because of inappropriate actions, inadequate sensitivity to the needs and demands of the internal opposition, or the dictates of different internal and external agendas. It must also be said that foreign donors have often supported far from democratic regimes in the past.

Is There a New Global Hegemony of Power and Discourse?

This raises the fundamental question of whether and to what extent the concern with democratisation on the part of the US and other western donors is genuine and deepseated. This will depend on the yardstick. The evolution of and adherence to western-style institutions and procedures – the essence of 'good governance' – is at best a very limited definition of democratisation.

Domestic struggles within SSA have often sought more lasting transformations of the structures of politico-economic inequality, poverty and underdevelopment. A more appropriate yardstick would therefore be whether empowerment of the poor, as a central tenet of democratisation and more balanced development, forms part of this new discourse and agenda for action. The answer would be negative in many cases, as this would conflict with the ultimate objective of a global free trade regime, as seen most recently in the frenzied climax to the GATT Uruguay Round in December 1993, which sought to secure such an objective. Amid the forecasts of doom if the deal were not to be concluded and the subsequent western euphoria when it was, the fact that the industrialised countries would gain disproportionately, and that the poorest countries would probably be worse off, was obscured or forgotten. This has been substantiated by recent calculations suggesting that, whereas other regions would benefit, SSA (and especially the Nigerian and South African economies) would suffer on account of the removal of tariff barriers on foreign imports competing with basic industries which are vital to the continent's manufacturing sector (*Africa South and East*, 1994).

External forces and processes may thus not be conducive to the struggle against poverty and for transformation in SSA. On the contrary, they may well prove disruptive and contradictory in the ways that they interact with domestic forces and processes. Alternative discourses articulated by the United Nations Economic Commission for Africa (UNECA), Organisation of African Unity (OAU), opposition political parties, other elements in 'civil society' (such as community-based organisations (CBOs)), new social movements and progressive academics have often been ignored, bypassed or undermined where they do not correspond to the agenda of foreign donors (e.g. Buijtenhuijs and

Rijnierse, 1993; Cornia *et al.*, 1992; Fowler, 1991, 1992; Harbeson and Rothchild (eds), 1991; Morss, 1991; Stewart, 1991; Stewart *et al.*, 1992; UNECA, 1989).

Although new windows of political and economic opportunity and spaces for grassroots social action are clearly being opened through the process of struggle, the continuing dramas still being played out in Cameroon, Kenya, Togo and Zaïre, for example, remind us that authoritarian regimes and kleptocracies generally cling to power at all costs. The future in South Africa seems far more promising since the ultimate success of the elections in April 1994 and the peaceful takeover by the ANC-led Government of National Unity, although a modest level of political violence continues. Namibia's record since independence provides one of the brightest examples on the continent, but even here, despite progress in health and education, there has been little tangible restructuring in favour of the previously disempowered and the poor. This symbolises the long-term nature of the structural challenges facing governments in SSA, although popular aspirations and external conditionalities often demand rapid results. Even when undertaken by governments enjoying newfound legitimacy, national strategies of development, adjustment and reconstruction commonly face internal opposition from those who perceive their interests to be adversely affected. However, where the very legitimacy of the state and/or its territorial limits is contested, the problems and conflicts engendered may be even more intense, precipitating repression and even violence rather than (or in parallel with) political and economic liberalisation. These dilemmas are well illustrated by the current or recent conflicts of varying intensity in regions as diverse as Cassamance in Senegal, northern Ghana, Nigeria, Rwanda, Burundi and Lesotho.

Overall, many progressive analysts find little cause for optimism. To wit, in their editorial in a recent issue of the *Review of African Political Economy*, provocatively entitled 'Surviving democracy?', Allen *et al.* (1992, p. 3) remind us that:

> The issue [of democratic struggle] has been of concern to African scholars in particular for well over a decade ... and has been linked by them to questions of development, class, human rights and security ... Mainstream contemporary interest in democratisation, however, has tended to diverge from such themes, rooted as it is in a process marked by the development of multiparty systems and liberal institutions, the influence of external actors and the role of civil society. Parallels with processes in eastern Europe have imported into the African debate aspects of anti-communism and post-Cold War triumphalism, as well as an indifference to the growing power of 'donors' in African political change and to the limitations of the present democratisation process.

Conclusions and Prospects for Democracy and Development

The adherents of neo-classical economics have consistently sought to perpetuate the fiction that the economic and political spheres of policy and action are somehow separate. Notions of political economy, so central to analysts in the Marxist tradition, have been branded as conspiratorial, perverse and worse. Ironically, however, the imposition by the international financial institutions (most conspicuously the IMF, World Bank and major western donors) of economic and more recently also political conditionalities on aid and budgetary support programmes have provided irrefutable evidence that they too deploy political economy in both theory and praxis.

This is not to suggest that previous policies by African governments were always appropriate or that radical remedial action was unnecessary. The central problems lie with the nature of the treatment and its method of administration. Structural adjustment policies have been extremely blunt tools, pressed in a blueprint fashion upon countries with widely differing characteristics and potentials, and imposing severe and widespread hardship, often on the weakest segments of society. While some measures, e.g. increasing agricultural producer prices and/or liberalising marketing procedures, have had beneficial effects on many peasants and small farmers, other measures have frequently undermined such gains. The price of adjustment has also been high in aggregate terms, with SSA's debt burden increasing during the 1980s to reach crippling proportions, given the prevailing economic structures and conditions (commodity prices, terms of trade, protectionism and institutional constraints) on the continent. On the other hand, external economic and political conditionalities – and the impact of structural adjustment policies – frequently amplified internal opposition to authoritarian regimes and thereby hastened moves towards democratisation which have now occurred almost continent wide.

Future Prospects

So what of the future for SSA as we enter the mid-1990s? Aid has arguably been deployed more effectively than in the past but alone is inadequate in terms both of scale and effect. Interregional competition for ODA is unprecedented – thus increasing the effective leverage exercised by donors through political conditionality. Unofficial aid through NGOs grew rapidly during the 1980s but is still equivalent to only about 6 per cent of ODA and may have peaked in the late 1980s.

One of the principal incentives proffered under the terms of structural adjustment and associated policies was the prospect of renewed private FDI once economic and political life had been liberalised. However, little new private money has arrived from abroad and structural adjustment can at best be regarded as a necessary but insufficient condition for renewed investor interest. The harsh reality is that SSA has, for some years, been far less attractive to FDI than Pacific Asia or central and eastern Europe. This is unlikely to change dramatically in the foreseeable future and most TNCs perceive no great role for SSA in their global investment portfolios. However, on the basis of recent evidence, use of joint ventures and turnkey arrangements, coupled with novel forms of FDI (franchising, leasebacks etc.) which reduce both investor risk and the extent of foreign ownership are likely to increase. The precise distribution of benefits will then depend on the details of individual contracts.

The pervasive economic plight of a large proportion of each country's population and the relative powerlessness of most governments will undermine any regime unable 'to deliver' and to meet at least some of the expectations raised by economic sacrifice and state concessions on democratisation, no matter how hard-won these have been.

Equally, the removal of authoritarian and/or corrupt regimes is welcome and a necessary but insufficient condition for democratisation and accountability. There are many relevant precedents, perhaps most conspicuously the Provisional National Defence Council (PNDC) of Jerry Rawlings in Ghana (Yeebo, 1991). Western notions and institutions of democracy, focusing on multiparty politics with regular elections at central, regional and/or local government level are narrow and limited (although potentially permissive). However, they are being promoted by western governments and international institutions in simplistic blueprint fashion, rather like structural adjustment policies. Neither by design nor by default do they take account of the diverse socio-political conditions across the countries of SSA.

Furthermore, implementation of these proposals or demands does not necessarily transform the status quo at either the macro or micro levels, as seems implicit in the new official discourse. The holding of multiparty elections and the presence of opposition parties in parliament do not necessarily lead to real participatory democracy at any or all levels. Such changes do not even guarantee a greater role for NGOs and CBOs or for civil society generally. Indeed, the effect might be to pre-empt such a role. The ability of wily autocrats to manipulate procedures and outcomes for their own ends has been clearly demonstrated in a number of African countries, in many of which civil society is often organised in ways very different from the western norm, but nevertheless commonly remains weak.

In economic terms adjustment and stabilisation policies are sometimes accelerating deregulation and privatisation in socially sub-optimal ways, e.g. through asset stripping and/or with direct sale or mortgaging (through debt–equity swaps) to TNCs or other external actors, especially if aid resources are subject to political as well as economic conditionality. Whereas moves to introduce some genuine worker participation and control, e.g. through shareholdings, would be a progressive reform, the loss of domestic sovereignty and economic leverage involved in debt swaps could easily be regressive.

Nevertheless, we should recognise that the adjustment and stabilisation policies advocated by the international financial institutions (IFIs) *may*, under the right conditions, promote greater community control over some local environments and environmental resources. This would be a significant form of empowerment (and a route to achieving the objectives of poverty reduction and the promotion of environmental sustainability set at the United Nations Conference on Environment and Development (UNCED) in Rio de Janeiro in June 1992).

Ultimately the policies of global institutions (still overwhelmingly located in the north) are still determined by, and primarily in the interests of, the major northern governments, especially the US – which is now unchallenged as the hegemonic superpower, although Japanese economic power continues to expand globally. The basic objectives of the 'new world order' are to modernise and reform but not to transform the world system. Genuine empowerment of the poor – in most of SSA and beyond – would threaten this in the short to medium term and is thus unlikely. Equally, there is little ground for optimism that a marked improvement in SSA's economic prospects is likely in the foreseeable future and could therefore provide the route to empowerment for most of the powerless. Indeed, despite (and in certain respects also *because of*) the economically and politically costly pursuit of structural adjustment policies by most SSA governments, the continent's overall poverty and global peripherality have increased during the 1980s and early 1990s.

Obviously, there is some diversity of conditions and there have been differing policy responses across the 45-odd countries of SSA. Moreover, there are methodological difficulties in isolating the impact of specific policies and, as Husain (1993) reminds us with respect to the contrasting recent experiences of Ghana and Zambia, the terms of trade for key primary export commodities can fluctuate significantly, thus compounding or masking the impact of state policy. However, in most countries, the conventional diagnosis and structural adjustment medicine have not worked, and there is increasing evidence that they can and/or will not work as envisaged on account of several embedded weaknesses and contradictions. No real evidence of widespread economic recovery is yet available, and a combination of endogenous and exogenous factors can explain the relative performance of African countries over recent years (Mosley and Weeks, 1993). SSA requires a different remedy, an alternative approach to development aimed at enhancing its autonomy and vitality, utilising its vast resource base sustainably and for Africans in the first instance, and conserving its environment in the process. In sum, participatory *human* development should form the central focus.

Importantly, alternative discourses *are* being actively promoted by influential African institutions (OAU, UNECA) and researchers, not just by outsiders *for* Africa. The necessary elements of such a framework are now emerging increasingly clearly (Cornia *et al.*, 1992, pp. 159–90; Logan and Mengisteab, 1993; Maganya, 1990; Nyang'oro and Shaw, 1992; Onimode, 1990; South Commission, 1990; Stewart, 1991; Stewart *et al.*, 1992; UNECA, 1989). In addition to the need for widespread acceptance and participation, the principal features required to give structural adjustment a human face have been summarised by the proponents of that approach as:

- First, long-term concerns for institutional change, income redistribution and broad-based, employment-intensive growth ... and the short- to medium-term emphasis of 'adjustment with the human face' for a non-deflationary and equitable approach to macro-economic stabilisation.

- Second, a neo-structuralist emphasis on structural changes (particularly the modernisation of the food-crop sector and the widening of the manufacturing base) without which balanced growth and long-term balance-of-payments stabilisation cannot be achieved.
- Third, the now widely accepted need for greater export substitution and regional import substitution. (Cornia *et al.*, p. 164)

Such an agenda involves a substantial reorientation of focus and objectives, geared to enhancing Africa's increasingly peripheral and poverty-ridden position and role within the world system. Greater autonomy is clearly vital, but autarchy has been shown to be an unviable strategy. A large measure of delinking from the world economy as advocated by Mahjoub (1990b) seems misplaced in the light of experience with autarchic experiments in the 1970s, when conditions were arguably more favourable, however appealing it might be theoretically. Equally, no simple policy changes, such as export substitution, are free of drawbacks or can guarantee dramatically better results *per se*.

Obviously, conditions and the precise policies necessary to effect changes such as those outlined above do and should vary between countries in a continent as diverse as SSA. However, at a general level, appropriate policies and changes can readily be identified (Adedeji *et al.*, 1991; Cornia *et al.*, 1992, p. 417; UNECA, 1989). Hopefully, such strategies will gain greater credence and acceptability under more popularly responsive democratic regimes, although current prospects are not particularly encouraging.

References

Adedeji, A., Teriba, O. and Bugembe, P. (eds) (1991) *The Challenge of African Economic Recovery and Development*. Cass, London.

Africa Confidential fortnightly. London.

Africa South and East (1994) no. 38, February. Johannesburg.

Allen, C., Baylies, C. and Szeftel, M. (1992) 'Surviving democracy?' *Review of African Political Economy*, no. 54, pp. 3–10.

Avramovic, D. (1991) 'Africa's debts and economic recovery'. *African Development Review*, 3, 2. Special issue on North–South roundtable on African debt, recovery and democracy, pp. 41–64.

Barratt Brown, M. and Tiffin, P. (1992) *Short Changed: Africa and World Trade*. Pluto, London.

Bennell, P. (1990) 'British industrial investment in sub-Saharan Africa: corporate responses to economic crisis in the 1980s'. *Development Policy Review*, 8, 2, pp. 155–77.

Buijtenhuijs, R. and Rijnierse, E. (1993) *Democratization in Sub-Saharan Africa 1989-1992: An Overview of the Literature*. African Studies Centre, Leiden.

Chirwa, C.L. (1991) 'Africa's bilateral debt'. *African Development Review*, 3, 2. Special issue on North–South roundtable on African debt, recovery and democracy, pp. 149–54.

Conway, P. and Greene, J. (1993) 'Is Africa different?' *World Development*, 21, 12, pp. 2017–28.

Corbridge, S. (1993) *Debt and Development*. Blackwell, Oxford.

Cornia, G.A., van der Hoeven, R., and Mkandawire, T. (eds) (1992) *Africa's Recovery in the 1990s: From Stagnation and Adjustment to Human Development*. Macmillan, London.

Dowden, R. (1993) 'Uganda slips through West's democracy net'. *Independent*, 27 March. London.

Economist Publications (1990) *How to Win in Emerging Stock Markets: Profitable Investment Strategies for the 1990s*. Special Report 1201, Economist Publications, London.

Economist, The (1993) 328, 7830, 25 September. London.

Fowler, A. (1991) 'The role of NGOs in changing state–society relations: perspectives from eastern and southern Africa'. *Development Policy Review*, 9, 1, pp. 53–84.

Fowler, A. (1992) 'Distant obligations: speculations on NGO funding and the global market'. *Review of African Political Economy* no. 55, pp. 9–29.

George, S. (1988) *A Fate Worse Than Debt*. Penguin, London.

George, S. (1992) *The Debt Boomerang: How Third World Debt Harms Us All*. Pluto, London.

Gibbon, P., Bangura, Y. and Ofstad, A. (eds)(1992) *Authoritarianism, Democracy and Adjustment: The Politics of Economic Reform in Africa*. Seminar Proceedings 26, Scandinavian Institute of African Studies, Uppsala.

Harbeson, J. and Rothchild, D. (eds) (1991) *Africa in World Politics*. Westview, Boulder and Oxford.

Helleiner, G.K. (1992) 'The IMF, the World Bank and Africa's adjustment and external debt problems: an unofficial view'. *World Development*, 20, 6, pp. 779–92.

Hoogvelt, A., Phillips, D. and Taylor, P. (1992) 'The World Bank and Africa: a case of mistaken identity'. *Review of African Political Economy* no. 54, pp. 92–6.

Husain, I. (1993) 'A comment on "The IMF, the World Bank and Africa's adjustment and external debt problems: an unofficial view"'. *World Development*, 21, 12, pp. 2055–8.

Husain, I. and Underwood, J. (1991) 'The debt of Sub-Saharan Africa: problems and solutions'. *African Development Review*, 3, 2. Special issue on North-South roundtable on African debt, recovery and democracy, pp. 65–98.

Jespersen, E. (1992) 'External shocks, adjustment policies and economic and social performance'. In G. Cornia, R. van der Hoeven and T. Mkandawire (eds) *Africa's Recovery in the 1990s*. Macmillan, London.

Kelley, A.C. (1991) 'The Human Development Index: handle with care'. *Population and Development Review*, 17, 2, pp. 371–24.

Killick, T. (1991) *Problems and Limitations of Adjustment Policies*. London: Overseas Development Institute, Working Paper 36.

Krueger, A.O. (1987) 'Origins of the developing countries' debt crisis 1970 to 1982'. *Journal of Development Economics*, 27, 1/2, pp. 165–87.

Logan, I.B. and Mengisteab, K. (1993) 'IMF–World Bank adjustment and structural transformation in sub-Saharan Africa'. *Economic Geography*, 69, 1, pp. 1–24.

Maganya, E.N. (1990) 'The African debt crisis: which way out?' In B. Onimode *et al.*, *Alternative Development Strategies for Africa, Vol. 1: Coalition for Change*. Institute for African Alternatives, London.

Mahjoub, A. (ed.) (1990a) *Adjustment or Delinking? The African Experience*. Zed, London, and United Nations University, Tokyo.

Mahjoub, A. (1990b) 'Structural adjustment or delinking: the question posed'. In A. Mahjoub (ed.) *Adjustment or Delinking? The African Experience*. Zed, London, and United Nations University, Tokyo.

McGillivray, M. and White, H. (1993) 'Measuring development? The UNDP's Human Development Index', *Journal of International Development*, 5, 2, pp. 183–92.

Mistry, P.S. (1991) 'African debt revisited: procrastination or progress?' *African Development Review*, 3, 2. Special issue on North–South roundtable on African debt, recovery and democracy, pp. 99–148.

Morss, E. (1991) 'The new global players: how they compete and collaborate'. *World Development*, 19, 1, pp. 55–64.

Mosley, P., Harrigan, J. and Toye, J. (1991) *Aid and Power: the World Bank and Policy Based Lending* (2 vols). Routledge, London.

Mosley, P. and Weeks, J. (1993) 'Has recovery begun? "Africa's adjustment in the 1980s" revisited'. *World Development*, 21, 10, pp. 1583–1605.

Nyang'oro, J.E. and Shaw, T.M. (eds) (1992) *Beyond Structural Adjustment in Africa: The Political Economy of Sustainable and Democratic Development*. Praeger, New York.

O'Connor, A. (1991) *Poverty in Africa: a Geographical Perspective*. Belhaven, London.

Okogu, B.E. (1992) *Africa and Economic Structural Adjustment: Case Studies of Ghana, Nigeria and Zambia*. Pamphlet series 29, Organization of Petroleum Exporting Countries Fund for International Development, Vienna.

Onimode, B. (1988) *A Political Economy of the African Crisis*. Zed, London.

Onimode, B. (ed.) (1989) *The IMF, the World Bank and the African Debt* (2 vols). Zed, London.

Onimode, B. (1990) 'Alternatives to World Bank and IMF programmes'. In B. Onimode *et al.*, *Alternative Development Strategies for Africa, Vol. 1: Coalition for Change*. Institute for African Alternatives, London.

Organization for Economic Co-operation and Development (1992) *Geographical Distribution of Financial Flows to Developing Countries: Disbursements, Commitments, Economic Indicators, 1987/1990*. Paris.

Overseas Development Institute/Save the Children Fund (1988) *Prospects for Africa*. Hodder & Stoughton, London.

Reed, D. (ed.) (1992) *Structural Adjustment and the Environment*. Earthscan, London.

Review of African Political Economy (1992) Special issue: Surviving democracy, no. 54 (July).

Riddell, R. (1992) *Losing the 90s: Another Declining Decade for African Development*. Briefing Paper, Catholic Institute for International Relations, London.

Schatan, J. (1987) *World Debt: Who is to Pay?* Zed, London.

Simon, D. (1992) *Cities, Capital and Development; African Cities in the World Economy*. Belhaven, London.

Simon, D. (1995) 'The demise of "socialist" state forms in Africa: an overview'. *Journal of International Development*, 7, 2 (in press).

South Commission (1990) *The Challenge to the South: The Report of the South Commission*. Oxford University Press, New York.

Stewart, F. (1991) 'Are adjustment policies in Africa consistent with long-run development needs?' *Development Policy Review*, 9, 4, pp. 413–36.

Stewart, F., Lall, S. and Wangwe, S. (eds) (1992) *Alternative Development Strategies in Sub-Sarahan Africa*. Macmillan, London.

United Nations Development Programme (1992) *Human Development Report 1992*. Oxford University Press, New York and Oxford.

United Nations Development Programme (1993) *Human Development Report 1993*. Oxford University Press, New York and Oxford.

United Nations Economic Commission for Africa (1989) *African Alternative Framework to Structural Adjustment Programmes for Socio-economic Recovery and Transformation*. Addis Ababa.

Woodward, D. (1992) *Debt, Adjustment and Poverty in Developing Countries* (2 vols). Belhaven, London.

World Bank (1981) *Accelerated Development in Sub-Saharan Africa: An Agenda for Action*. Washington, DC.

World Bank (1989) *Sub-Saharan Africa: From Crisis to Sustainable Growth*. Washington, DC.

World Bank (1990) *World Development Report 1990*. Oxford University Press, New York and Oxford.

World Bank (1992) *World Development Report 1992*. Oxford University Press, New York and Oxford.

Yeebo, Z. (1991) *Ghana: The Struggle for Popular Power*. New Beacon, London.

CHAPTER 3

Fighting Fire with Petrol: How to Counter Social Ills in Africa with Economic Structural Adjustment

Anders Närman

Perspectives on Structural Adjustment

For Africa, the last decade has been characterised by an ever-deepening crisis. If we look at the economic, social, environmental and political conditions, all trends seem to demonstrate a deterioration. A complex reality is also driving us into some kind of theoretical crisis on development thinking as a whole. Researchers are somehow becoming confused over the question of what are the causes and what are the effects in a perpetual process of underdevelopment, and whether structural adjustment will bring any relief.

Only economists seem to have a clear picture of what to do in the present situation. Following on the traditions of Smith and Ricardo, they argue that the panacea is to be found in a world of free markets and free trade. According to the Harrod and Domar model development, or at least economic growth, can be seen as a function of investment. The Keynesian necessity of growth is still stressed in neo-classical economics: a world of endless resources was envisaged by Rostow in his stages of growth. Within this same culture of economics, the high priests of development strategies push for structural adjustment programmes (SAPs). Efficiency, privatisation, trade liberalisation and monetary reforms are the buzz-words translated into policies. With the arrogance of the almighty, any criticism is brushed aside due to the alleged lack of alternatives.

It is high time to try to oppose the tools with which the economists seem virtually to control global development thinking. After all, what are their theories worth in a real-world situation? Can we trust that some kind of 'invisible hand' will come to sort out the present inequalities, which lie at the core of under-development? In light of the knowledge that no development is taking place, especially not involving the most disadvantaged strata of the world's population, we must try to find out why. This is especially important for the people suffering

45

most from the effect of present economic policies. The following observations about the Kenyan situation are apposite:

> The current turmoil in the country's monetary sector and the upward spiral of prices has in some way something to do with the matter of the government's relations with donors. The public has a right to know what is the basis of these relations and what the nation is being asked to do by donors. Though economic experts may have a technical answer as to what needs to be done to get the country out of its present economic crisis, itself not a very reasonable supposition, it is the people of this country who will swallow any prescriptions the economists, Kenyan or foreign, are writing out. The people have a right to know what those prescriptions are. (*Weekly Review*, 19 March 1993)

However, to these economic advisers it seems that economic growth takes clear precedence over development, and from that perspective the only way forward is to accept the global rules of the game. An easy way out for policy makers is to pretend that economic growth and development are actually, by definition, nothing but two sides of the same coin. Thereby globalisation is: 'a reality which countries wishing to move into the fast lane of rapid growth and development can no longer ignore' (Hawkins, 1993, p. 39).

As a prerequisite to becoming active players on the stage of the global market, all African countries have to accept some kind of economic structural adjustment. However, an obvious question must be why it is necessary to be in the highest league before being ready to play, and not even playing the same game. Is it not basically part of a hidden agenda, so that we can satisfy the needs for cheap raw materials in the North? Against this it is claimed that we in the rich world have no great demand for products from Africa. However, Africa's marginalisation within world trade owes more to the fact that we are paying only a pittance for its products, rather than a lack of need for them. Imagine that African farmers or farm-workers were to be paid for their real productive work in the same manner as a Swedish worker – the price of a kilo of coffee, for example, would increase to some US$200–300. What is it in the international economic structure that prevents the Africans from negotiating a deal that will close the gap of paying the true cost of productive work instead of widening it?

With most African countries having a similar pattern of cash-crop agricultural production, the price for what is sold is constantly falling. At the same time the continent, or at least some countries, will have to continue depleting its mineral and fuel resources to be able to earn foreign exchange. This has been expressed in a very precise manner by a Zimbabwean minister, Fay Chung (1990, p. 27):

> The economic rules of the game are determined by the international division of labour. In terms of these rules, manufactures are produced in the industrialised countries whilst raw materials are supplied by the poorer countries. The prices of raw materials have fallen whilst generally the cost of manufactures have risen.

To believe that Africa can export itself out of the crisis is rather optimistic, especially if this is to be based on the production of commodities from manufacturing industries. Two decades ago, Nyerere (1973, p. 116) warned about Africa venturing into some kind of capitalist industrial development: 'First, where in our lands are those citizens who have sufficient capital to establish modern industries; and second, how would our infant industries fight other capitalist enterprises?' Because of this, Nyerere argued for an alternative path through socialist development, based on African ideals. Any other strategy chosen would only lead to a continued outside dependence. To this day there is nothing to show that the Tanzanian leader was wrong in his analysis. Manufacturing industries are still contributing only a fraction of Africa's aggregate GDP in the early 1990s. To expect radical progress in this respect from the SAPs can be nothing but a dream (or worse, a con trick played by the rich on the poor).

If we compare the gross national products it can be noted that, for 1990, fewer than nine million Swedes produced commodities and services measured at a market value of 30–40 per cent higher than 500 million Africans. Either we in Sweden must have an enormous productive capacity or there is something wrong in this kind of a calculation. Only some five years earlier, the aggregate African GNP was almost double that of Sweden.

In addition to this it has been claimed that Africa's urban population, comprising only 20–25 per cent of the continent's total population, is generating 80 per cent of the aggregated national income. Does this mean that the hard-working rural woman is a myth, as her production is insignificant compared to that of the urban civil servant, as measured in economic terms? If so it would be absurd to cut down on the bureaucracy, as this is obviously an extremely productive sector of the economy. African economic growth at the end of the 1980s was characterised by a substantial downswing. For the period 1965 to 1990 the annual per capita growth was as low as 0.2 per cent, which came down to a negative 1.2 per cent annually during the 1980s.

As the colonial period is now long gone, other means are utilised to keep up the prevailing dependency structures. Most important here is the debt relationship. Sub-Saharan Africa (SSA) had, up to the early 1990s, accumulated a total official debt of close to US$200 billion. According to various sources the debt servicing at the same time was to be somewhere between 20–25 per cent of the total exports of goods and services. Considering the fact that – as Simon showed in Chapter 2 – the total debt is more than three times the value of total exports and in excess of SSA's aggregate GNP, it is impossible to imagine repayment of this money. As long as this debt is accepted by the global community there is no way that we can expect African nations to achieve anything close to a sound economic balance. Therefore, to believe in such a development as a result of SAPs can be nothing but window-dressing. Furthermore, it is doubtful how we in the North will ever be able to justify this kind of debt from a moral standpoint. Africa has been systematically exploited for more than four centuries, and still any claim for compensation is met with a cold shoulder. This point was made by Professor Ali Mazrui during an African Association of Political Science (AAPS) seminar in Harare on 1 February 1993.

If the African people have been able to accumulate these enormous debts, which have more than trebled in the 1980s, we could assume some kind of development as a result. All empirical evidence, however, points towards another reality. Debt has been generated from an intercourse between the North and the local elites maintaining a structure of dependence. Often the money borrowed has been used for grandiose large-scale projects (with little benefit for the poor in the society), militarisation, or even outright kleptocracy among a corrupt leadership (Raikes, 1988, pp. 36–40). It is pathetic to see how the former mentors of the masterly ruler Mobuto of Zaïre are now blocking 'his' assets held in parts of Europe.

In 1990 Tanzania was able to pay back interest and reimbursements of some 8 per cent of its total debt. How many years would it take for this country to pay back all of its loans, even if it did not take out any new ones? A country with a more diversified economy, such as Kenya, was paying less than 20 per cent in the same year. Compared to their annual exports, Tanzania and Kenya paid back 26 and 34 per cent respectively. For both countries, a substantial share of the export earnings was generated from agricultural production, while essential foodstuffs and agricultural inputs had to be imported simultaneously. Where are the long-term economic development trends, or the demand for sustainability in this?

Realising that the Africans will never be able to pay back the alleged debts, it would be natural to write them all off, were they not badly needed for strategic economic reasons. To maintain the charade of altruism, the OECD countries have built up a system of global social welfare. Like similar national approaches, this will primarily create passive receivers. Still, at an early stage, development assistance was to be regarded as some kind of push to initiate a process of self-help: 'A keynote of aid policy should be the achievement of long-term and self-sustaining development' (Pearson, 1969, p. 124).

Unfortunately the overall effect of development assistance is often counter-productive and Africa is somehow forced into a situation of enormous aid dependence. In the long run it will be as difficult to get out of this as it is to be rid of the debt burden. It is something of an irony that Tanzania, with a clear vision of self-reliance, became one of the countries most squeezed in the trap of aid dependence, with development assistance in 1990 roughly half the level of GNP. Five years previously it was standing at only 8 per cent. A similar trend, if not of the same dimension, can be found all over SSA.

At independence Zimbabwe was brought in as one of the new project aid countries of Sweden with the stated objective of alleviating some initial barriers in the development process. However, after more than a decade this aid relationship seems to have become permanent. At the same time Zimbabwe has been sliding down to take its place among what are classified as low-income countries. Is this in spite of, or because of, the international 'help' received? In the same geographical region is Botswana, a country with enormous economic growth over the last 15–20 years. With this in mind, it is an absurdity that Botswana actually includes aid funds in its development plans. Regrettably, in a few years time this might be justified, as even this country is expecting to reach a stage of zero growth in the not very distant future.

From a possibly sincere desire to help some three to four decades ago, present development assistance can be seen in a much more doubtful light: 'the international aid process became a seething pot-pourri of humanitarianism, commercial self-interest, strategic calculation and bad conscience – a perfect recipe for all the contradictions, confusions and pathological disorders with which aid-giving is afflicted to this day' (Hancock, 1989, p. 72).

Maybe it is time to realise that traditional development norms might not be the same in the North and the South, except among the elite with whom we co-operate, and who also constitute an image of success for the poor to live up to. However, this illusive modernisation can never be part of a sustainable development process. In this context it is necessary to find a new model of development, built on the traditional community and the downgraded concept of self-reliance. It is basically to us in the North that the actual application of a more self-reliant style of government in Africa represents a threat. Self-reliance is not an impossible strategy on its own account, but only so from the point of view of dependence, which it was supposed to overcome. As commented, rather belatedly, by one of the prime proponents of the *dependencia* school, A.G. Frank (1991, p. 25), the Third World 'cannot escape dependence'. However, it is only by accepting that this kind of determinism is ruling the global structures that nothing can be done about it.

One crucial issue related to the SAPs is the severe social consequences, such as deterioration in educational standards and a growing unemployment. This might not only be an indicator of the crisis, but also in itself a cause of the same. In most discussions related to the South East Asian miracle (see Chapter 11), it is noted that the strategic lessons to be drawn from this are unclear, apart from the acute need to improve on education and institution-building. What if it is the neglect of educational achievements that lies at the very core of the underdevelopment process? Human capital is an essential requirement not only for a modernised process, but also to recreate the human resources for mobilisation towards a common goal. Still it is found that:

In most countries, despite economic improvements in a few areas, there has been a decline in the extent and quality of education and health care, and the formal sector employment has fallen, sometimes drastically. Much of the blame rests with the economic crises that preceded structural adjustments, but clearly the adjustment measures themselves contributed significantly to this decline. (Adepoju, 1993, p. 6)

Let us look at what has happened to the two interlinked factors of education and the labour market, and to what extent another approach can contribute to an alternative development.

Education

During their formative years, many of the former colonies were squeezed between the popular internal demand for 'education for all' and a multitude of often contradictory advice from a donor community. A substantial share of the national budgets has been allocated to live up to high expectations. Often education was to take second place in government spending, behind the military and security forces. At the end of the 1980s the average share of public expenditure on education in SSA was some 18 per cent. In addition to this, the direct community contribution to the educational structure has been substantial. In Addis Ababa in 1961 the common objective of Universal Primary Education was decided upon, a target to be reached in 1980.

In a very short period of time many African countries greatly expanded primary school enrolment. Within one or two decades many countries were noted for a statistical intake well above 100 per cent in relation to relevant ages, indicating a substantial number of over- and under-aged children in school, coupled with repetition. Even with a calculation of 100 per cent enrolment, this does not mean that educational facilities have been equally distributed among the people. Economically-disadvantaged regions, such as those inhabited by pastoralist people, have normally been found to have an average far below the national total (Närman, 1990). Furthermore, in most countries the proportion of girls undergoing schooling is considerably lower than that of boys.

Looking at the growth in retrospect, we can ask what has actually been achieved. For SSA primary school enrolment was only 69 per cent in 1989. However, if we take the anomalies included in this figure into account the net enrolment is below half (47 per cent). Thus the objective of basic schooling for all is an unfulfilled dream. The situation at the secondary level is even more gloomy, with an enrolment of less than 20 per cent in 1989. Here Zimbabwe stands out with above 50 per cent, while Tanzania achieved a paltry 4 per cent. Expressed in another way, some 80 million children are currently not absorbed into the school system. Furthermore, less than two-thirds are actually able to complete primary schooling. At the same time it has been estimated that, out of the total adult population in SSA, some 110–120 million people are illiterate. A substantial majority of these are females.

SAPs might not directly include education as such, even if a World Bank (1988) policy paper on SSA education pointed in that direction. Combined direct and indirect quantitative effects of the programmes are distinctly negative. Newly reintroduced school fees and increased costs for school uniforms, books etc. (so-called 'cost sharing'), coupled with a general decrease in family income, will make it difficult for many to afford education for their children. During the early 1980s enrolment rates started to decline for the first time in a number of countries (Committee for Academic Freedom in Africa, 1992, pp. 51–2). The problems have been frequently commented on in the press, e.g. in the following headline: 'Nyanga school loses pupils due to high fees' (*Parade*, June 1992, p. 41), and the more general situation in Zimbabwe was recently described as follows:

> Educational provision has also suffered. Although government has suspended a planned increase in fees because of the difficulties associated with the drought a rise in costs of school books, uniforms, exam fees etc. has meant the removal of many children from school. Families are now being forced to choose between children as to who should receive education or not, claimed one headmaster who indicated that it was usually girls who suffered as a result. (*New African*, April 1993, p. 32)

Thus the already precarious situation for girls tends to be accentuated even more. Structural adjustment will perpetuate the glaring inequalities, whether expressed in gender relations or between regions, ethnic groups or classes.

From the time of independence, the objective of quantitative growth has grossly overshadowed the highly neglected concern for qualitative issues. To a large extent, the educational system promoted has been a poor replica of the western educational model. Few attempts are being made to question this philosophy in practical applications and in most cases the education offered is rather academic in character. Within secondary education, only a low proportion of pupils is selected for any kind of vocational stream. One pertinent question here would be why this is so, especially in view of the new demands on a manufacturing sector for export production as 'advised' within the SAPs. Does not that kind of development create a need for all kinds of skilled and semi-skilled craftsmen and technicians? Calculations from the World Bank on cost efficiency seem to be nothing but a smokescreen to cover up for vested interests. If Africa is to industrialise, the continent cannot forever be dependent on foreign experts and volunteers:

> many industries cannot expand due to a shortage of skills at the professional, technical and artisan levels. In the Government itself, shortage of skills hampered the implementation of projects which could generate substantial employment opportunities for both the skilled and the unskilled labour. One of the consequences of this imbalance is the importation of expensive expatriate personnel even in skills for which Kenya is well poised to produce. (Republic of Kenya, 1983, p. 12)

This kind of problem in Kenya was being experienced simultaneously with a gradual increase in unemployment among secondary-school-leavers (Närman, 1988). Another specific problem with school-leaver unemployment is that 'the education they receive divorces them from the rural setting, without preparing them adequately for urban living' (Grey-Johnson, 1990, p. 104).

On the drawing board have been numerous innovative ideas, either tried out only partially or not at all. Among the more indigenous African educational ideologies, it would be possible to find the impetus for a more genuine discussion on future policy options in the field. Many of the alternatives developed from Africa in actual fact constitute a serious challenge to the whole perception of development as it is identified in the North. In Tanzania the concept of Education for Self-reliance was introduced as a national policy by the then president, Nyerere, through which the virtues of community co-operation were to be emphasised. The new educational system opposed values and knowledge as not being part and parcel of Tanzanian socialist ambitions (Nyerere, 1967).

Education with production as developed for Botswana by Patrick van Rensburg (1982) is another example, which has inspired numerous experiments in alternative education all over Africa. Unfortunately in many cases the actual implication has moved far away from the original pedagogical advantages of the method, leaving it as nothing but a way of cost sharing. Initially, however, the productive element was supposed to change negative attitudes towards manual labour and the so-called Botswana Brigades were to form an integral part of local community development.

Instead of just branding various methods in African alternative education as outright failures, it might be worthwhile analysing to what extent they can contribute positively to the development process. Not least would it be essential to study how various educational measures can avoid the individualistic attitudes fostered in mainstream modern schooling. After all, in this context, African traditions are often portrayed as placing a far greater emphasis on collective, as distinct from purely individual values.

Another important task within education is the consciousness-raising component. This is found in the specific dialogue methods as established by Freire (1970). Within a tradition of oral literature, it is possible to utilise popular theatre as a means of critical education. One example of such activities was taking place in the Kenyan village of Kamiriithu at the end of the 1970s. This has been expressed by one of the key personalities involved, Ngugi wa Thiong'o (1981, p. 1), thus: 'Education and culture can play a decisive role in the social transformation so vital and necessary for a victory over the neo-colonial stage of Imperialism.'

Given limited government resources for education, one potential local community response could be to provide for alternatives. This would be a natural field in which non-governmental organisations could co-operate with civil society. Within this context, foreign voluntary organisations would contribute towards a sustainable development process. However, many of their present activities seem merely to smooth over some of the negative social effects of structural adjustment.

One aspect that needs to be explored further is how education (mainstream and alternative) is linked to the world of work (formal as well as informal). So far it is obvious that the modern labour market has not been able to keep up with the output from formal schooling. It seems that the present formal education offered in Africa neither equips people for the modern labour market nor for a role in the mobilisation towards 'another development'. Self-reliance is a theme to be considered not only in connection with education, but also related to the labour market and the interaction between the two.

The Labour Market

At the end of the 1980s there was a total labour force of close to 200 million (including the unemployed) in SSA. An absolute majority are directly dependent on agriculture for their survival. A decreasing trend in opportunities within this sector has only been masked by new work in the service sector. During the three decades since 1960 there has been no proportionate growth in manufacturing employment on the African continent. Agricultural development in Africa has been focused on modernisation. One result of this is the emergence of a small number of comparatively well-to-do farmers, while the rest are crammed on to unproductive land or forced into the crowded cities, where there are virtually no job vacancies.

In a 1982 Kenyan survey on unemployment the total labour force was estimated at 6.8 million. Eleven per cent of these were reported as comprising a residual labour force, in reality unemployed. Among the others we find 18 per cent in modern wage employment and 3 per cent in the urban informal sector. An absolute majority was still in small-scale agriculture (Republic of Kenya, 1983, p. 27). Until 1988 the only significant change seems to be a declining proportion for formal wage earning and a corresponding growth in the informal sector (Republic of Kenya, 1991, p. 18).

By 1990, the number of waged employees reached 1.4 million, an increase of 280,000 (25 per cent) since 1982. During the same period an estimated 2.5 million left education to compete for employment. It seems that the government is absolving itself of the responsibility, relying on structural adjustment for renewed growth:

> Historically, educated youth have sought urban, often white-collar employment. Although this tendency will certainly continue, it is clear that the modern sector will be unable to raise enough capital to employ more than a fraction of Kenya's workers from now to the end of the century. (Republic of Kenya, 1986, p. 54)

Of the people in formal employment in 1990 no less than 40 per cent were to be found in the public service sector, which is supposed to undergo drastic reduction in terms of SAPs. At the same time the manufacturing industries are supposed to become more efficient, e.g. move from labour- to capital-intensive techniques. Both these actions will boost the unemployment figures further. In an African context, the Kenyan situation is not among the worst cases. It was estimated that in 1980 only 9.5 per cent of the total labour force were to be found inside the formal labour market (Grey-Johnson, 1990, p. 35). With the present strategies of SAPs the negative results are obvious: 'The repercussions of these measures on the social sector have been grave. Millions of jobs have been lost and as a result the rise in unemployment has increased poverty and hardship in many African households' (ibid., p. 42). If this is related to education it can be claimed that 'scarce resources which are spent on human resource development are not yielding the expected social returns' (ibid., p. 38). One conclusion from this could be that the value of World Bank cost-benefit calculations on education itself will be devalued.

Under the present circumstances considerable thrust is being given to the urban informal sector. In the case of Kenya it has been estimated that 75 per cent of all new jobs up to the year 2000 will be within the urban informal sector (*Weekly Review*, 30 August 1991, p. 29). To a large extent this sector is made up of various kinds of general service, transport and trade activities, with manufacturing constituting only an insignificant share. The informal sector is often regarded as merely a way of surviving, but it could also function as a means to mobilise the civil society for development from within. A government policy to co-opt the informal sector and partly formalise it would hamper the inherent popular power.

The informal sector activities, as measures of empowerment within the political and economic sphere to strengthen the civil society in relation to the state machinery, could also be a reaction to the global dependency structures and the dominance of western capitalism.

> Employment was a social activity for the community in which everybody had a more or less defined role to play, and the object of the production was to satisfy the basic needs of the community. Only the left-over surplus was exchanged with the neighbouring communities.
>
> Colonialism destroyed this 'natural economy' of African societies, and integrated them to demands of world economy. From now on, Africa's role in the global economy was to produce the so-called primary products for exchange in the world market. The best lands, the best resources, and the best labour were to be used for the purpose of satisfying the demand of the world market. All this has been documented. (Tandon, 1987, p. 23)

Even if it is now difficult to return to what used to be, the question still remains whether there are no alternatives to structural adjustments for the future of the African people. To continue organising the people for production for a world market in return for alms from the rich can hardly be considered an alternative. An educational structure functioning only to promote this inequality can hardly be conducive to the real needs of Africa.

It seems that the alternative to the policies now pursued on the 'advice' of the north must be some kind of indigenous self-reliance, built on (but not a copy of) a traditional way of life. The only factor working against this is what we in the North are trying to protect with a new, refined neo-colonialism.

Conclusions

During the 1970s a theme in development thinking was related to the creation of a New International Economic Order, it being obvious that the existing system was basically unjust. However, the forces in favour of maintaining these structures were stronger than the ones trying to achieve a world of greater equality. Today we can hardly be unaware of the injustices within the world economy, but instead of trying to reform it we are forcing the poorest countries to adjust to it. While the positive effects of these programmes are seriously in doubt, the disastrous social consequences are more than obvious. Under these circumstances we, as development researchers, are not only risking our own intellectual credibility, but also agreeing consciously to be a party to the ongoing exploitation of the most disadvantaged members of the global society.

With an ever more complex global situation it is increasingly difficult to tell the causes from the effects objectively. All of us involved in development have to accept the role of normative values in the formulation of long-term strategies as well as the short-term planning. Development research will have to redirect much of its efforts away from being an instrument for donor agencies or governments, themselves part of the process of underdevelopment, towards an analysis of the gap between theory and practice.

Irrespective of whether you are a proponent or opponent of SAPs as presently being implemented in Africa, there is no doubting that they are having profound consequences within the social sector. Educational standards and access to schooling will dwindle, while at the same time unemployment will reach even higher proportions than today. This in itself is a serious issue, but it could be justified with potentially positive future effects.

On the other hand, if we regard the human element of education as central, these aspects can be viewed from another perspective. In the successful development models found in South East Asia, from a modernistic and economic point of view, a central theme has always been to safeguard education and to build institutions. This is also admitted to by those calling themselves development experts.

The crucial question is therefore whether SAPs are not only instrumental in inflicting serious social suffering on the poor, but whether this will also undermine any future attempts to move towards some kind of independent and sustainable development in Africa. Through the present neglect of human development, there is a grave risk that we, consciously or unconsciously, are mortgaging the future of the African continent.

References

Adepoju, A. (ed.) (1993) *The Impact of Structural Adjustment on the Population in Africa.* James Currey, London.

Chung, F. (1990) 'Thoughts on the political economy of development, and the role of education, in relation to unemployment'. *Defusing the Time-bomb?* International Foundation for Education with Production, Gaborone.

Committee for Academic Freedom in Africa (1992) 'The World Bank and education in Africa'. *Race and Class,* 34, 1, pp. 51–60.

Frank A.G. (1991) 'No escape from the laws of world economics'. *Review of African Political Economy* no. 50, pp. 21–32.

Freire, P. (1970), *Pedagogy of the Oppressed.* Seabury Press, New York.

Grey-Johnson, C. (1990) *The Employment Crisis in Africa: Issues in Human Resources Development Policy.* Southern Africa Political Economy Series, Harare.

Hancock, G. (1989) *Lords of Poverty.* Mandarin, London.

Hawkins, A.M. (1993) 'The African economy in the 1990s'. *Southern African Political and Economic Monthly,* 6, 5, Harare.

New African (1993) April, London.

Nyerere, J. (1967) *Education for Self-reliance.* Government Printers, Dar es Salaam.

Nyerere, J. (1973) *Man and Development.* Oxford University Press, Dar es Salaam.

Närman, A. (1988) *Practical Subjects in Kenyan Academic Secondary Schools: Tracer Study II: Industrial Education (Three-year Follow-up).* Education Division Documents no. 39, Swedish International Development Authority, Stockholm.

Närman, A. (1990) 'Pastoral peoples and the provision of educational facilities: a case study from Kenya'. *Nomadic Peoples* no. 25–7, Uppsala, pp. 108–21.

Parade (1992) June, Harare.

Pearson, L. (1969) *Partners in Development: Report of the Commission on International Development.* Praeger, New York.

Raikes, P. (1988) *Modernizing Hunger.* Catholic Institute of International Relations, London.

Republic of Kenya (1983) *Report of a Presidential Committee on Unemployment 1982/3.* Government Printers, Nairobi.

Republic of Kenya (1986) *Economic Management for Renewed Growth.* Government Printers, Nairobi.

Republic of Kenya (1991) *Development and Employment in Kenya: A Strategy for the Transformation of the Economy.* Government Printers, Nairobi.

Tandon, Y. (1987) *Priority Needs and Regional Co-operation Concerning Youth in English-speaking Africa.* UNESCO, Paris.

Van Rensburg, P. (1982) *The Serowe Experience.* Seminar paper, Gaborone.

Wa Thiong'o, N. (1981) *Education for a National Culture.* Zimbabwe Publishing House, Harare.

Weekly Review (1991) 30 August, Nairobi.

Weekly Review (1993) 19 March, Nairobi.

World Bank (1988) *Education in Sub-Saharan Africa: Policies for Adjustment, Revitalization and Expansion.* Washington, DC.

CHAPTER 4

Regional Food Trade and Policy in West Africa in Relation to Structural Adjustment

Leo De Haan, Andries Klaasse Bos and Clemens Lutz

Regional Food Trade and Structural Adjustment: No Clear Relationship

This chapter presents a review of the debate on regional food trade, food security and food policy in West Africa, since these elements return to the discussion on the objectives of structural adjustment, such as improvement in the balance of payments, liberalisation of trade and deregulation of (food) markets (see Chapters 1 and 2). Structural adjustment programmes (SAPs) do not contain specific targets with respect to growth of external or regional trade; implicitly the instruments used may affect such external trade flows.

It is not our purpose to explain here in detail how SAPs have affected regional food trade, food security and food policy in West Africa. First, because the large and growing number of country studies of the impact of a SAP are remarkably obscure with respect to the effects on trade flows, more particularly within the region concerned. On the other hand, the many documents dealing with regional (food) trade and economic integration keep silent with respect to the impact of structural adjustment. Apparently researchers do not consider the relationship to be important. Second, hardly any data collection has been undertaken to conduct an analysis of food trade and food policy in West Africa with respect to structural adjustment. Third, many analyses have been made of the various SAPs in different countries and they have proved that general conclusions on their effects cannot be drawn; much depends on the specific position of a country and on the type of instruments and measures comprising the SAP (Mosley *et al.*, 1991; Netherlands Ministry of Foreign Affairs, 1994). Various evaluations of SAPs lead to contradictory results.

Having said this, it is useful, within the framework of this volume, to make a number of remarks concerning the relationship between SAPs and their impact on food trade and food security. SAPs are seen primarily as national macro-economic policies that are used to re-establish national stabilisation and national growth mechanisms. The policy instruments chosen and specified in the Economic and Financial Policy Framework Paper (the essential document in each SAP) deal with national and sectoral entities, not with aspects beyond national boundaries. This may also explain why some government policies under the influence of a SAP have become even more inward looking than before. It may also provide the key to the apparent contradiction between the recently flourishing phenomenon of workshops and conferences being organised on the theme of regional co-ordination and integration in sub-Saharan Africa on the one hand and the lack of progress in actual policies to co-ordinate or integrate regional trade on the other. We will return to this at the end of this chapter.

A major imbalance attacked by a SAP is the large, structural deficit of the balance of payments. Devaluation of the national currency will be a major instrument to get prices 'right'. If not constrained by structural factors, agricultural production, particularly of export goods, will increase. Although export products will benefit most, the production of food crops will also become more profitable, favoured by other SAP policies undertaken by the government (a general result from a SAP is the improvement of the rural/urban terms of trade). For example, Nigeria had become a huge importer of cereals from non-African countries, but as a result of structural adjustment it developed into a large exporter of food products to neighbouring countries and regional food trade was boosted as a result of Nigerian policies (Egg and Igué, 1993). On the other hand, countries of the CFA franc zone must look for ways to dampen the negative trade effects of the large depreciation of the Nigerian naira and slow down the 'informalisation' of their economic activities, trends which run counter to their SAPs.

One study deals particularly with the relationship between SAPs and regional development in Africa (Coussy and Hugon, 1991). Its starting point is the relative failure of various forms of regional integration before the implementation of SAPs, and the weak links in interregional relationships when SAPs are being implemented. The regional impact of SAPs is studied and the opportunities they offer for encouraging regional interdependence and co-operation are discussed. However, conclusive evidence of how precisely the relationship works out is again missing in this document.

The thesis has been defended that large disparities in monetary and trade policies between neighbouring countries have stimulated (illegal) cross-border trade in food and other products, the illegal cocoa export from Ghana through Côte d'Ivoire being a notorious case. Since the various SAPs in African countries would lead to less disparity between policies, a decrease of such informal trade would result. However, at the same time, the formal trade flows between these countries may be boosted.

SAPs are supposed to lead to a liberalisation of trade. The various tariffs will be lowered and non-tariff barriers may disappear. Even so it remains to be seen whether or not the regional food trade between West African countries will grow, or whether, due to international competition, western cereals will be imported to meet the additional food demand.

Another central element of all SAPs is deregulation of the market. Governments withdraw from various fields, including the food markets. Marketing boards are being dismantled and private agencies have a free hand in moving food along the most profitable channels, including supranational regional ones. As a general tendency one would expect the expansion of regional and international food trade to make for better overall food security. However, countries that suffer from structural food deficits may still find ways to protect their national food producers, even under the implementation of SAPs. One such method could be the buying of certain volumes of local cereals at guaranteed prices in order to build up a government buffer stock for food security reasons, as has been the usual practice in all Sahel countries.

With these observations we want to suggest that SAPs may affect *de facto* regional food trade, but the actual direction and volume of trade flows would depend on various country-specific factors. Whether or not they would contribute to policies of regional co-operation or integration is another question.

This chapter will first explain the concept of food security. Then the current discussion on the relationship between food trade and food security in West Africa will be summarised and consequently the discussion on the world market orientation of national food production will be reviewed. Attention will also be paid to the debate on the possible benefits and constraints of the creation of a regional, i.e. West African (food) market.

An important question is whether sustainable food security in West Africa can be achieved by protection measures for national food production, or by a liberalisation of food trade that facilitates 'cheap' imports of food, which in turn may promote food security. The answer to this question is highly relevant, since the liberalisation of trade is one of the elements in most structural adjustment policies being implemented in West African countries.

The Concept of Food Security

During the 1970s, when serious concern arose with regard to the cereal balance at the national and local level in Sahel countries, the term food security was hardly used at all. It certainly did not have the connotation of food shortages at the household or individual level which it has today. Food security was dealt with in a limited sense, i.e. it had a supply-oriented connotation. This is clearly demonstrated by the serious efforts of food donors and Sahel governments in those days to build up national and sometimes local cereals security stocks, to be used during periods of drought and crop failure. Thus, in most cases, food security referred to increasing the total food supply situation at the national level.

A radically different analysis of the hunger problem which caused a breakthrough in scientific and policy thinking was launched by Sen (1981), who stressed

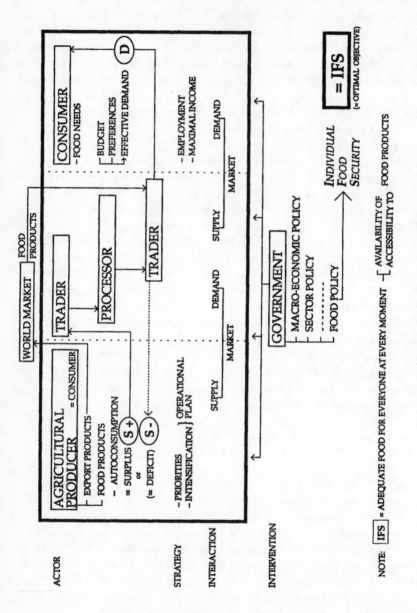

Figure 4.1 A simplified agro-food system

the demand-side at the household level by introducing the concept of entitlement. The emphasis on accessibility which characterises many documents on food security nowadays, including the authoritative 1986 World Bank report on Poverty and Hunger, is directly derived from this entitlement issue.

'Access for everybody at all times to sufficient food to live an active and healthy life' (World Bank, 1986) is nowadays the broadly accepted definition of food security. Defined in this way, the concept of food security has two important dimensions, i.e. availability and accessibility. In this context 'availability' refers to the adequacy of the food supplies, and 'accessibility' to the degree to which these food supplies are accessible to consumers. 'Availability' covers the fields of production, imports and distribution; 'accessibility' covers consumer prices, incomes, purchasing power and consumption patterns such as taste and cooking habits.

To understand the meaning of these dimensions, one has to look further into the various aspects of the food system. Figure 4.1 illustrates the national food system of a typical West African country. A food system is the sum total of all actions, interactions and underlying strategies of each of the agents involved in the food chain. These agents include producers, traders, processors, distributors and consumers. The system is in constant flux and can vary according to place and time. For example, when there is a change in the economic position of the producer who consumes part of his food production, his strategy will also change. The same may be said for the trader and for the consumer. The consumer needs security with respect to a definable minimum quantity of food, and this can be expressed quite specifically in calories, proteins, fats and vitamins. However, a person's actual food package in terms of amount and composition is a variable determined by their income level, prices and personal preferences. Garcia (1984, p. 26) stresses that properties of the system arise not merely from the properties of the agents but from their relationships. Timmer *et al.* (1983, p. 7) point out that the relationships between the actors in the food chain are to a large extent market relations. An important factor in the food system is the influence of the wider geographical context, especially that of the world market on the national food system and that of the regional market on the food system of the village.

The food system can be defined without taking the government into consideration as an actor. Theoretically, the system will work on the basis of individual initiatives by those who supply food and those who want to buy it, i.e. the market system. But in practice the market cannot function on its own, while less than 'perfectly' functioning markets may raise obstacles which may have negative effects on the household food security. In that case, the government is allotted certain roles in improving food security. First, the government may intervene indirectly by regulating food prices and foreign exchange rates. Second, it may provide the necessary public services and infrastructure. Third, it may intervene directly by selling and buying food.

For many years food security was thought to be an area reserved exclusively for the government and its policies and instruments. As Hirsch (1987, p. 105) stated, 'food security seems to have suffered for this over-narrow interpretation and for the state's de facto monopoly over it.' Disappointing results with respect to food security targets were attributed to government failure. On the other hand, we agree with Killick (1989, p. 22) that arguing 'the inevitable impotence of government' is an overreaction. The balance of the arguments about 'controls versus markets' has recently shifted against government controls, which has major implications for the design of food policies. It is accepted that markets perform an important allocation function in the economy, while being recognised that market failures should be corrected by government interventions. The present debate focuses on the types of market failures (imperfections) and how they can be solved. We would argue that a proper functioning of the private sector, particularly the good performance of the food trade in all places and all seasons, contributes greatly to food security as defined above. If the state refrains from direct and indirect interventions in the food market and focuses instead on the provision of public services, this will lead to better functioning of food markets and thus to higher food security.

It should now be clear why an analysis of the food trade is relevant from the point of view of food security. Such an analysis may reveal the shortcomings and bottlenecks that prevent a smooth functioning of the food market, which can jeopardise food security. Various distortions may occur, such as blockades in trade, rent-seeking behaviour, traders' oligopolies and problems for producers in the surplus areas to find a market and for consumers in the deficit areas to buy food. Government restrictions on food trade may considerably increase these distortions, possibly even leading to a switch from official trade to parallel or clandestine trade.

Food Policy in West Africa

Following the great Sahelian drought of the 1970s discussions about the causes of food shortages in this region among researchers and policy makers were characterised by a conflict between climatic and economic reasoning. Nowadays it is widely accepted that drought does play a role, but one also has to admit that it is not the only cause of food shortages.

Economic factors are important in explaining food shortages in West Africa, but over time the economic argument has shifted. As Dioné (1990, pp. 1–2) clearly points out, in the 1960s and 1970s the colonial structure of the West African economies was to blame for the emphasis on export production of tropical non-food crops and a consequent neglect of food production. West African governments therefore committed themselves to reconstructing their national economies. In restructuring the colonial orientation of the economies they centred their efforts on industrialisation by import substitution. Policies, including food policy, favoured non-agricultural sectors and urban areas. As a result, the terms of trade deteriorated to the detriment of the agricultural sector. So-called parastatals, i.e. (semi)-government organisations taking the lead in and often monopolising certain sectors of the economy, became important tools in the implementation of new government policies. The performance of virtually all parastatals was very poor and required increased subsidisation from the state budget. Thus, in the 1980s, the parastatals were blamed for the worsening food crisis.

The policy of urban bias, leading to relatively low prices for agricultural products (which is nowadays considered to be a disaster for West African agriculture), was accompanied by a debt crisis. To overcome this nearly all West African governments sooner or later turned to the International Monetary Fund and the World Bank. Under their aegis, so-called SAPs were forced upon the West African economies. As far as the food sector is concerned, these are characterised by trade liberalisation and privatisation and by the elimination of subsidies. The short-term effects have already become clear, especially in the urban areas (Mosley *et al.*, 1991). The suspension of food subsidies, together with declining incomes because of loss of employment and salary freezes – all parts of SAPs – have affected the buying power of most urban groups. The long-term effects are as yet less clear.

The Controversy between Protection and the World Market

The sustained availability of adequate food in the Sahel is threatened by a number of serious problems. Great fluctuations in the annual harvests are caused by unreliable and variable rainfall in combination with low soil fertility and an unfavourable soil structure. Moreover, land use in many regions has reached the limits of sustainable exploitation of natural resources, a situation which has often resulted in overexploitation. During the 1980s a serious debate arose among researchers on the potential for food production in the Sahel, and because the debate has far-reaching implications for West African food policy we will discuss the arguments in detail.

According to Shapiro and Berg (1988), food production in the Sahel can never guarantee the general availability of food, a necessary condition to fulfil food security at reasonable cost. They think the Sahel should specialise in those fields of production in which it has a comparative advantage and should import part of their food requirements at low prices from the world market. Raising cereal production in the Sahel would, in their opinion, be too costly; importing rice from Pakistan or Thailand would be much cheaper. They are criticised by Gentil and Ledoux (1989), who are much more optimistic about the possibilities for increasing local food production in the Sahel and who reject a radical choice between food production and export crop production.

Shapiro and Berg base their view in the first place on the absence of drought-resistant, high-yielding varieties of millet and sorghum. For that reason they believe that a large increase in food production is impossible. One might argue that the deficiency in soil fertility could be overcome by applying chemical fertilisers, but the authors judge that the marginal returns on the application of chemical fertilisers are too low to become economically feasible. Gentil and Ledoux oppose this view. They claim that new, drought-resistant varieties of millet and sorghum have already proved to be successful and that in the wetter parts of the Sahel (precipitation $\geq$ 600 mm) chemical fertilisers can also be used economically. They add that, above a precipitation level of 1,000 mm, the cultivation of maize with ox-drawn ploughs and the application of chemical fertilisers could raise food production considerably.

'World market advocates' tend to consider irrigated rice as the only crop with a high-yielding potential in the Sahel. However, again they argue that imported rice would be much cheaper. 'Protectionists' argue against this, claiming that the production costs in irrigated rice projects could be lowered considerably if double cropping were achieved, less expatriate personnel were involved and more responsibility given to the farmers themselves, which would mean increasing local participation in project management. In addition, they maintain that rain-fed rice production is a viable alternative to irrigated rice. World market advocates maintain, however, that these kinds of efforts and investments will have a substantially higher economic rent if spent on a crop for which the Sahel holds a comparative advantage.

They also have little confidence in market incentives that should stimulate the peasants to produce and sell more food. Shapiro and Berg consider their price responsiveness to be low, leaving little room for a price or subsidy policy to stimulate food production. Their opponents argue that, once peasants are able to operate in a guaranteed market and with inputs available on time, they do show considerable price responsiveness.

With regard to food consumption, world market advocates claim that low prices of imported food like rice and wheat flour (caused by low world market prices and sometimes by foreign food aid and local subsidies) have given them a solid place in West African food consumption, especially in urban areas. In their opinion this trend can no longer be reversed, because a change of taste has already taken place. Moreover, these food products have a high status and are much easier to prepare than local grains. In urban areas women especially will no longer have time available for the laborious preparation of meals consisting of sorghum or millet.

Protectionists think that these trends can still be reversed. They claim that the performance of food markets can be improved and that distribution costs of local cereal trade can be lowered. This may cause lower prices for sorghum and millet and consequently an increase in demand. In addition, they plead for more research on the processing of local food crops in order to make them more attractive to urban consumers.

World market advocates say that protection is always more costly than free trade. But protectionists show that a large part of the supply of grain and meat on the world market is subsidised. They pose the question why West African countries should expose their agricultural production to unfair competition. Moreover, prices and demand on the world market show considerable fluctuations, which makes it dangerous for countries to rely entirely on the world market for their food supply. In fact, this will not promote food security in the long run and protectionists therefore argue for a selective use of protection, with the aim of counterbalancing the negative effects of world market integration.

In this review of standpoints we have reproduced opinions in a somewhat simplified form. For example, even the World Bank does not always condemn protection (World Bank, 1991). However, the problem with evaluating the different arguments is that they are difficult to weigh up. The research findings to support them are only partially tested and it seems that many arguments are ambiguous. To illustrate this, we limit ourselves to some observations based mainly on our own findings.

First of all, there seem to be very few products which the Sahel can export at competitive prices. Cotton may be one, and perhaps groundnuts and cattle too. But meat from the Sahel, for example, currently suffers from severe competition on the urban markets of the West African coastal countries from meat imported from Argentina and the European union. Although Sahelian meat is of superior quality it has lost the lower strata of the market to cheap, imported meat, often mere cuttings. However, this picture is distorted from a comparative advantage point of view because the meat from the European Union is subsidised. Already some governments of the West African coastal countries have taken measures against these cheap imports, because they not only compete with Sahelian meat but also with meat originating from their own northern provinces.

Second, the debate on the use of chemical fertilisers is obscured by the fact that knowledge from the 'sustainable land use discussion' has not yet been taken into account. Our research in northern Benin (De Haan, 1992) shows that the introduction of chemical fertilisers enables farmers to cultivate the same plots for many years. This causes a deterioration of the physical structure of the soil, resulting in increased soil erosion. Moreover, because ox-drawn ploughs are used, almost all trees have been cleared from the fields, again promoting erosion. However, it is not easy to assess these remarks on sustainability from a food security point of view. Experience from northern Togo (De Haan, 1993) shows that considerable (and thus profitable) increases in yields could be obtained when applying fertilisers in the right way. In fact, entire districts in that area depend on chemical fertilisers to assure a minimum level of subsistence food production. Farmers in this area are much more conscious of the environmental effects of their type of land use than are their colleagues in northern Benin, but their agricultural production does not yet seem sustainable in the long run.

Third, the production costs in the irrigation schemes for rice are too high. This is caused by investment in dams and other infrastructure in large-scale irrigation schemes. In some cases these costs are not entirely passed on to the farmers and are thus not fully reflected in the production costs. Most of these schemes also suffer from high management costs, owing to the large scale and complexity of the operations. Double cropping, which could boost production and lower production costs considerably, is the exception rather than the rule. This reflects various problems, such as lack of water, mismanagement of input supply, labour shortages at the farm level and low prices of the output when compared to more remunerative activities outside the scheme. That is why the development strategy in this field has moved in the direction of small-scale irrigation, which is more in line with farmers' experience of traditional irrigation and therefore easier for them to manage. No large investments are needed for these activities, which should result in lower production costs and thus in the greater competitiveness of West African rice. But recently (Lekanne dit Deprez, 1992) it seems that exploitation costs in these kind of projects are rising as they become older, whereas yields start decreasing.

Taking the argument of taste preference, every observer admits that western foodstuffs have a great attraction for African consumers. It is not difficult to find a Burkinabe mother putting her baby on a diet of exclusively French stick (*baguette*) and condensed milk, which she considers to be superior foodstuffs but which in fact lead to qualitative undernourishment of her child and shows how obstinate taste preferences can be. In addition, one cannot deny that rice and bread are easy to prepare. Thus it remains to be seen whether lower prices of Sahelian cereals will precipitate a substantial increase in demand in urban areas.

One important argument of the world market advocates remains unanswered by protectionists. As we know, many Sahelian peasants depend partly on the market for their food. Not only do they have to buy food in times of crop failure, but in most years they sell part of their food crop immediately following the harvest in order to obtain badly needed cash; in many cases this means that they have to buy food before the next harvest. Reardon *et al.* (1988) have shown that, in fact, a significant number of Sahelian peasants are net buyers of food. World market advocates therefore conclude that, because Sahelian peasants are in sum structural net buyers (which is especially true of the poorer rural strata), their food security depends on the lowest possible food price, i.e. that of imported food.

One has to bear in mind that these findings are limited to Sahelian peasants and perhaps also apply to peasants in the drier, northern parts of the coastal countries, such as northern Togo. However, that leaves large groups of peasants in the wetter parts of West Africa who are usually able to produce enough subsistence food. In Nigeria, considerable increases in food production have been achieved thanks to fertilisers.

Regional Food Trade and the Common West African Cereal Market

The debate between world market advocates and protectionists is often presented as a controversy between institutions like the World Bank and United States Agency for International Development (USAID) on the one hand and French

development agencies on the other. In the mid-1980s the French tried to coun-
terbalance the anti-protectionists by introducing the idea of a common West
African cereal market (*espace céréalier*). This market would be selectively closed
to the world market so as to combine the supposed advantages of protectionism with those of a large internal market, i.e. where supply and demand could
be more easily attuned to each other and where food security could be fostered.
The discussions on the common cereal market have resulted in growing attention
for regional food trade, i.e. between countries, in West Africa.

The French initiative started in 1986, at a conference of the Comité Permanent
Inter-Etats de Lutte contre la Sécheresse dans le Sahel (CILSS), an organisation
of nine mainly francophone Sahelian states and the Club du Sahel (the donors
of CILSS countries), at Mindelo on the Cape Verde Islands. This conference
recommended the encouragement of regional food trade and the establishment
of a regional cereal market, and a number of studies were initiated to enumerate
cross-border food flows.

The advantage of a protected West African cereal market seemed obvious: it
could reduce a possible food deficit in one country by taking advantage of a surplus
in another country and it could realise encouraging prices to farmers. In this way
the dependence on food imports from the world market could be diminished.
This initiative should not be limited to the Sahelian countries alone, as some
West African coastal states have more favourable climatic conditions and hence
food surpluses to offer to the Sahel. Moreover, because most Sahelian countries
are landlocked, legal and illegal food imports from the world market are being
transported via the harbours. Effective protection of local production could more
easily be achieved with the help of the coastal countries (CILSS/Club du Sahel,
1989).

Although official national statistics in West Africa show imports and exports
between countries, experts agree that there are substantial but non-registered,
often illegal, flows too. This applies especially to those cases where governments
intervene in the market. To obtain a better insight into what was actually going
on, following the Mindelo conference a number of studies on cross-border trade
were undertaken by a team supervised by Egg, Igué and Coste, respectively of
the National Institute of Agronomic Research (Institut National de Recherche
Agronomique (INRA)) in Montpellier, the National University of Benin
(Université Nationale du Bénin (UNB)) and the Institute of Research and
Application of Development Methods (Institut de Recherche et d'Application
des Méthodes de Développement (IRAM)) in Paris (Coste, 1989; see also
Dioné, 1990, for a summary).

Of course, there is nothing new in highlighting cross-border trade in West
Africa. As Hopkins (1975) made clear, long-distance trade routes have existed
for centuries all over West Africa (see Figure 4.2), and authors such as Coquery-
Vidrovitch (1976) developed the concept of an African mode of production based
on a combination of subsistence village production and long-distance trade. With
regard to the long-distance trade between Ashante and Hausaland crossing

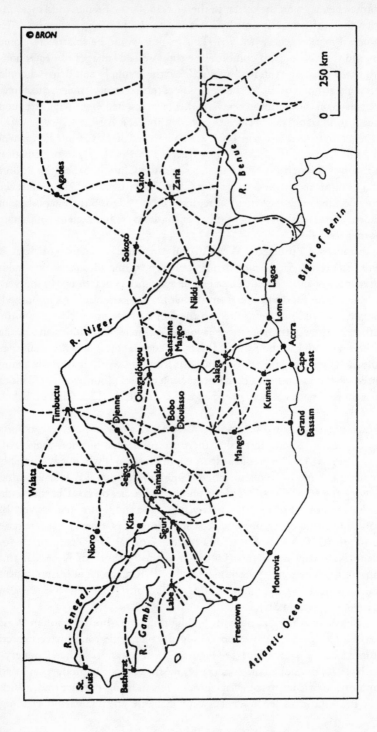

©BRON

Figure 4.2 Major trade routes in West Africa in the nineteenth century

Togo, we know from Arhin (1979), De Haan (1983) and Norris (1984) that these trade routes did not disappear once colonial boundaries had been established. We personally saw truckloads of Thai rice imported illegally but in broad daylight from Benin into Niger (Van Der Krogt and Klaasse Bos, 1991; Fanou *et al.*, 1991) and headloads of subsidised chemical fertiliser transported from Togo to Benin. In East Africa, the Intergovernmental Authority on Drought and Development commissioned a study on the potential for intraregional trade in cereals, which concluded that unofficial intraregional trade was approximately three times the magnitude of official trade (European University Institute, 1992, p. 168).

At a conference in Lomé in 1989 a large number of studies on cross-border trade were presented. Egg and Igué (1990) conclude that these flows are very important in quantitative terms, but that they are mostly not declared at customs. According to Coste (1989), in 1987/8 the cross-border trade of cereals alone amounted to 1,250,000 tonnes for the whole of West Africa, stretching from Senegal to Chad and Cameroon; this figure represented some 20 per cent of the total cereal trade in the area. Coste estimated that about one-third of this cross-border trade was made up of cereals produced in West Africa, meaning that two-thirds consisted of (re-exports of) cereals imported from the world market. In Figure 4.3, the most important cereal trade flows in West Africa for 1988/9 are indicated. Rice is a very interesting example. Produced in various West African countries, rice is losing its market share due to the growing volume of imports, much of which crosses the borders illegally, irrespective of the protective measures taken by countries with a considerable local rice production (INRA/IRAM/UNB, 1991).

Border trade is most intense around certain development poles and also between countries with large disparities in economic policies, notably between CFA franc zones and non-franc zones, the trade from and to Nigeria being a case in point. A difference between the real value of the currency and the official value, the so-called overvaluation of the national currency, distorts official trade flows between countries and will lead to the growth of unofficial or clandestine trade. Furthermore, large discrepancies in import and export policies between countries are expected to stimulate cross-border trade.

The Lomé conference concluded that the Sahel countries did not form separate, closed markets, but were more or less open to products from neighbouring countries and the world markets. Food products from the Sahel had always, to some extent, been in competition with food from neighbouring countries and the world market. However, this competition is not efficient, because of the high transaction costs, which are partly the result of the illegal and non-transparent structure of cross-border trade. Fanou *et al.* (1991) calculated that the transaction costs of the cross-border maize trade in Benin could be reduced by 30–50 per cent if these inefficiencies were eliminated.

As a result of these studies it is recognised that a certain market integration already exists in many border zones; it can be characterised as a market-driven

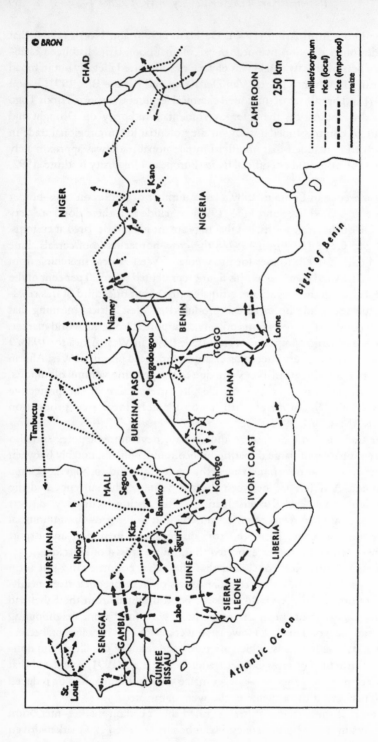

Figure 4.3 Cereal trade in West Africa 1988/9

de facto integration along many international trade routes. This market-driven integration depends to a large extent upon international trading networks which perpetuate long-distance trading traditions, on having a good information system and on trying to benefit as much as possible from the various government regulations and interventions in the food trade. Although one would expect that new policies under SAPs would lead to a decrease in both tariff and non-tariff barriers, in actual fact such changes may not come about. This is demonstrated by Nigeria's policy of establishing a number of measures aimed at the selective protection of the agricultural sector (Egg and Igué, 1993).

Despite the traditional trade links and the need for larger intraregional cereal trade, it is evident that a consensus between the governments on the incentives for the promotion of regional trade is still lacking. The use of conventional instruments to develop a regional market and to stimulate trade amongst neighbours, such as the harmonisation of tariffs and trade regulations and the setting up of preferential trade treaties, has not been successful. Existing tariffs on imports and exports have not been lowered. On the contrary, policy disparities continue to exist. Since the larger part of government revenue originates from duties on foreign trade this is understandable; it would be against a government's own interests to lower the duties.

Expanding the West African Market: An Ongoing Debate

It seems rather unsatisfactory that much time and energy continue to be spent on the expansion of trade through regional co-operation and policy integration, and for which many regional workshops and conferences have been organised. During 1992 there were at least five (see bibliography). By contrast nothing has yet been undertaken in the field of intergovernmental trade agreements. 'In most cases West African governments have, so far, hardly been putting their regionalist rhetoric into practice' (Brah *et al.*, 1993, p. 11). Those who were inspired by the idea of creating a West African regional market have become discouraged because of the lack of regional co-operation between governments. The situation of non-co-operation, which is characteristic of that current in the region, leads to a scenario of growing dependence on western markets and outside assistance (Egg, Igué and Coste, 1991). Hopefully, such impending dependence may eventually motivate the governments of the countries within the region to co-operate, which explains why some researchers are reluctant to give up their support for regional trade co-operation.

Berg (1991), whom we have characterised as a 'world market advocate', defends a pragmatic view with respect to the creation of a regional market. In trying to answer the question of how West Africans could bring about the closer ties that are desirable, he distinguishes four approaches:

1. The 'standard' or 'dominant' approach that builds on preferential trade arrangements but aims at a future fully integrated 'economic community';
2. A production-oriented 'global' approach, championed especially by the Economic Commission for Africa;
3. An outward-oriented, minimal protection approach as put forward especially by economists and others who believe that more outward looking is what is needed, not a focus on regional preferences. This view has its most articulate champions in the World Bank;
4. A new strategy just launched by the French government, which proposes to build integration vertically, by increasing the functional co-operation between France and the CFA franc zone countries.

In his review, Berg criticises the first approach because, within a preferential trade area of developing countries, trade has rarely expanded. The second approach does not consider the market as the main driving force in fostering production. Instead, it concentrates on the production side and tries to expand regional production and infrastructure. Apparently this view is not favoured by Berg or by others who believe that the main constraints are in the market channels and not in production and the infrastructure. Neglect of marketing problems by governments will preclude any solution. The third approach aims at a minimum level of trade protection. The underlying idea is that economic integration schemes based on regional trade preferences have not contributed to any increase in trade. What really matters is to encourage growth and to make West African economies more efficient. Countries should aim at trade liberalisation, thus ending up with low common external tariffs. A main criticism is that this works against the less-developed countries, favouring those which are already more developed (Berg, 1991). Remarkably, the fourth approach aims at closer links between the industrialised metropolitan power of France and its less developed monetary zone associates, with which it shares its language and institutions. This strategy was developed in the last three years by the French Ministry of Co-operation and approved by the Ministers of Finance of the CFA franc zone. The objective is to transform this zone into a genuine economic and monetary union and a large unified market (Berg, 1991; Kabore, 1992).

We end this review of the debate with some practical measures as suggested by Berg (1991), on which general agreement seems to exist:

•   The potential for intraregional trade can be exploited more effectively and relatively non-contentious barriers should be attacked more vigorously. These include burdensome customs procedures and disparate regulations, lengthy and complicated transit procedures, the lack of standardised product norms, the lack of transport norms, heavy informal transaction costs at frontiers (i.e. corruption or, more politely, 'rent-seeking' actors), the lack of trade information and inadequate trade financing facilities. Governments can contribute to greater intraregional trade by progressively eliminating these barriers and limitations.

- Governments and donors should not restrict their regional programmes to conventional organisations and channels as the existing 'economic communities' have proved ineffective; the pace of change is determined by the least enthusiastic member state, or the most bureaucratic.
- The focus of integration efforts by governments as well as by donors should therefore include any group of willing states without reference to membership of larger regional organisations. *Ad hoc*, partial agreements, such as the potential Mali–Burkina Faso–Côte d'Ivoire accord on the trade in red meat, promise quicker and better results.

Conclusions

The introduction of SAPs during the 1980s in virtually all West African countries has considerably changed government priorities and policies. However, such policies are so concerned with national objectives of stabilising and restructuring the economy that they have been unable to broaden the governments' horizons towards developing regional trade policies; nor do they promise change towards larger food trade flows between countries of the West African region.

West African economies are highly dependent on export markets, largely outside the region, for the sale of their agricultural products. On the other hand, there is a growing dependence on cereal imports due to a declining self-sufficiency ratio. Achievements in regional integration policies are therefore important in order to achieve better food security. However, existing trade, including the food trade, between West African economies is still hampered by official policies.

Recent research on the cross-border trade of food products and on related government policies has brought two results. First, despite a lack of data, the actual trade along unofficial channels is believed to be considerable. One could therefore conclude that a *de facto* market integration exists. Second, disparities between government policies are considered a severe handicap for arriving at a more efficient organisation and expansion of regional trade.

One would expect positive effects of the implementation of SAPs on the development of a regional market. Deregulation and liberalisation seem to be basic characteristics of SAPs and should foster international and regional trade. However, in practice this relationship cannot be identified. Since independence African governments have attached great importance to regional co-operation and integration. This has resulted in the creation of a number of regional organisations and institutions, supported by various donors, and the organisation of many seminars. However, there continues to be a wide gap between, on the one hand, the need for more regional co-operation based on expected economic benefits, and, on the other, the apparent lack of action to establish such co-operation. Despite six years of continuous discussion on cereal trade integration, the results in the field of policy co-ordination and harmonisation in West Africa are negligible. The inward-looking attitude promoted by SAPs is partly responsible for this outcome.

References

Arhin, K. (1979) *West African Traders in Ghana in the Nineteenth and Twentieth Centuries*. Routledge & Kegan Paul, London.

Berg, E. (1991) *Strategies for West African Economic Integration: Issues and Approaches*. CILSS/Club du Sahel, Paris.

Brah, M., Pradelle, J.-M. and D'Agostino, V. (1993) *Regional Cooperation and Integration in West Africa*. Banque Africain de Développement/Organization for Economic Co-operation and Development, Abidjan/Paris, SAH/D (93) 401.

CILSS/Club du Sahel (1989) *Les Espaces Céréaliers Régionaux en Afrique de l'Ouest*. Séminaire de Lomé (Togo) SL 89/01–SL 89/29, Documents provisoires, Paris.

CILSS/Club du Sahel (1992) *Conférence sur l'Intégration des Marchés Agricoles en Afrique de l'Ouest: Enjeux pour les Pays Sahéliens et leurs Partenaires Commerciaux*. Saly Portudal, Sénégal, December.

Coquery-Vidrovitch, C. (1976) 'The political economy of the African peasantry and modes of production'. In P. Gutkind and I. Wallerstein (eds) *The Political Economy of Contemporary Africa*. Sage, London, pp. 90–111.

Coste, J. (1989) *Esquise Régionale des Flux de Céréales en Afrique de l'Ouest*. Séminaire CILSS/Club du Sahel, Lomé.

Coussy, J. and Hugon, P. (eds) (1991) *Programme d'Ajustement Structurel et Intégration Régionale en Afrique Subsaharienne*. Centre de Recherche d'Economie de Développment, Nanterre, France.

De Haan, L. (1983) 'Die kolonialentwicklung des Deutschen Schutzgebietes Togo in räumlicher perspektive'. *Erdkunde*, 37, pp. 127–37.

De Haan, L. (ed.) (1992) *Rapports entre Agriculteurs et Eleveurs au Nord Bénin: Ecologie et Interdépendance Transformée. Rapport Final*. Commission des Communautées Européennes/Université d'Amsterdam/Université Nationale du Bénin. Amsterdam.

De Haan, L. (1993) *La Région des Savanes au Togo. Les Paysans, l'Etat et l'Intégration Régionale*. Editions Karthala, Paris.

Dioné, J. (1990) *Sécurité Alimentaire au Sahel: Point sur les Études et Projet d'Agenda de Recherche*. Document de Recherche. CILSS/Institut du Sahel, Paris/Bamako.

Egg, J. and Igué, J.O. (1990) *Espaces Régionaux d'Échanges et Politiques Agricoles en Afrique de l'Ouest*. Séminaire CIRAD/Club du Sahel/OCDE, Montpellier.

Egg, J. and Igué, J.O. (1993) *Market-driven Integration in the Eastern Subregion: Nigeria's Impact on its Immediate Neighbours*. INRA/IRAM/UNB–CILSS/Club du Sahel, Paris, SAH/D (93) 400.

Egg, J., Igué, J.O. and Coste, J. (1991) *Approaches to Regional Cooperation in West Africa: Discussion Based on Work Conducted by INRA/IRAM/UNB*. CILLS/Club du Sahel, Paris, SAH/D (91) 387.

European University Institute (1992) *Promoting Regional Co-operation and Integration in Sub-Saharan Africa*. Workshop, Florence, 26–8 February.

Fanou, L., Lutz, C. and Salami, S. (1991) *Les Relations entre les Marchés de Maïs du Bénin et les Marchés Avoisinants au Togo, au Niger et au Nigéria*. Université Nationale du Bénin/Université d'Amsterdam. Réseau Néerlandais de Recherche Working Paper WP-91-01. Amsterdam/Cotonou.

Garcia, R. (1981) *Food Systems and Society: A Conceptual and Methodological Challenge*. UN Research Institute for Social Development/81/C.37, Geneva.

Gentil, D. and Ledoux, G. (1989) *Commentaires sur l'Etude 'The Competitiveness of Sahelian Agriculture Shapiro-Berg'*. IRAM, Paris.

Hirsch, R. (1987) *Trends and Development in Cereals Policy in the Sahel*. Acts of the Mindelo Conference, CILSS/Club du Sahel, Paris.

Hopkins, A.G. (1975) *An Economic History of West Africa*. Longman, London.

INRA/IRAM/UNB (1991) *Cereals Trade and Agricultural Policies in the Western Sub-market: Regional Processes and the Prospects for Integration: Summary Report*. INRA/IRAM/UNB, CILLS/Club du Sahel. SAH/D/91/367, Paris.

Kabore, T.H. (1992) *Cooperation Economique Régional et Développement Durable*. Séminaire sur l'Intégration Economique en Afrique de l'Ouest. Abidjan.

Killick, T. (1989) *A Reaction Too Far: Economic Theory and the Role of the State in Developing Countries*. Overseas Development Institute, London.

Lekanne dit Deprez, B. (1992) 'Irrigatielandbouw in Afrika'. *Derde Wereld*, 2, pp. 86–8.

Mosley, P., Harrigan, J. and Toye, J. (1991) *Aid and Power: The World Bank and Policy-based Lending*. Routledge, London.

Netherlands Ministry of Foreign Affairs (1994) *Structural Adjustment and Beyond*. Proceedings of an international seminar on structural adjustment and long-term development in sub-Saharan Africa; Research and Policy Issues (edited by Rolph van der Hoeven and Fred van der Kraay). James Currey, London.

Norris, E.G. (1984) 'The Hausa Kola trade through Togo, 1899–1912: some quantifications'. *Paideuma*, 30, pp. 162–84.

Reardon, T., Matlon, P. and Delgado, C. (1988) 'Coping with household-level food insecurity in drought-affected areas of Burkina Faso'. *World Development*, 16, 9, pp. 1065–75.

Sen, A.K. (1981) *Poverty and Famines*. Clarendon, Oxford.

Shapiro, K. and Berg, E. (1988) *The Competitiveness of Sahelian Agriculture*. Elliot Berg Associates/OCDE/Club du Sahel, Alexandria.

Timmer, C.P., Falcon, W.P. and Pearson, S.R. (1983) *Food Policy Analysis*. World Bank Publication, The Johns Hopkins University Press, Baltimore/London.

Van Der Krogt, S. and Klaasse Bos, A. (1991) *Les Échanges Frontaliers de Quelques Produits Vivriers entre le Bénin et le Niger.* Université d'Amsterdam, Réseau Néerlandais de Recherche, WP-91-02, Amsterdam.

World Bank (1986) *Poverty and Hunger: Issues and Options for Food Security in Developing Countries.* Washington, DC.

World Bank (1991) *World Development Report 1991: The Challenge of Development.* Washington, DC.

PART TWO

Structural Adjustment and Urban Basic Needs

The Medicine that Might Kill the Patient: Structural Adjustment and Urban Poverty in Zimbabwe

Dan Tevera

Introduction

The 1980s was a decade of economic crisis and a development disaster for most of sub-Saharan Africa (SSA), during which average per capita income plummeted by a quarter (Jolly, 1988). The essential dimensions and features of this crisis were discussed fully in Chapters 1–3. The situation has forced many African countries to turn to international financial institutions such as the International Monetary Fund (IMF) and the World Bank for assistance. By 1992 more than 30 countries were implementing World Bank-directed structural adjustment programmes (SAPs), which are viewed by the national governments involved as the appropriate response to the crisis being experienced (Stoneman and Cliffe, 1989).

However, the growing body of literature on SAPs in Africa and elsewhere in the Third World shows that not only do the expected economic benefits not always materialise, but that there are major social costs involved with notable impacts throughout the space economy (Cornia *et al.*, 1987; Hodd, 1987; ILO, 1993; Onimode, 1989; Stewart, 1991; Riddell, 1992; Robinson, 1992). Onimode (1989) makes several critical observations, among which are that SAPs have hindered African development by linking the local economies more firmly with the capitalist system, thus inhibiting local industrialisation and perpetuating traditional trade patterns, whereby these countries have provided markets for manufactured goods produced in the North and sources of raw materials. In addition, while SAPs have a generally negative effect on national economies, they particularly hurt the import-based segments of the economy compared with those segments which are less dependent on foreign inputs.

Riddell (1992) argues that the expectation that the devaluation demanded by the SAPs will serve to spur production, because lowering the international value of a country's currency means the reduction/removal of cheaper, imported food, is unlikely to materialise because it does not follow that farmers will necessarily increase the current area of land under the cultivation of staples.

In this chapter, an attempt is made to contribute to the policy debate on Zimbabwe's SAP and assess its impact on basic needs provision in urban areas. The paper is divided into four sections. Section one provides an overview of the economy since independence. Section two outlines the objectives of the SAP and the measures that were adopted to achieve them. Section three examines the impact of the SAP on the vulnerable groups, especially the urban poor. Finally, Section four draws some tentative general conclusions.

The Economy since Independence and Government Policies

Zimbabwe is a low-income developing country in southern Africa with a population of 10.4 million. Its economy since independence in 1980 has been characterised by fluctuating rates of annual growth, ranging between 10.7 per cent and -4.2 per cent, and high levels of unemployment (Durevall, 1991). At the time of independence, the socialist-inclined ZANU–PF government inherited a typical, underdeveloped economy characterised by racial inequalities with about 4 per cent of the population earning 60 per cent of the national income in 1979 (Cliffe and Munslow, 1981; Davies and Sanders, 1987; Riddell, 1984). During the 1980s government policies aimed to transform the economy (Drakakis-Smith, 1986).

The Three Year National Development Plan and the First Five Year National Development Plan had annual growth targets of 8 per cent and 5.1 per cent during their respective plan periods, but both plans have run their course without achieving these targets. At least two main factors beyond the government's control have hindered the attainment of the intended targets, fulfilment of the objectives of rectifying the distortions inherited from the previous regime and of dealing with the most glaring problems of underdevelopment. The targets appear to have been based on the unrealistically high economic growth rates achieved soon after independence and in 1981 due to demand-led growth. Persistent droughts since 1982 and the international recession of the mid-1980s have been blamed for the low rate of economic and employment growth and have constrained the government's efforts to promote development. In 1985 Zimbabwe's national debt amounted to 32.2 per cent of the GNP (Government of Zimbabwe, 1981, 1982, 1983, 1986; Ministry of Finance, 1987).

From 1983 to the end of 1990, Zimbabwe was implementing an IMF-inspired stabilisation programme, the main goal of which was to manage aggregate demand in order to reduce domestic absorption. The adoption of the programme highlighted the beginning of a gradual process whereby 'hardline socialist policy has been abandoned for a market-cum-social welfarist policy' (Moyo, 1991, p. 1).

The Structural Adjustment Programme

As a follow-up to the stabilisation programme in October 1990 a 'home-grown' SAP was officially launched in Zimbabwe. According to the government the main objective of the programme is poverty reduction through changes in the production structure of the economy. According to the policy document on the SAP Zimbabwe will move to an open economy during the 1991–5 period (Government of Zimbabwe, 1991a). The politicians were at pains to emphasise that the programme was not instigated by external forces such as the IMF or World Bank. However, analysts wondered why the government decided to introduce the SAP at that time since the economy was not then in crisis.

For economists like Durevall (1991), the move was not at all surprising because, despite the tremendous progress in the provision of social services (e.g. post-independence primary school enrolment and basic health indicators, which were good), per capita income remained low and the potential for raising the income of the vulnerable groups remained small. He argues, in fact, that several factors made Zimbabwe an ideal country for implementing an adjustment programme with a reasonable chance of success. First, its import substitution strategy has been successful and has contributed to the growth of a largely privately-owned manufacturing sector. Second, Zimbabwe possesses a well-developed banking sector, a stock market, insurance companies and building societies which are all privately owned and hence more responsive to the liberalisation of the economy. Finally, Zimbabwe did not have a severe economic crisis as had been the case in some African countries where structural adjustment was the last straw, leading to social upheavals and political instability which made new investments risky (Nsingo, 1988).

The objectives of the Zimbabwean SAP include the expansion of goods for trade, the removal of balance-of-payments constraints and the restoration of a sustainable balance between aggregate demand and aggregate supply of goods. In a policy document entitled *Zimbabwe: A Framework for Economic Reform (1991–1995)*, the government declared its commitment to a programme of economic policy reform aimed at sustaining higher medium- and long-term growth and at reducing poverty. The document states that the objective of the programme is the improvement of living conditions, especially of the poorest groups. The programme proposes to increase real incomes and lower unemployment by generating sustained higher economic growth by transforming the economy to make it more competitive and productive. This transformation involves departing from a highly regulated economy to one where market forces play a dominant and decisive role.

The following steps have been taken in implementing the structural adjustment programme. The economy was first opened up by sequentially putting goods, which were previously imported under a barrage of import restrictions, on the Open General Import Licence Scheme and decreasing import taxes from about

29 per cent in 1991 to 23 per cent by 1995. The currency was then devalued in order to increase the competitiveness of local goods on the international market and to encourage domestic production of goods; as imports become more expensive this encourages switching to domestically-produced alternatives. This was followed by the relaxation of investment controls and the abolition of the foreign exchange allocation system. Finally, the budget deficit is being reduced from 10 per cent of GDP in 1989 to 5 per cent by 1994–5, mainly through the reduction of subsidies given to parastatals (which, in the 1980s, were as high as 4 per cent of GDP per annum) and by reducing the civil service salary bill from 16.5 per cent of GDP in 1990/1 to 12.7 per cent in 1994/5. The government has expressed its intention to reduce the size of the civil service from 104,000 to 78,000 by 1995.

The principal challenge is to develop and implement a combination of macro-economic and sectoral policies that will lead to growth with equity and the protection of the vulnerable groups in society such as the poor, women and children. The Social Dimensions of Adjustment (SDA) programme, instituted in November 1991, is a crucial component of the Zimbabwean SAP and its aim is to mitigate the social costs of adjustment during the economic reform period.

The major areas targeted for action are employment and training, food subsidies, cost recovery and social services, poverty monitoring and evaluation. To co-ordinate the first three activities a Social Development Fund is being established to operate two main programmes: the Employment and Training Programme and the Social Welfare Programme (Government of Zimbabwe, 1991b).

The Structural Adjustment Programme and Poverty Alleviation

This section addresses the question whether the programme has alleviated poverty or has hurt the poor even more. In other words, is the medicine curing the patient? Is the urban population finding it easier or harder to meet basic needs? One has to be cautious in that 1994 is only three years since the introduction of the SAP and this makes it difficult to isolate the effects of adjustment policies from those of the 1991/2 drought and a generally ailing economy. There are, nevertheless, sufficient indicators to enable one to draw preliminary conclusions about the short- to medium-term effects on the population of Zimbabwe's SAP.

Issues to be examined include the following: access to jobs, access to medical care and education, and food and nutrition. Since the introduction of the SAP, the economy has shown signs of a deepening crisis characterised by higher inflation, intensified de-industrialisation, increased unemployment, stagnant salaries and inability by the vulnerable groups to meet basic needs.

Worker Retrenchment and Unemployment

Worker retrenchment, in both the public and private sectors, has been one of the cruel aspects of the Zimbabwean SAP. Official retrenchment figures show that 10,840 positions were lost in the private sector and parastatals from January 1991 to the end of February 1993. In addition there were 6,543 job losses in the public sector for the period June 1991 to November 1992. The total number of jobs lost in the three sectors during the period in question represent about 1.5 per cent of formal sector employment or 10 per cent of the annual number of school-leavers (ILO, 1993).

According to the president of the Confederation of Zimbabwean Industry, although many workers had already been laid off, the liquidity crisis was going to cause employment to shrink a further 25–33 per cent in the manufacturing sector, which employed almost 200,000 workers in 1990. It is anticipated that between 50,000 and 60,000 people will lose their jobs in both the public and private sectors because of retrenchment.

Zimbabwe's dilemma is that massive retrenchments are occurring at a time when the school system is producing almost a third of a million school-leavers each year, the majority of whom have little prospect of formal employment. Furthermore, most of the retrenchees have been unskilled and semi-skilled workers with little formal educational qualifications or certificate experience in specific skills. This vulnerable group has been the principal victim of the programme because the retrenchment packages have been low and insufficient investment has occurred to provide further training or alternative sources of formal employment.

Medical Care

In 1981 the government introduced free medical care to all those whose monthly incomes were less than Z$150 and to those outside formal employment with the objective of providing 'health for all by the year 2000'. However, throughout the 1980s, the Z$150 threshold was not reviewed, despite increases in nominal wage levels, due to inflation. This reduced the number of people eligible for free medical care. Wage distribution patterns for the period 1982 and 1992 reveal that in 1982 about 46 per cent of formal sector employees qualified for free health care, while by 1992 less than 2 per cent were eligible. Although by 1991 inflation had eroded an income of Z$150 to just Z$80 in real terms, thereby placing many more people in the tariff-paying group, collection of fees was lax and many low-income people (albeit earning more than the threshold income) continued receiving free medical care. In 1992, however, a new exemption limit of Z$400 per household was introduced.

A consequence of the SAP was severe cuts in health expenditure which occurred in 1991 and 1992, thereby reversing the continuous upward trend that had occurred since independence. The programme affected the health sector in several ways. First, the government cut real recurrent expenditure on health by 11.8 per cent during the 1991/2 financial year and by an additional 14.5 per cent during the 1992/3 financial year. The major consequence of these cuts was a fall of 10 per cent in the number of nurses per person employed by the Ministry of Health between 1991 and 1992 – from more than 9 per 10,000 to just over 8 per 10,000 (ILO, 1993). By mid-1992 about 800 health workers had been retrenched and 400 nursing posts had been abolished. Another consequence was the substantial decline in the public funding of drugs. Second, systematic collection of user fees was initiated from the beginning of 1991 as part of cost recovery and with the intention of raising 5 per cent of the health expenditure through fees by 1993 and 8 per cent by 1995.

The introduction of the various cost recovery policies outlined above has made access to medical services much more difficult, especially for the poor, who are not on medical welfare and cannot afford the cost of hospitalisation and medicines. Sanders (1992) has identified some of the impacts of the SAP on the population: the implementation of the fee collection system involving advance payment, particularly for maternity care, is likely to cause a sharp drop in the number of people utilising modern health services. The introduction of charges for medicines has made the drugs very expensive and well beyond the reach of many patients and this has made life particularly difficult for those with chronic diseases requiring long-term drug therapy (e.g. for hypertension, diabetes, psychiatric illness). The introduction of drug charges coincided with a period of rapid devaluation of the Zimbabwean dollar and this has magnified the increase in drug prices. Indicators are showing a steady increase in deaths from diseases which in the past had been brought under control, partly because access to both preventive and curative medicine is now restricted and partly because of other factors such as poor nutrition, unhealthy living conditions and infection by the deadly HIV/AIDS virus. The long-term implications of this are a quantitative and qualitative decline in health care provision at all levels.

Education

As part of the SAP, severe cuts in education expenditure have been made since 1991. The programme affected the education sector in the following ways. Real recurrent educational expenditure fell by 8 per cent in 1991/2 and by a further 11 per cent in 1992/3 (ILO, 1993). Cost recovery measures were also increased in education in 1992, with the introduction of school fees for primary schools in urban areas, and for secondary schools throughout the country. There was a substantial increase in international examination fees owing to the devaluation of the Zimbabwean dollar.

Fees at the (non-boarding) primary school level were introduced and set at Z$12 per year in rural areas, Z$60 in high-density urban areas, and Z$210 in low-density areas except for children whose parents or guardians earn less than Z$400 per month. At the secondary school level, the annual fees now range from

Z$150 in rural areas to Z$210 in high-density urban areas and Z$450 in low-density urban areas. Boarding fees at government primary and secondary schools were set at Z$220 and Z$250 respectively. However, the government insists that no students will be turned away on the grounds that they cannot afford to pay fees provided that they can prove this.

Sanders (1992) identified four main impacts of the SAP on the education sector. First, the increased costs have 'already contributed to increases in drop-out rates, particularly amongst girls' (Sanders, 1992, p. 61). Second, there has been a gradual deterioration in the quality of and access to educational opportunities since 1991, especially in the communal areas and the low-income urban suburbs. Third, females have suffered particularly from the introduction of fees because most parents reason that if they cannot afford to educate all of their children due to lack of money then it is the daughters who have to be sacrificed. This explains the disproportionately high drop out from school by female students. Enrolments in some rural schools declined by almost 20 per cent between 1991 and 1993. Finally, the reduction in the number of teachers in primary and secondary schools resulted in the pupil–teacher ratio increasing by about 5 per cent in primary schools in 1991 (Chisvo, 1993).

Food and Nutrition

The devaluation of the Zimbabwean dollar has sharply increased the costs of inputs, particularly where there is a significant foreign exchange component (e.g. processed foods, transport). Furthermore, the progressive removal of subsidies and deregulation of prices of a range of basic commodities like foodstuffs has been inflationary. The rate of inflation increased from 16.1 per cent in 1990 to 23.3 per cent in 1991 and 42.1 per cent in 1992 but dropped to just less than 30 per cent in 1993. In July 1991 consumer prices for lower-income urban families were on average 235 per cent higher than in July 1990. The price of subsidised plain maize meal rose by over 100 per cent between January 1991 and January 1994, while the price of bread rose by between 100 and 175 per cent during the same period.

Lower-income households have suffered more because the inflation rate for this group was 47 per cent in 1992 while that for the higher income households was 35.9 per cent (ILO, 1993). During the 1991–2 period food prices for lower-income urban households rose by an incredible 534 per cent. According to the Central Statistical Office surveys, over half of the budget of lower-income urban households is spent on food items alone, unlike the high-income urban wage earners who spend only 20 per cent of their budget on food. This shows clearly that, in urban areas of Zimbabwe, lower-income households have suffered much more from the effects of inflation than those with higher incomes.

The removal of consumer subsidies is likely to have more devastating effects on the urban population than on the rural population, who depend less on purchased foodstuffs. Within the urban areas, however, the high food prices will most harm the poor and squatters, whose efforts to produce their own food on municipal soil are often thwarted by local authorities (Mbiba, 1994).

Although the full impact of inflation on the low-income families has not been comprehensively studied, preliminary indicators suggest that there has been a deterioration in diets and nutritional status, especially of poorer groups (ILO, 1993). The introduction by the government of 'a transparent commodity-specific subsidy' on a maize meal product, targeted to cover those low-income groups who can only afford to pay a proportion of the full production cost of maize meal, has had minimal impact so far because only a few have benefited from the facility.

Survival Strategies of the Urban Poor under the Structural Adjustment Programme

This section provides an overview of the survival strategies of the urban poor in Zimbabwe under the ESAP. The low-income groups are less fortunate because they have few options available. Their coping strategies have taken the following forms: increased involvement in informal sector activities, walking to work instead of boarding a bus, standing in long queues for buses instead of taking the quicker but more expensive 'commuter omnibuses' or 'emergency taxis' and resorting to cheaper traditional medicines instead of relying entirely on expensive western medicines. For the middle-income families who have lost their jobs the coping strategies have been the following: moonlighting, sub-letting rooms, cultivation of vegetables and raising chickens in the backyard, involvement in informal sector activities on a part-time basis, and/or abandonment of highly mortgaged houses in the low-density areas in favour of cheaper houses in the less exclusive medium-density areas. The last two strategies will have adverse effects on the low-income groups because the many new entrants in the informal sector will probably depress incomes, and the increasing pressure on low-income housing stock will force the cost of shelter to increase further.

The hardships are manifested by the proliferation of backyard accommodation, largely because many people can no longer afford to rent formal accommodation; the emergence of a variegated fabric of street trading activities in the central business districts of most urban areas in the country; and the growing number of so-called 'street children'.

A visible effect of the current economic hardships has been the massive expansion of the informal economy, especially street trading, small-scale manufacturing, waste scavenging, cross-border trade and personal services. Street vending in Harare, especially in the central business district and the adjacent transitional zone, has now become widespread despite the fact that the authorities are determined to contain the activities. Police consider the activities illegal and regularly confiscate the goods and arrest the vendors. Harare's street traders engage in a wide variety of activities including selling fruit and vegetables, sweets, books, newspapers, flowers and so forth. The street traders are predominantly young, male and poor (Tevera, 1993). Most have been operating for less than three years and have experienced declining incomes during the past twelve months mainly because of increased competition, decreased consumer purchasing power and frequent raids by the police. Furthermore, about three-quarters mentioned 'police harassment' (in the form of Z$25 fines, confiscation of goods and arrests) as their biggest problem.

A common sight in the streets of Harare these days are the 'street kids', children who patrol the parking areas offering various services for a small fee. Poverty, homelessness and inappropriate socialisation compel these youngsters to turn to the streets for a livelihood (Muchini and Nyandiya-Bundy, 1991). The number of street children has increased rapidly from about 200 in 1988 to more than 1,000 in 1993. Police often round up street children and place them in correctional institutions (e.g. the Highfield Probation Hostel). However, the approach does not seem to be working because the street children soon return to the streets. The spectacular rise in their numbers is attributable to the rapid growth of the city at a time when employment generation has been very low and unemployment high. According to a survey of street children in Harare by Tevera (1993), the majority share a number of characteristics:

- being male and aged between 11 and 20 years;
- having no fixed abode;
- having not more than primary education;
- earning between Z$11–20 on a good day and using most of the money to buy food and clothing;
- having been in the streets for less than three years;
- feeling that the two things they wanted most in life were housing and employment; and
- claiming that the biggest problems in their day-to-day activities were 'harassment by police' and street gangs.

Conclusions

In Zimbabwe, as elsewhere in SSA, the SAP has been especially harsh, with investment and economic growth remaining stagnant while living conditions of the vulnerable groups have worsened significantly. The most hard-hit groups are female-headed households whose insecure means of support have been further undermined (Maya, 1989) and the children of the poor, many of whom have now become street children.

The main conclusions from this analysis of the Zimbabwean case can be summarised as follows. First, the SAP has resulted in the further economic marginalisation of the poor groups. Second, there has been considerable decline of employment in the formal sector. Third, public services such as health and education have been cut sharply, thereby worsening the plight of the poor. The hardships have been compounded by the fact that low-income families typically have many children.

Poor and vulnerable groups, especially children and women, are most susceptible to the shocks caused by SAPs. Casual evidence shows that the burden of coping with the consequences of the SAP rests mainly on women, who invariably still have more limited access to family income than men. The drop in real wages and the increased expenditure on school and health fees have put women under even greater stress.

Although the focus of this chapter is on the impact of the SAP on urban poverty in Zimbabwe, it is worth noting that the rural population have been exposed to similar effects. Both urban and rural households have been severely affected by declining real wages, declining formal sector employment and the phased abolition of the roller mill maize subsidy.

To counteract the harsh effects of the programme, the government implemented the SDA programme to benefit the unemployed and poor families. The various measures implemented by the government to protect the poor in terms of the provision of compensatory mechanisms, e.g. subsidised mealie meal, no fees in rural areas and lower fees in high-density areas, are essentially short term and palliative and have not yet been the sugar-coated pill that will counteract the bitter medicine of structural adjustment. The adjustment programmes aim to remove impediments on growth in the private sector. Unfortunately, human beings and their needs are given low priority in many of these programmes.

References

Chisvo, M. (1993) *Government Spending on Social Services and the Impact of Structural Adjustment in Zimbabwe*. United Nations International Children's Emergency Fund, Harare.

Cliffe, L. and Munslow, B. (1981) 'The prospects for Zimbabwe'. *Review of African Political Economy*, no. 18, pp. 1–6.

Cornia, G.A., Jolly, R. and Stewart, F. (eds) (1987) *Adjustment with a Human Face: Protecting the Vulnerable and Promoting Growth*. Clarendon Press, Oxford.

Davies, R. and Sanders, D. (1987) 'Adjustment policies and the welfare of children: Zimbabwe, 1980–1985'. In G.A. Cornia *et al.* (eds) *Adjustment with a Human Face*, pp. 272–99. Clarendon Press, Oxford.

Drakakis-Smith, D. (1986) 'Urbanisation in the socialist Third World: the case of Zimbabwe'. In D. Drakakis-Smith (ed.) *Urbanisation in the Developing World,* Croom Helm, London.

Durevall, D. (1991) *The Zimbabwean Economy in the 1990s: Trade Liberalisation and Land Reform*. Macroeconomic Studies Series, Dept of Economics, Gothenburg University, Gothenburg.

Government of Zimbabwe (1981) *National Manpower Survey*. Ministry of Manpower, Planning and Development, Harare.

Government of Zimbabwe (1982) *Transitional National Development Plan 1982/3–84/5*. Government Printer, Harare.

Government of Zimbabwe (1983) *Annual Review of Manpower 1983*. Ministry of Labour, Manpower Planning and Social Welfare, Harare .

Government of Zimbabwe (1986) *Socio-economic Review of Zimbabwe 1980–1985*. Government Printer, Harare.

Government of Zimbabwe (1991a) *Zimbabwe: A Framework for Economic Reform (1991–1995)*. Government Printer, Harare.

Government of Zimbabwe (1991b) *Social Dimensions of Adjustment (SDA): A Programme of Action to Mitigate the Social Costs of Adjustment*. Government Printer, Harare.

Hodd, M. (1987) 'Africa, the IMF and the World Bank'. *African Affairs*, 86, 344, pp. 331–42.

International Labour Organization (1993) *Structural Change and Adjustment in Zimbabwe*. Geneva.

Jolly, R. (1988) 'Poverty and adjustment in the 1990s'. In J.P. Lewis (ed.) *Strengthening the Poor: What Have we Learned?* Transaction Books, Oxford.

Maya, R.S. (1989) *Structural Adjustment in Zimbabwe: Its Impact on Women*. Zimbabwe Institute of Development Studies, Harare.

Mbiba, B. (1994) 'Institutional responses to uncontrolled urban cultivation in Harare: prohibitive or accommodative?' *Environment and Urbanization*, 6, 1, pp. 188–202.

Ministry of Finance, Economic Planning and Development (1987) *Annual Economic Review of Zimbabwe*. Government Printer, Harare.

Moyo, S. (1991) *A Preliminary Review of Zimbabwe's Structural Adjustment Programme*. Zimbabwe Energy Research Organisation Working Paper no. 14, Harare.

Muchini, B. and Nyandiya-Bundy, S. (1991) *Struggling to Survive: A Study of Street Children in Zimbabwe*. Department of Psychology, University of Zimbabwe, Harare.

Nsingo, K. (1988) 'Problems and prospects of economic structural adjustment in Zambia'. *Courier*, 111, pp. 78–84.

Onimode, B. (ed.) (1989) *The IMF, the World Bank and the African Debt*. Zed Books, London.

Riddell, J.B. (1992) 'Things Fall Apart Again: Structural Adjustment Programmes in Sub-Saharan Africa'. *Journal of Modern African Studies*. 30, 1, pp. 53–68.

Riddell, R.C. (1984) 'Zimbabwe: the economy four years after independence'. *African Affairs*, 83, 333, pp. 463–76.

Robinson, P. (1992) 'What is structural adjustment?' In N. Hall (ed.) *The Social Implications of Structural Adjustment Programmes in Africa*. School of Social Work, Harare.

Sanders, D. (1992) 'Social aspects of structural adjustment: health'. In N. Hall (ed.) *The Social Implications of Structural Adjustment Programmes in Africa*. School of Social Work, Harare.

Stewart, F. (1991) 'The many faces of adjustment'. *World Development*, 19, 12, pp. 1847–64.

Stoneman, C. and Cliffe, L. (1989) *Zimbabwe: Politics, Economics and Society*, Pinter, London.

Tevera, D.S. (1993) 'Urban poverty, street activities and policies in Harare'. Paper presented at the National Workshop on Urban Poverty in Zimbabwe, Harare.

CHAPTER 6

The Impact of Structural Adjustment on Intermediate Towns and Urban Migrants: an Example from Tanzania

Mogens Holm

Introduction

Neo-liberal macro-economic policies have been enforced even more strongly since the political demise of state socialism in eastern Europe, which left the initiative concerning development policy to organisations dominated by western countries and the principal industrialised nations, especially the US (Slater, 1993). Even in the last years of the USSR's existence the socialist bloc provided alternatives to western development strategies for socialist-oriented developing countries like Tanzania, Angola and Mozambique. Recently the International Monetary Fund (IMF) and World Bank have enforced their 'conditionalities' for involvement, originally contained in their structural adjustment programmes (SAPs) in the early 1980s. Further details were provided in Chapters 1 and 2.

The examples presented in this chapter are drawn from research in two intermediate towns in Tanzania, namely Makambako in Iringa region and Babati in Arusha region (see Figure 6.1), and highlight the ways in which external shocks and national policy changes are mediated through local circumstances in their impact on the lives and living conditions of rural–urban migrants in particular. The pressures on the intermediate towns have been enormous in the last decade, as indicated in the population censuses of 1978 and 1988 (United Republic of Tanzania, 1990) and, indeed, the pressure on infrastructure and urban facilities is growing rapidly, especially as an increasing number of migrants are taking up permanent residence in intermediate towns.

Initially, pressure was most pronounced with respect to transport and settlement. In recent years macro-economic adjustment programmes have led to a reduction in local administration and especially in local planning and land survey, where the possibilities of surveying land in accordance with the demand for plots is now extremely limited. The district planning staff members are well qualified to implement a planning scheme but, unfortunately, have only very limited

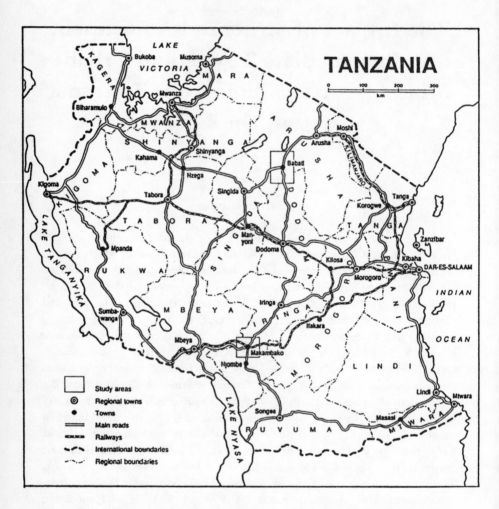

Figure 6.1 Political geography of Tanzania indicating location of study areas

resources and equipment with which to conduct land surveys and therefore they do not provide plot applicants with sufficient information for registration.

Evidently, urban dwellers – especially migrants – have few alternatives to squatter housing, often erected on locations with direct access to markets and other urban facilities. Examples can be given of squatter settlements on plots originally reserved for manufacturing, industrial development or different public facilities. As migrants are innovative and adaptable people, migrating to areas where they have an appropriate social and political network with relevant ethnic ties, they find ways to set themselves up on non-registered plots and establish squatter settlements. Unlike squatters in many other parts of the world, most Tanzanian migrants have the resources to build their residences as permanent homes from the beginning and the planning authorities generally respond by updating their development or land use plans rather than by bulldozing the houses to implement the original land use plans (Hardoy and Satterthwaite, 1981).

The authorities in Njombe district (Iringa region) argue that an upgrading of squatter areas is the only realistic solution and consequently elaborate town plans are regarded more as pieces of blueprint paper to satisfy local government and the planning commission than something actually to be implemented. A paradox exists in that the local government planning system is very hierarchical and includes strict lines of command for confirmation of planning decisions, yet the actual implementation of plans is poor. The outcome is dramatic, with far-reaching consequences for the quality of urban development and for future allocation of urban facilities. This applies especially in intermediate towns as they are seldom covered by the legislation for urban development and planning authorities consequently have limited prospects for controlling the nature and direction of urban expansion.

A principal 'conditionality' within adjustment programmes is reduced government spending and governmental involvement in economic production and supporting activities. As explained above, this also affects urban development planning. Surprisingly, a reduction of public spending on domestic services (education, health, environment and planning) is always recommended by the IMF, World Bank and bilateral donors, yet nobody advocates a reduction in spending on defence, police or intelligence agencies (Gibbon, 1992, p. 59; Maliyamkono and Bagachwa, 1990, p. 24; Therkildsen and Semboja, 1992, p. 1108).

Local Development and Decentralisation in Tanzania Since Independence

Decentralised government and regional development were two key features of socialist policy in Tanzania after independence. These principal objectives were introduced in the five year plans and included in political declarations at the end of the 1960s and the beginning of the 1970s. Tanzania's socialist government had declared its own road to self-reliant development. However, resources were limited and, furthermore, the political system was weak and based primarily on the urban elite. Very limited resources were available, especially for spatial development, and consequently there was heavy reliance on donations and the involvement of expatriate experts. Involvement of donor organisations in planning and resource allocation was certainly risky as it involved donors' 'conditionalities', especially in the case of the IMF and World Bank (Riddell, 1992, p. 53).

Within the first three years of independence in 1961 the first National Development Plan, recommended by the World Bank and adopting the sectoral approach in regional planning, was introduced. A few years later, in the Arusha Declaration (1967), rural development became a national priority. Three main strands in Tanzania's development programme were introduced during those years: decentralised planning, a growth centre concept in terms of which nine urban centres were chosen to receive first priority for investment and industrial development and, finally, the villagisation programme with the establishment of community villages, *ujamaa* villages. These key elements in the socialist programme reached their zenith in 1972/3. This approach to regional and planning policy was based on an idea of the priority of national investment, equity in public services for all Tanzanians and decentralisation of planning in remoter parts of the country with few resources.

Although the policy was clearly in line with an African model of socialism, it became evident that it was rather difficult to achieve under prevailing conditions. The decisions regarding decentralisation and the development of communities in *ujamaa* villages were taken by a centralised political and urban elite. As Tanzania was a young nation, local participation in political organisation and decision-making was very limited. The administrative bodies and political organisations at the local level (districts, divisions and wards) were operated primarily by party officials transferred from the Chama cha Mapinduzi headquarters in Dar es Salaam. To prevent corruption party officials were often recruited from other parts of the country and from other ethnic groups than the ones dominating locally. Under these circumstances, local government had limited foundations among the local population and functioned as a controlling hand from party headquarters. Consequently the distance between government and those who were governed was growing and local participation in decisions was limited.

From the beginning of the 1970s government functions were decentralised, and in order to exercise decentralised planning a regional planning machinery was created to contribute to national planning. However, this structure operated in a hierarchy of command from village level to the Prime Minister's Office in Dar es Salaam. Impatience among the party elite with the slow progress of voluntary resettlement of farmers in *ujamaa* villages led to the adoption of the villagisation programme where more centralised control and mobilisation seemed to be needed to implement the policy (Rakodi, 1990, p. 131). In consequence of the strategy decided in the Arusha Declaration in 1967 the regional administration took over the local government from 1972 to 1984. This recentralisation also provided the government with an opportunity to translate the ideas of the Arusha Declaration into development planning proposals as set out in regional integrated development plans (RIDEPs), where physical and economic planning were to be integrated at all levels under the supervision of the Prime Minister's Office.

In the event, the *ujamaa* policy never proved very successful at the national level as a significant number of the new villages were poorly sited in relation to soil and water. Although the aim of the villagisation programme was to enforce the provision of public services for rural dwellers, a lack of funds for transport, construction and maintenance hindered its realisation. The concentration of population led to deforestation and to a tendency to cultivate fields near the village on a long-term basis, with detrimental effects on soil fertility. Fields and fruit trees further away from the new villages were often abandoned, with an adverse impact on nutritional levels in some cases.

When the national government found that centralisation led to mismanagement and miscalculations of local resources a redecentralisation policy with local government was decided on in 1984. However, the regional administration established during 1972–84 remained basically the same and the new system included unclear divisions of responsibilities, authority and accountability. Consequently it also became difficult to make rational allocations of resources among ministries, regional administration and governments (Therkildsen and Semboja, 1992, p. 1103).

The main elements of spatial planning in Tanzania under the decentralised system suffered from poor implementation. Donor organisations were invited to participate in the planning process but little enthusiasm could be identified in practice. The majority of donors and development agencies – including the Danish DANIDA – were not interested in infrastructure or in participation in the investment plan elaborated by the Tanzanian government. Consequently very little was implemented and a long phase of infrastructural breakdown started which persists today.

'Conditionalities' for Development Aid

At the beginning of the 1980s the World Bank and the IMF were involved in investments in Tanzania but these became subject to macro-economic preconditions embodied in the SAP and the Economic Recovery Programme (ERP) which operated from 1983 to 1985 and 1986 to 1989 respectively. The latter was reviewed from 1990 to 1993. These programmes were expected to run simultaneously with the national development plans, while amendments were also introduced into the national five year plans and the planning process.

It was recommended that the Tanzanian government pay attention to economic balance within the national economy and to increased economic growth. It was probably the intention of the government to address the development crisis through fiscal measures, thereby indirectly solving some of the spatial development problems; i.e. disparities between urban and rural areas. Unfortunately, some antagonism arose as the government had not considered the interests involved in existing land use and land tenure systems and the land survey process. Many cases where customary land use conflicted with formal title deed and/or traditional clan ownership came to court (Downs and Reyna, 1988). The Local Authorities Act, 1982, the National Land Use Planning Act, 1983, the National Environment Management, 1984, and the Government Guidelines on Plan Preparation Survey and Plot Allocation, 1988, are examples of legislation passed to address the spatial dimension of the process of development and conflicting interests concerning access to land.

Increased responsibilities were handed over to local government but remained under the ultimate control of central government. However, local government lacked appropriate revenues to provide adequate public services, i.e. land survey, road maintenance, water supply, health service and education. In addition, the laws mentioned above have not been properly co-ordinated and apparently constituted the source of most of the confusion in the responsibilities among the spatial planning institutions (Therkildsen and Semboja, 1992, p. 1106).

In response to the increasingly severe problems and economic crisis the Tanzanian ERP was announced in a cabinet speech in July 1986. Its aims were to restore the national economy, to accommodate it to the SAP, to combat inflation and falling foreign exchange earnings as well as to achieve a balance between export earnings and import payments (Wagao, 1988). The objective was to stimulate an economic recovery in order to achieve fiscal balance and enable the rehabilitation of industry and infrastructure.

The ERP was also introduced to enable the Tanzanian economy to meet the 'conditionalities' demanded by donor organisations (Maliyamkono and Bagachwa, 1990, p. 19). The main features of Tanzanian economic development will be discussed in the following paragraphs, especially in relation to standards of living for migrants in the intermediate towns investigated in this survey. Despite Tanzania's socialism requiring a centrally planned economy, the first demand from the international donor organisations to get Tanzania on the track to 'development' was to introduce a liberal market economy. It has been introduced step-wise since 1984 and at the end of the 1980s private retail and wholesale businesses were legalised. The consequences of this for food marketing have been studied by Bryceson (1993, pp. 61-91). However, to obtain a private business licence for export/import was extremely complicated, as permissions were needed from numerous levels of bureaucracy. The procedure could eventually invite nepotism and corruption.

Western donor organisations still expected developing countries to introduce liberal economic policy. As confirmed by Sir Geoffrey Howe, Britain's former Foreign Secretary:

that only by agreeing to terms of the 'international institutions' would African countries find willing donors in Europe and the US. 'There is ever wider recognition that peace and reconciliation, political stability and the discipline of economic liberalism are the key to national recovery.' (*Guardian*, September 1988, quoted in Maliyamkono and Bagachwa, 1990, p. 115)

Liberalisation of the market economy caused rapid price increases, which benefited producers but imposed an additional burden on poor rural and urban consumers in particular. Liberalisation was a necessary step to motivate farmers and non-agricultural producers to supply markets with provisions but, at the same time, the strategy of liberalisation increased social inequity. Shortly after the liberalisation was carried out more supplies appeared on shop shelves and commercial activity increased radically. A wider variety of consumer goods was available for those who could afford them and business people increased their incomes markedly. Eventually the poorest section of the population was unable to interact with the market economy to any significant extent and consequently they were forced back to reliance on the subsistence economy.

Macro-economic Programmes and Social Inequity

The socialist policies pursued by the Tanzanian government until the early 1980s were explicitly committed to the promotion of equity and the satisfaction of basic needs. Through public subsidies on food – especially imported grains – consumer prices were kept at a reasonable level and the planned economy made it possible for the same prices to be charged countrywide. Furthermore, farmers were assured a politically-determined price for their products through the National Milling Corporation (NMC) and Tanzanian Farmers' Association. As the economic situation in Tanzania changed, and also as a result of mismanagement, the co-operative organisations became bankrupt and food prices in the market economy increased much more than the prices paid by co-operatives. In the late 1980s government subsidies were still given to the NMC and Grain Marketing Board primarily to cover their total losses and debts to the National Bank of Commerce rather than reducing consumer prices (Booth, 1991, p. 16; Therkildsen and Semboja, 1990, p. 1109). The current economic liberalisation programme includes a reduction of public subsidies and leaves consumer prices for the free market to determine. The outcome is that prices have increased radically – possibly to a more realistic level compared to real costs – but a large proportion of the population can no longer satisfy their basic needs as their ability to pay is too limited. Malnutrition is spreading within the country, not least in urban areas.

Although the strategy of the new economic order is to establish free market conditions, a consequence could be a new divergence between a free market mechanism for the better-off and a subsistence economy for the poor. The strategy in the new economic programme is to cut government subsidies and leave demand and supply to the free market (Riddell, 1992, p. 57; Gibbon, 1992, p. 79).

Donor organisations clearly intend to reduce public spending, accelerate private income earning activities and increase capital accumulation. It is hoped this will be reinvested, especially in local development, thereby also increasing private employment. Initially it was a miscalculation to count on private investment as a compensation for public investment in roads, infrastructure or water supply, since no private capital was available for regional infrastructure. In the 1970s and 1980s only limited private capital was productive in Tanzania; accumulation occurred mainly in business, only to be invested – illegally – abroad or to be used in domestic private luxury consumption. In these years a rich urban elite developed, and especially around Dar es Salaam private construction, to accommodate Asian and African business families in 1,000 square metre mansions including ten bathrooms, swimming pool and private water supply, was observed along the beachfront. Everything was designed in Hollywood style, including the main gate. On the public side of the gate, however, a four-wheel drive car was needed to pass over the potholes while driving to the city centre.

A final component of donor 'conditionalities' is the freeing of the exchange rate to float on the international market, something hitherto avoided by the Tanzanian government in order to maintain a reasonable balance of payments. The value of the Tanzanian shilling (Tsh) has decreased radically over the last ten years and the present devaluation can be regarded as an adjustment to 'reality'. However, the price for this adjustment is being paid by domestic buyers as all imported provisions or those processed with imported goods become more expensive, while local producers selling for export gain from devaluation. This adjustment of the exchange rate also leads to inequity among those dependent on buying imported provisions and those receiving the benefit of selling to export.

'Conditionalities' and the Collapse of Local Government

Since independence local government has faced serious problems of access to appropriate resources in order to implement its plans. This reduced ability directly weakens local government. Local administration and planning author- ities are highly dependent on central/regional decisions and consequently have limited power (Rakodi, 1990). Furthermore, where local finances lag far behind local needs, local governments have only limited opportunities to support local activities or to enforce local initiatives. Too often local government bodies find themselves operating primarily as a 'control body' to punish illegal activities on behalf of central government, and acting as their representative rather than as a public body representing the interests of the local population.

These events are an outcome of the political system and, moreover, affect the political situation in respect of authoritarian decision-making, disastrously mismanaged development projects, the debt burden, opposition to the one-party system and the hierarchical structure of the party (Booth, 1991, p. 22). These circumstances restrict the ability of public authorities to make and implement decisions concerning local development, and reflect the weakness and, in some cases, even the collapse of local government.

There is interaction between the rural and urban elite and local government bureaucrats. The elite are dependent on the bureaucrats and, conversely, this dependency provides the legal basis for the power of urban bureaucrats (Gibbon, 1992, p. 85). Bureaucrats in urban administration are powerful in as much as they are responsible for all kinds of licences, permissions and title deeds etc. In reality, they have limited possibilities to initiate activities themselves but in land use and market activities they have the power to give permissions and to control ongoing activities.

Consequently, it is difficult to involve local government when it comes to the administration of donor projects. Implementation through donor organisations (the IMF, World Bank or non-governmental organisations) requires strong public administrative bodies, especially in areas where local participation and interaction with local authorities are prerequisites for successful development projects. Many cases have been observed where appropriate governmental administrative bodies either do not exist or do not function; hence *ad hoc* groups are organised to satisfy donors' demands for local participation.

Donors recommend reduced governmental involvement. However, this leads to weak local government and therefore creates a paradox, namely that the 'conditionalities' recommended by donor organisations undermine the 'conditionalities' for successful development projects. The collapse of local government has been on the agenda since the beginning of the 1980s and especially since local government was reinstated by law in 1984 without co-ordination between responsibility, resources and decision-making. Land use regulations provide an illustrative example of the consequences of a weak local administration.

Plot clearance cannot keep pace with demand and plot applications are queuing up. As an alternative to waiting for years, impatient applicants work out an agreement with local division or ward leaders – in return for other favours – to get away with illegal construction on the plot, expectantly looking forward to a regular title deed and construction permission. This example illustrates the weakening of local government and, accordingly, the weakening of prospects for upgrading public infrastructure and institutions, especially at district and division levels. There are only limited possibilities in local areas and intermediate towns of introducing development programmes and implementing the local exploitation and processing local resources. Furthermore, under the circumstances described, intermediate towns are not attractive to private investors.

The Decline of Local Development

The study of Makambako and Babati has been undertaken with reference to the understanding of the central role of intermediate towns in regional development in developing countries. In much recent literature it has been argued that intermediate towns perform an important role in regional development because they are rural dwellers' first point of urban contact, they provide centres for interaction between rural hinterland and city centres and they represent an alternative to larger urban centres for the absorption of urban migrants. Theoretically the development of intermediate towns should lead to decentralised urban development and form a background for reliable local development, with the local population processing available resources.

Local resources are identified and processed from the intermediate towns; demand for labour power, infrastructure and services is directed to the local intermediate market. The intermediate towns serve as focal points for interaction where rural and urban people meet and communicate, exchange agricultural products for non-agricultural products, services and other kinds of urban resources (Hardoy and Satterthwaite, 1986).

Obviously effective local government requires power, resources and trained personnel, otherwise the flow of local resources will merely pass through and leave intermediate towns with a limited role as transit trade centres while processing and distribution will be located in bigger cities. Development in intermediate towns is based on access to appropriate local infrastructure and urban facilities. The prerequisites for launching local innovators as small-scale entrepreneurs in processing, construction or business are access to transport, communications, water and electricity on a reliable basis and with an adequate capacity. There are further preconditions to be satisfied if private investment is to be attracted and private employment increase.

Evidently the collapse of local government and reduced public spending on infrastructure and urban facilities lead to a 'standstill' in local development. In this study, very little processing was found in intermediate towns and the majority of the migrants interviewed have limited possibilities of engaging in income-generating activities. The urban areas do not provide migrants with appropriate facilities to achieve an adequate level of living. The macro-economic adjustment strategy to reduce public spending on infrastructure affects urban living standards along with other spheres of life, as will be made clear below.

Do Macro-economic Programmes Affect Intermediate Towns?

As stated before, reduced public investment results in the running down of existing infrastructure and urban facilities. These cannot be extended in accordance with population growth and increases in demand. Intermediate towns are particularly short of resources since, in the heyday of socialist policies, the national government and donor organisations concentrated their investments and development programmes on larger cities and villages in view of the growth centre programme and the villagisation programme respectively. As a result, development activities are still concentrated in larger urban centres where infrastructure and other urban public facilities have survived since the end of the 1960s, although these days they are relatively run down.

The intermediate towns are being left behind in development terms and their function as a link in the chain for exchange between rural agricultural products and urban non-agricultural products is collapsing. Consequently, a high proportion of the local population is unable to survive on its urban income-earning activities and they are under pressure from a 'reproduction squeeze' which is depressing their standard of living.

Urban Migrants' Living Conditions in Relation to the Collapse of Infrastructure and Urban Facilities

This section offers some observations from an investigation of Makambako and Babati to indicate the standards of local government's (non-)fulfilment of urban migrants' basic needs. Three indicators will be presented:

- migrants' access to income-generating activities;
- access to public health services; and
- water supply and how it is affecting mortality.

Migrants' Access to Income-Generating Activities

Urban migrants expect an adequate level of facilities to enable them to establish income-generating activities. An investigation into their survival strategy in two intermediate towns will be presented as examples of urban dwellers' living conditions when urban facilities have collapsed. Both areas are seriously run down (as is the case with the majority of Tanzanian intermediate towns) in terms of the infrastructure required for effective local development.

The majority of urban migrants were motivated to take up urban residence to escape the subsistence economy and become involved in the market economy. However, less than 3 per cent of all migrant households in the interviewed sample were engaged in processing and it was explained that inadequate supply of electricity and water, and lack of financial support, were the main reasons. Furthermore, one-third were engaged in business and another quarter undertook waged labour. More than half of the investigated households (57.1 per cent) undertook farming, even as urban dwellers (Table 6.1), a large proportion to ensure survival. The migrants often combined several occupations characterised by different modes of production and distinct economic relations. The majority of migrant households were involved in both market and subsistence economies, and participated in farming, manufacturing and capitalist waged labour (Kongstad, 1986). These multi-active households faced a continuing threat to their social reproduction since access to appropriate resources remains limited.

Table 6.1: Migrants' Occupations, Head of Household (% of total sample; N = 571)

	N	%
Farming	326	57.1
Business	206	36.1
Wage labour	169	29.6
Civil servant	24	4.2
Others	14	2.5
No occupation	5	0.9
Total	744	

Even with urban residence the standard of living of the migrants was often below what they had experienced in the rural areas on account of higher living costs coupled with limited access to income-earning activities. Consequently, urban migrants continue a rural lifestyle by many means, e.g. by cultivating food for their own consumption as supply of marketed food is short or too expensive. It appears from this that intermediate towns do not meet the local resource needs of urban migrants.

Access to Public Health Services

Access to public health services in Tanzania is considered an important factor among basic needs. After independence, free universal public health services became a cornerstone of the Tanzanian government's policy and a principal argument for community life in *ujamaa* villages. Although health policy has received high priority in Tanzania, public expenditure cuts in recent years have affected public health services and in the investigated towns a large proportion of migrants attending health services have to pay for medical examinations and treatment such as tablets and injections (Table 6.2).

Table 6.2: Payment in Tsh in health institutions (% of total attending each institution)

	Public in town N = 268		*Private in town N = 237*		*Private outside town N = 78*	
Payment	N	%	N	%	N	%
No payment	179	66.8	8	3.3	10	12.8
200 or less	23	8.6	80	33.8	5	6.4
201 – 400	21	7.8	54	22.8	13	16.7
401 – 1500	37	13.8	80	33.8	27	34.6
over 1500	8	3.0	15	6.3	23	29.5
Total	268	100.0	237	100.0	78	100.0

As indicated in Table 6.2, less than one-half of all cases seeking health care received it from the public sector and one-third of these had to pay although, in principle, it should be free of charge. Only one-third of all patients received totally free treatment. Because of increased pressure on health care, the majority of patients pay something for their medical treatment. Health services are expensive and therefore a considerable proportion of migrant households do not seek treatment, not because their health is excellent but because they simply cannot afford it. The public health centres in Makambako and Babati are totally run down. Their supply of medicine is not appropriate in relation to the demand, their equipment does not function, in-patient facilities are very restricted and the operating theatres are out of order.

Water Supply and How It Is Affecting Mortality

A third basic need of fundamental importance to the standard of living of the households is water supply. In both study areas the supply can be considered very poor, since only one-fifth of the sample households have private water on tap (Table 6.3). Babati, an old town, has a better piped-water supply than Makambako, which only became a 'town' within the last twenty years.

Table 6.3: Water supply in migrant households in Makambako and Babati

Water supply	Makambako		Babati		Total	
	N	%	N	%	N	%
Private tap	19	6.7	95	33.0	114	20.0
Public tap	5	1.8	159	55.2	164	28.7
Dams/wells	254	89.8	33	11.5	287	50.3
Water kiosk	4	1.4	–	–	4	0.7
Missing	1	0.3	1	0.3	2	0.3
Total	283	100.0	288	100.0	571	100.0

Local government water provision to town dwellers is clearly insufficient, since nine-tenths of migrant households in Makambako obtain water from dams and wells, and in Babati only one-third are supplied with water from private taps, whereas approximately half of the households are supplied from public taps.

Water supply is presented here as a basic need on account of its importance to households' health situation. Certainly there is a demonstrable relationship between health status, death in the households and infection from water. A higher death rate within households supplied with water from dams or wells than from piped water has also been indicated in other investigations (Heggenhougen *et al.*, 1987).

Table 6.3 indicates that one-half of all households in this sample are provided with water from dams or wells. Approximately three-fifths of all deaths registered in 1990 occurred in these households (Table 6.4). Children in particular are sensitive to infection from water. One-third of all deaths were children aged five or under (32.9 per cent; $N = 85$) and the majority of child mortality (20 out of 28 cases; 71.4 per cent; $N = 28$) occurred in households without piped water. The data provided here indicate the importance of urban families having access to clean water and this applies especially to urban migrants, who lack adequate funds to pay for a safe lifestyle.

Table 6.4: Water supply from dams and wells by mortality within households (% of total number of death cases in 1990; counting to more than 571)

Somebody died in 1990	Water from dams/wells					
	Yes		No		Total	
	N	%	N	%	N	%
Yes	49	57.6	36	42.4	85	100.0
No	240	48.3	257	51.7	497	100.0
Total	289	49.7	293	50.3	582	100.0

Conclusion

In the three examples given from the two study areas it was observed that urban dwellers' basic needs were not fulfilled. Local government institutions at district and division levels have very limited ability to initiate development projects or to support private entrepreneurs in establishing businesses.

Urban migrants are regarded here as multi-active innovators in development, and in their strategy to increase their living standards they are 'kicked' back to at least partial reliance on the subsistence economy, apparently because substantial infrastructural resources are lacking. Finally, the lack of appropriate water supply was observed and the risk to health standards was indicated, especially for child mortality.

The aim of this chapter has not been to draw a direct link between donor 'conditionalities' and the collapse of local government and intermediate towns. Since the introduction of the redecentralisation policy in 1984 little attention has been paid to local government revenues. Rather the aim has been to highlight the collapse of local administration at present and the lack of resources required to fulfil the conditionalities of public development projects in local areas. Under these circumstances the macro-economic policy recommended by donor organisations creates an enforced 'standstill' in local development and consequently leads to increased inequity in development between intermediate towns and larger cities.

The strategy of modernisation in the adjustment programmes recommended by donors, introducing a very different balance between public and private sectors, has proved very damaging to local government and urban development in Tanzania. There is no private capital to fill the gap left by the government and future private investor interest depends on support from local resources.

To avoid 'the medicine killing the patient', donor 'conditionalities' should turn away from the reduction of government involvement and towards giving first priority to the organisation of local resources. As Simon argued in Chapter 2, donors should also turn away from the western concept of democracy to models which promote effective decentralisation and fuller local participation.

References

Booth, D. (1991) *Structural Adjustment in Socio-political Context: Some findings from Iringa Region*. Research Report III, Tadreg, Dar es Salaam.

Bryceson, D.F. (1993) *Liberalizing Tanzania's Food Trade*. UN Research Institute for Social Development, Geneva.

Downs, R.E. and Reyna, S.P. (1988) *Introduction to Land and Society in Contemporary Africa*. The University Press of New England, London and Hanover, NH.

Gibbon, P. (1992) 'A failed agenda? African agriculture under structural adjustment with special reference to Kenya and Ghana'. *Journal of Peasant Studies*, 20, 1, pp. 50–96.

Hardoy, J.E. and Satterthwaite, D. (1981) *Shelter: Need and Response*. John Wiley, Chichester.

Hardoy, J.E. and Satterthwaite, D. (1986) *Small and Intermediate Urban Centres*. International Institute for Environment and Development, London.

Heggenhougen, K. *et al.*, (1987) *Community Health Workers: The Tanzanian Experience*. Oxford University Press, Nairobi.

Kongstad, P. (1986) *Work and Reproduction: How to Survive in Third World Countries*. Working Paper no. 50, University of Roskilde, Roskilde.

Maliyamkono, T.L. and Bagachwa, M.S.D. (1990) *The Second Economy in Tanzania*. Eastern African Studies, Dar es Salaam.

Rakodi, C. (1990) 'Policies and preoccupations in rural and regional development planning in Tanzania, Zambia and Zimbabwe'. In Simon, D. (ed.) *Third World Regional Development: A Reappraisal*. Paul Chapman, London.

Riddell, J.B. (1992) 'Things fall apart again: structural adjustment programmes in Sub-Saharan Africa'. *Journal of Modern African Studies*, 30, 1, pp. 53–68.

Slater, D. (1993) 'The geopolitical imagination and the enframing of development theory'. *Transactions of the Institute of British Geographers, New Series*, 18, 4, pp. 419–37.

Therkildsen, O. and Semboja, J. (1992) 'Short-term resource mobilization for recurrent financing of rural local government in Tanzania'. *World Development*, 20, 8, pp. 1101–13.

Wagao, J. (1988) 'Tanzania's trade policy'. In M. Hodd (ed.) *Tanzania after Nyerere*. Pinter, London.

United Republic of Tanzania (1990) *Tanzania Sensa 1988*. Bureau of Statistics, Dar es Salaam.

PART THREE

The Differential Rural Impact of Structural Adjustment: Case Studies from Tanzania

Structural Adjustment, Sugar Sector Development and Netherlands Aid to Tanzania[1]

Jan Sterkenburg and Arie van der Wiel

Following Tanzania's initiation of its socialist development policy in the late 1960s, it embarked upon an ambitious plan to expand its sugar industry. The principal objectives were to increase sugar production to meet rising consumer demand and to expand employment and incomes in hitherto undeveloped parts of the country through the establishment of ten new plantations in addition to the existing four. This would increase the country's sugar production from 80,000 tonnes per annum to 470,000 tonnes. The sugar companies were nationalised and brought under a parastatal holding corporation. Producer and consumer prices were strictly controlled and sugar was distributed according to a quota system. Personnel policy was supervised by the sole political party. The fundamental changes in the country's development policy after the adoption of the structural adjustment programme (SAP) also affected sugar policy. A number of crucial measures were implemented which heavily influenced the performance of the sugar industry, in which the Netherlands was a major donor.

The objective of this chapter is to analyse the experiences of Tanzania's structural adjustment policy and its effects on the sugar industry, and the role of Netherlands development assistance in policy formulation and the performance of the sugar industry. The chapter addresses three main questions:

1. What are Tanzania's experiences with the implementation of the structural adjustment policy and how has it affected the country's sugar policy?

1. This contribution is based on an evaluation study by the Operations Review Unit (IOV) of the Directorate-General for International Co-operation, Ministry of Foreign Affairs, the Netherlands. The results of the study were published in an IOV report (IOV, 1992). The authors of this chapter directed and co-ordinated the study.

2. How has the sugar industry performed since the 1970s and what was the effect of the country's structural adjustment policy on the performance of the sugar industry?
3. In what way has Netherlands aid influenced the policy and the performance of the sugar sector?

Macro-economic Policy and the Role of Foreign Aid

During the years immediately after independence, i.e. in the period 1961–67, Tanzania retained the free market economy it had inherited from the colonial period. In the agricultural sector commercial private estates and progressive smallholders were encouraged and agricultural production was oriented towards export promotion. The manufacturing sector was dominated by private capital, both local (mainly Asian) and foreign, and production was based on import substitution. During this brief period the Tanzanian economy experienced an increase in its per capita GDP and a relatively favourable balance-of-payments situation. Although the Tanzanian government encouraged investment by foreign and local private capital, it was also sensitive to demands for rapid Africanisation and it accelerated the expansion of the co-operatives in order to strengthen the position of the African population in the economy.

A fundamental reorientation of Tanzania's development policy was announced in the Arusha Declaration of 1967. In that year the Tanzanian leadership officially set the country on a course of socialism and self-reliance. The main objective of the new policy was the creation of an egalitarian socialist society without exploitation and with improved human welfare. State provision of basic services – i.e. health, education, sanitation and water – was pursued to ensure access for all Tanzanians to at least minimum standards of these services. Self-reliance implied that the country would rely on its own resources to develop the economy and that the role and significance of foreign aid would be reduced. It also meant state control over the main sectors of the economy. Consequently, the Arusha Declaration was followed by increased government intervention in production, marketing and distribution. Traditional co-operatives were brought under state control and later replaced by parastatal institutions. The banking and insurance system was nationalised, large private trading companies and industrial enterprises were taken over by the state and certain types of agricultural estates were turned into state farms. A new strategy for rural development was another key element of the socialist policy. *Ujamaa* villages with communal forms of production became the basic rural economic and social unit. Slow progress in developing voluntary *ujamaa* villages led the government to initiate compulsory villagisation in the early 1970s. This resulted in the resettlement of large segments of the rural population within a very short period of time.

The rapid changes in the institutional framework and the intensification of government control had an unfavourable impact on the economy. Economic growth slowed markedly after the Arusha Declaration from slightly more than 4 per cent per annum between 1967 and 1973 to 2.3 per cent between 1973 and 1978. The trade deficit during this period worsened steadily, resulting in a severe foreign exchange crisis in 1974/75, which led to quantitative import restrictions including the introduction of an all-embracing import licensing scheme. Economic stagnation was the result of external and internal factors. The 1973 oil crisis, the second oil price shock at the end of the 1970s, the subsequent world recession and fall in the prices of Tanzania's major export commodities and the war with Uganda contributed to a severe economic crisis. Total output declined on average by about 1 per cent per annum. Industrial capacity utilisation went down to 20-30 per cent, and the country's physical infrastructure collapsed. The situation was undermined further by the pricing policies of parastatal monopolies entrusted with the marketing and export of crops. To reduce their losses the parastatals lowered crop purchase prices. Farmers discouraged by the low prices abandoned or neglected their export crop plantations or switched to domestic food crops, thus further aggravating the balance-of-payments situation. Finally, the crisis sharply reduced the government's revenues and eroded its ability to maintain community services (World Bank, 1990).

Until the early 1980s, Tanzania considered the cause and extent of the economic difficulties to be principally due to exogenous factors rather than to domestic policies. This view was endorsed by the donor community, including the World Bank, as Tanzania was given extensive development aid without the condition of policy reforms. At the end of the 1970s, donors were gradually becoming more critical and argued that, however valid external causes might have been, mistaken domestic policies and institutional weakness were important contributory causes of the economic crisis. Initially Tanzania rejected the economic reform measures requested by the donor community, but later reluctantly accepted the conditions for the expansion of support. In the early 1980s aid levels started to drop from about US$700 million per annum to below US$500 million in 1985. The reduction in foreign aid coincided with a substantial decline in export revenue, and therefore contributed to the aggravation of the economic crisis.

In 1986 an agreement was signed between Tanzania and the International Monetary Fund (IMF) to support a three-year economic recovery programme (ERP) intended to restore the basis for a market-oriented economy. Policy measures arising from the agreement included the reduction or removal of subsidies, an increase in agricultural producer prices, the gradual abolition of a wide range of parastatals, the liberalisation of trade, the reduction of government expenditure and a series of devaluations. The 1986 agreement was extended in 1990 by a three-year economic and social action programme (ESAP or ERP II) with similar objectives and policy measures, but with more attention focused on alleviating the social costs of the economic adjustment programme.

The 1986 agreement led to a sharp expansion of donor aid to Tanzania from US$500 million before ERP to over US$1,000 million annually after ERP. The official development assistance (ODA) amounted to US$50 per capita in 1992, and equalled more than 40 per cent of Tanzania's GDP and almost 85 per cent of its imports. This made Tanzania one of the most aid-dependent countries not only in sub-Saharan Africa but in the world (see Simon, Chapter 2). Not only did the volume of the aid flow increase, but the type of assistance granted also showed a significant change. Since the mid-1980s, commodity import support (CIS) has become the dominant form of aid. Donors have considered CIS to be the most effective instrument in supporting the restructuring of the Tanzanian economy. At the end of the 1980s, almost 40 per cent of the development assistance was being made available in the form of non-project aid. The remaining 60 per cent was divided into capital investment type of projects (35 per cent) and technical assistance (25 per cent). Whereas, at first, most of the CIS funds were allocated administratively by Tanzania and donors to beneficiaries, since the early 1990s about 80 per cent of these funds have been channelled through a more market-oriented allocation system, such as the open general licence (OGL) facility. OGL provided foreign exchange to importers of raw materials, industrial inputs and spare parts for which import licences were issued automatically, provided that the shilling equivalent is deposited with the Bank of Tanzania. Luxury goods and foods and beverages, including sugar, were not allowed to be imported under the OGL system. A number of practical problems have prevented the OGL system from operating optimally. In mid-1993 the OGL was abolished and the government unified the exchange rate and introduced foreign exchange auctions (Doriye *et al.*, 1993).

World Bank (1991, 1993) assessments of the performance of the Tanzanian economy under the SAP indicated respectable growth in both output and per capita income. In the period 1986–92 the economic growth rate exceeded 4 per cent per annum. However, there are several areas where macro-economic performance continued to be unsatisfactory. Export performance, for instance, lagged behind expectations and, as a result, foreign exchange reserves continued to decline and arrears on debt repayments to increase. The trade deficit grew by about 40 per cent from 1985 to 1992, or in actual terms from about US$700 to $1,100 million. The two main reasons for this growing deficit were the boom in private consumption on the one hand, and imports and stagnation in export earnings on the other. The lower export growth was primarily caused by a deterioration in the external terms of trade for Tanzania's main export products (especially coffee). Increased imports were financed principally by external assistance. At present official exports in value terms amount to only one-third of imports. In an evaluation of the performance of the structural adjustment policies in Tanzania, Rattsoe (1992), therefore, seriously questioned the sustainability of the ERP in terms of import capacity, macro-economic stability and production capacity.

Tanzanian Sugar Policy

Self-reliance Policy

At independence Tanzania was importing about half of its domestic consumption of sugar. Since sugar was considered an essential food item in high demand in the country, the Tanzanian government decided to pursue a policy of domestic self-sufficiency. Domestic consumption considerably exceeded local production at four privately-owned estates located at Arusha (TPC), Kilombero, Turiani (Mtibwa), and Kagera. Plans were formulated for a sizeable expansion of local production and various studies were conducted to assess the viability of domestic sugar production. The government decided to implement the expansion primarily through large estates, although formally an important contribution to total production was expected from peasant farmers. The expansion programme designed in the mid-1970s aimed at a sugar production level of 470,000 tonnes by 1990. In addition to some expansion at the three existing estates, a spectacular expansion of Kagera was planned, and new areas for sugar development were identified in Mtwara region (Maharunga and Tunduru), south of Kilombero (Ruipa, Mahenge and Kiberege), the Usangu plains west of Mbeya, around Malagarasi in the west along the Tabora–Kigoma railway line, areas around Kahe and Same south-east of Moshi and at Ikongo near the Kenyan border east of Musoma (see Figure 7.1). This meant that the objective of domestic self-sufficiency was coupled with that of regional economic development in remote and isolated parts of the country, including border areas. In this way the expansion of sugar production would strengthen the economic and political integration of these areas in the newly independent state. The 1977 sugar survey reviewed the programme and proposed the expansion of sugar production at TPC, Kilombero and Mtibwa, the development of Kagera and the establishment of new estates at Ruipa and Ikongo. In addition, the sugar industry was brought under government control, which was exercised through the National Agricultural and Food Corporation (NAFCO) and, from 1974 onwards, through a new parastatal for the sugar industry, the Sugar Development Corporation (SDC or Sudeco). This intensive government control also involved the nationalisation of the sugar estates, strong representation for government ministries on the Sudeco board and the fixing of consumer and ex-factory price levels.

From the outset Tanzania opted for a system of estate production with a highly capital-intensive and relatively complex modern processing technology. It is estimated that more than 90 per cent of the total world cane output is processed in this way. The choice of a plantation system with modern technology was based on the following considerations. First, the period between cutting and processing has to be as short as possible in order to minimise the loss in sucrose content. This places high demand on efficiency, which is best achieved through the estate system. Second, modern technology is cheaper in terms of production costs because of the higher extraction rates (8–12 per cent) as compared with traditional

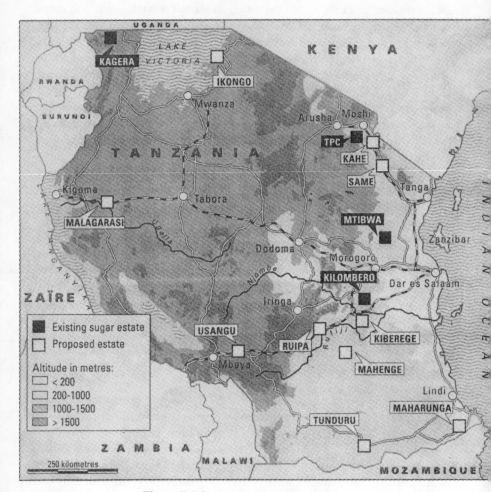

Figure 7.1 Sugar estates in Tanzania

processes (4.5–5.5 per cent). Third, the financial conditions imposed by donors, who tied supplies of import-intensive technology to their own manufacturing industries, were restrictive (Chambua, 1990).

Although the estate form of production had a high priority in Tanzania's sugar development policy, a substantial contribution of outgrowers to total output had been planned from the outset, varying from 30–50 per cent between Kilombero, Kagera and Mtibwa. Outgrower sugar cultivation was seen as an important instrument in raising the incomes and the standard of living of the farmers in the rural areas surrounding the estates. However, in the implementation of government policy, the outgrowers did not receive the required attention and support. Both Sudeco and the estate managers, including the foreign advisors, doubted the potential role assigned to the outgrowers. Their main arguments were the outgrowers' alleged lack of reliability in the supply of cane, their inability to provide the required crop husbandry standards, their reluctance to accept extension advice, their preference for food crops and their low price responsiveness (Coulson, 1979). The outgrowers' actual role was discouraged by the low ex-farm prices and the inadequate services provided by the estates, which needed all their resources to maintain their own output levels during the 1980s.

Because of the high world market price for sugar following the oil crisis in the early 1970s, feasibility studies commissioned by Sudeco considered expansion of sugar production very profitable for Tanzania. As a result, the Tanzanian government decided to accelerate and expand its earlier plans for the intended growth in the sugar industry. The high world market prices of the mid-1970s decreased rapidly again, but this did not lead to changes in the plans for expansion. In any case, implementation of the plans lagged considerably behind planning. Until 1975, policy conditions were quite favourable for the sugar estates. Prices were relatively stable and high enough to allow for sufficient reinvestment in capital equipment. Field, transport and factory equipment could be kept in good condition and production was not seriously hampered by breakdowns and lack of equipment. Moreover, the Tanzanian foreign exchange position was such that capital equipment and spare parts could be obtained from abroad within a short period. There were many well-stocked local dealers and items temporarily not obtainable were supplied by Kenyan trading firms and the estates did not therefore have to keep large stocks of goods. From 1976 onwards, i.e. in the very period of planned expansion, production costs began to rise and ex-factory price increases were too low and too late to cover the costs. In addition, the estates received a relatively small share of the price increases when compared to the organisations involved in distribution, and the Tanzanian foreign exchange position deteriorated seriously, especially from 1977 onwards. The imports required by the sugar industry were tied to opening a confirmed letter of credit, a process that took six to nine months in the early 1980s. Consequently the estates faced an acute shortage of spare parts which affected maintenance unfavourably and which caused increasingly frequent breakdowns. All in all, the very period during which a substantial expansion of the sugar industry had been planned was characterised by a deteriorating macro-economic environment and discouraging sugar production policies.

The consequences of government policy for the sugar industry were serious losses to the estates due to low ex-factory prices – although these were still above import parity for most years – and, consequently, a shortage of finance for rehabilitation and maintenance. The increased dependence on donor assistance for the rehabilitation of the sugar industry sparked off a discussion about the need for fundamental changes in Tanzania's sugar development policy between the Tanzanian government and Sudeco on the one hand and donors involved in the sugar industry on the other. The Netherlands, as the main donor, participated intensively in this discussion. The willingness to introduce major policy changes in the sugar sector was accelerated by the agreement between Tanzania and the IMF/World Bank in the mid-1980s to implement an economic reform programme.

Restructuring Issues

During the second half of the 1980s, major adjustment measures were taken which also affected the sugar sector with regard to pricing policy, domestic trade liberalisation, foreign exchange regime, fiscal policies, import liberalisation and parastatal reform.

Pricing policy
Till the mid-1980s, prices were established by the government for each stage of the marketing chain. The annual fixing of the ex-factory and consumer prices of sugar was a cumbersome procedure, chiefly because the sugar price was a politically sensitive subject. The pricing policy was based primarily on the principle of protecting the consumer from too high a price. From there, a downward calculation was made to arrive at the ex-factory price by subtracting sales taxes and Sudeco wholesalers' and retail margins. In this procedure for price setting the factories usually had to sacrifice most. This resulted, in fact, in consumer prices far below production cost levels, i.e. an implicit consumer subsidy by the government. In this period the industry could survive financially primarily on account of donor assistance.

Since 1988 Sudeco and the sugar companies have obtained the authority to determine producer prices on the basis of projections of production costs and desired profit margins. In this way the ex-factory price covers the full costs of production and reinvestment requirements. Sudeco discusses these prices with the government to arrive at the necessary consumer prices after adding the taxes, levies and marketing margins. As a result of these increases, consumer prices multiplied sixfold between 1988 and 1992. The new price setting system has been accompanied by more regular payment and a better system of sugar removal on the part of Sudeco and, consequently, by an improvement in the companies' liquidity position.

Domestic trade liberalisation

The growing disparity between supply and demand in recent decades as a result of relatively low consumer prices and stagnating domestic production levels, forced the government to introduce a rationing system whereby target groups and areas were allocated specific quotas. The implementation of the quota system was in the hands of Sudeco. A recent report observed considerable differences between quotas and actual distribution. This indicates that financial considerations superseded social goals in the implementation of the system. Under the scarcity conditions the system was, of course, also rather prone to corruption (Netherlands Economic Institute (NEI), 1991).

The liberalisation of the economy had far-reaching consequences for the sugar marketing policy. In 1992 the government of Tanzania decided to deregulate sugar marketing and to abolish the pan-territorial pricing system. Under the present arrangement private traders can purchase sugar either directly from the estates or from Sudeco's Dar es Salaam-based go-down, at a fixed price arranged between Sudeco and the government. Sudeco attempts to regulate sales in such a way that the total production processed in a six-month period is dispatched over the full twelve months, and the various parts of the country receive quantities roughly corresponding with their previous quotas. To facilitate the functioning of the system, Sudeco prefers to have a network of official dealers, i.e. private trading firms purchasing on cash terms. Under the new system, the inefficient regional trading companies (parastatals), many of which have considerable arrears in payments to Sudeco, are circumvented.

Foreign exchange regime

Before 1985 the sugar industry was dependent on the government or donors for its foreign currency requirements. Because of the scarcity of foreign currency, the allocation of these funds by the government to the sugar sector was restricted, and the main flow of foreign currency was provided by donors, the Netherlands in particular. Since the mid-1980s, a number of measures have been taken to liberalise the foreign exchange regime. Measures of relevance to the sugar sector are the introduction of an own-exchange window, export retention schemes and the OGL facility. In 1986, as one of the first measures under the SAP, private transfers of foreign exchange were liberalised. During the period 1986 to 1990, these private transfers (also called own-exchange window) constituted one-quarter to one-third of the import licences issued. It is likely that a substantial part of these own funds is derived from illegal exports. The window is instrumental in the import of sugar. In 1986 the export retention scheme had been extended to three categories of exports, including traditional agricultural exports. These exports allowed retention of about 10 per cent of export earnings in general (Maliyamkono and Bagachwa, 1990). The sugar industry acquired an exceptional position, as it obtained the right to use 100 per cent of its foreign exchange revenues to finance imports of inputs and capital equipment. Annually, the sugar industry exports 10,000 tonnes of sugar to the European Union (EU) under the Lomé Convention and it earns some foreign exchange through the export of molasses.

Fiscal policies

The sugar industry has always been an important source of revenue for the Tanzanian government. The main instrument has been a sales tax, although excise duties and other taxes have also been added to the ex-factory price for short periods of time. The sales tax fluctuated sharply during the 1980s as a proportion of the ex-factory price. In general, there was a high level of taxation in the period 1980–6, i.e. varying from 40–78 per cent after a sharp upward trend during the second half of the 1970s, and a gradually decreasing trend after 1986, following the implementation of the SAP, to about 20 per cent in 1991. Yet, in absolute terms, the sales tax per tonne increased up to 1990 and total tax revenue went up from Tsh220 million in 1980 to Tsh3,065 million in 1993, which equals a fourteen-fold increase over the decade. The sugar taxes' contribution to total sales tax revenue fluctuated between 5 and 10 per cent during most of the 1980s.

Import liberalisation

Till the mid-1980s the importation of sugar was controlled by Sudeco. However, since the introduction of the ERP, the importation of sugar by private traders has been liberalised. Imports come from neighbouring countries in the south (Malawi and Zambia in particular) and from overseas, especially Thailand, via Dar es Salaam. Import duties on sugar were about 30 per cent till the late 1980s, but have been reduced recently as part of a further liberalisation of the market. This has resulted in domestic prices exceeding the import parity price because development levies and taxes on the locally produced sugar are considerably higher than import duties. As a result of this, consumer prices in Dar es Salaam are below the officially set price of Tsh 185 per kg. Furthermore, traders have no advantage in buying directly from the estates as the ex-factory price is the same as Sudeco's ex-warehouse price in Dar es Salaam, which includes the transport cost between the estate and Dar es Salaam. Under these conditions it is more attractive for traders to import sugar than to buy from the local sugar companies. In 1993 the Tanzanian government was reviewing the price structure of both imported and local sugar to protect and provide incentives to domestic production.

Parastatal reform

After the Arusha Declaration the nationalised sugar estates became subsidiary companies of Sudeco. The structural adjustment policy has also led to a drastic reform of the parastatal sector. The parastatal policy statement of 1991 announced a divestiture programme under which all commercial state enterprises would become open to foreign and local private participation. The sugar industry has not been mentioned in the most recent Policy Framework Paper (1992–4), which indicates that full privatisation of this industry is not envisaged, and that the production of sugar on commercial lines to enhance efficiency should be pursued by means other than privatisation (World Bank, 1992). The contract signed with Newsco for the lease of Kagera is a form of privatisation being tested at present. In addition, Sudeco's role will be reduced to that of a management agent, and it will no longer be the holding corporation for the sugar companies. This implies that Sudeco will cease to perform its monopoly marketing–distribution function in the near future.

After the nationalisation of the sugar industry personnel, policy was subject to regulations governing the parastatals as laid down by the Standing Committee on Parastatal Organisations (SCOPO). This extensive list of regulations covered conditions of employment, restrictions on hiring and firing, levels of wages and salaries, procedures for promotions and grievance procedures. These SCOPO regulations were checked by Chama cha Mapinduzi party branch offices established at each estate, through which party officials interfered in various ways in the management of the estates. The SCOPO regulations and political intervention limited the estate management's capacity for flexible and effective labour-power development and personnel policy, and led to overemployment, promotion not related to merit and employment on political criteria rather than qualifications. This situation is subject to drastic changes at present. With the formal introduction of the multiparty system, the party branch offices have been closed down and the abolition of the SCOPO regulations has been announced for the near future.

The preceding description of Tanzania's sugar development policy reveals the fundamental change of policy by the middle of the 1980s. Before 1986 policy was characterised by a priority for expansion of production by means of the creation of new estates, a low level of ex-factory prices, high taxation and a high degree of government intervention in the day-to-day management of the estates. After the introduction of the ERP, the production environment has been deregulated and the sugar-producing companies have obtained more room for improved management and operations on commercial lines.

Production and Distribution System

The sugar industry is one of the largest agroprocessing industries in Tanzania and contributes approximately 35 per cent to the gross output of the food manufacturing sector. It is a major employer, with a labour force of about 20,000, including casual labour for cane cutting. The dominant sugar-cane production system is that of the plantation which combines cane cultivation with sugar processing. At present, the industry consists of five sugar factories and estates, owned by four companies: TPC limited, the Kilombero Sugar Company, Kagera Sugar Limited, and the Mtibwa Sugar Estate. The Kilombero Sugar Company operates two estates and factories. A holding corporation, the Sugar Development Corporation or Sudeco, holds 100 per cent of shares in TPC, Kilombero and Mtibwa, and majority shares in Kagera.

Sugar production was introduced in Tanzania at the beginning of this century by Asian and Arab traders. It was mainly produced for the manufacture of jaggery, a kind of brown fondant, locally known as *sukari guru*. It is particularly popular in the Asian and Arab communities, both for cooking and in sweetmeats. Jaggery factories were usually small and simple. The cane is crushed to extract the juice which is then boiled until it is thick enough to set in moulds when cooling. When, after independence, the Asians left the countryside and took up residence in the larger towns, jaggery more or less disappeared from the rural areas. This disappearance was also stimulated by the Tanzanian government's prohibition on the operation of jaggeries within a 50 km radius of the sugar estates. At present, jaggery sugar is only occasionally available in the market. It seems that, even in scarcity situations, jaggery was not seen by the local population as a substitute for sugar, its main use being for the brewing of local beer and for the distillation of spirits.

Plantation production of white sugar in Tanzania started in the early 1930s. In 1931 the Tanganyika Planting Corporation (TPC) was established at Arusha Chini in the Kilimanjaro region and operated by private Danish interests until the end of the 1970s when it was taken over by the government of Tanzania. TPC was, from the outset, an irrigated estate in a rather dry area, where rain-fed smallholder cane could not be grown. Initially, the installed milling capacity was 350 tonnes per day; during the mid-1950s this was increased to 1,550 tonnes. Also in the 1950s, a new private estate was opened in the Bukoba area in West Lake District to cultivate rain-fed cane. At the time of independence in 1961, these were the only two sugar factories in the country. Plans devised during the colonial period to expand sugar production were adopted after independence, and two new estates were developed during the early 1960s in the Morogoro region, one at Kilombero and the other at Mtibwa. As a result of this, sugar production rose steadily during the 1960s, from approximately 40,000 to 80,000 tonnes per annum. The production increase during the 1970s was less spectacular and, moreover, showed significant fluctuations. The average annual output in this period was around 100,000 tonnes. The production increase at the end of the 1970s was probably mainly the result of a new expansion of the production capacity at Kilombero II. During the 1980s there was hardly any output growth. The average production in this period was just over 100,000 tonnes. In the years since 1985, sugar production has fallen to levels below 100,000 tonnes, but showed a healthy recovery to over 110,000 and 120,000 tonnes in the period 1990–2.

The export of sugar has been quite stable over the past ten years. Under the Lomé Convention Agreement, Tanzania has a quota of 10,500 tonnes to export annually to the EU. In the 1970s these exports went to the UK, whereas during the 1980s their destination was France. The price received for sugar exports is almost twice the world market price, with income amounting to US$6 million in 1990/1. Since 1983 total sugar export proceeds are allocated to the sugar industry via the SDC. In some years small quantities of sugar have been exported to neighbouring countries. To supplement domestic supply Sudeco also imported sugar regularly, and over the last ten years this has amounted to some 10,000–15,000 tonnes annually. Since 1986 private traders have also been permitted to import sugar, provided they can mobilise foreign exchange. As sugar is on the negative list of the OGL system, importers have to get foreign exchange from their own resources, for example in the form of retention on exports. In spite of this obstacle, sugar imports have increased recently and compete seriously with domestic production.

It is estimated that sugar consumption in Tanzania amounted to approximately 130,000 tonnes in 1990/1 (NEI, 1991), based on adding domestic production and imports and subtracting exports. Domestic production of sugar amounted to some 110,000 tonnes in 1990/1. In that year Sudeco imported 11,500 tonnes while some 20,000 tonnes were imported by private traders, some of which entered Tanzania unofficially from the neighbouring sugar-surplus countries of Zambia and Malawi. Local production and imports lead to a per capita consumption of slightly more than 5 kg, against a peak in the early 1970s of almost 10 kg per capita. This fall in per capita sugar consumption was mainly caused by supply constraints. Whereas the population more or less doubled between the late 1960s and the early 1990s, the supply of sugar on the local market remained fairly stable at around 130,000 tonnes.

The importance of sugar to dietary habits in Tanzania has been confirmed by studies which indicate that sugar ranks very highly among essential consumer items. After clothes, sugar is second on the list of priority goods (Cooksey *et al.*, 1987). Sugar is also classified as an essential food commodity by the Tanzanian government. It is considered a basic item in the local diet and an important source of energy in the food supply. To prevent sugar becoming too expensive and out of reach of the majority of the population, the sugar price was regulated by the government, whose estimates of the demand for sugar (or, more accurately, sugar requirements) were based on some desired level of per capita consumption. It appears that the main basis for this estimate of 'demand' was the consumption level of Tanzania's northern neighbour, Kenya, where per capita consumption amounted to some 20 kg. On the basis of this principle, Sudeco estimated the demand for sugar at the end of the 1980s at more than 400,000 tonnes.

The large disparity between supply and demand over past decades forced the government to introduce a rationing system whereby target groups and areas were allocated a specific quota. Based on the availability of sugar for the local market, annual quotas were fixed for different types of consumers, including industrial users (breweries, food companies), consumers in Dar es Salaam and consumers in the regions. For political reasons the quota for Dar es Salaam was very high in comparison with that for the other regions, permitting a per capita consumption of about 25 kg per year. Quotas for the regions were based on their populations. The distribution over these three main categories of consumers was roughly as follows: 20 per cent went to industrial users, 50 per cent was allocated to Dar es Salaam and the remaining 30 per cent was distributed among other regions.

Considerable differences between quota and actual distribution could be observed (NEI, 1991). Large quantities of sugar were sold on the open market at prices higher than the official one, with the actual price being more than twice as high as the official price in the rural areas (Maliyamkono and Bagachwa, 1990).

Performance of the Sugar Industry

The ambitious expansion plans for the sugar sector of the late 1960s were scaled down during the early 1980s. The main reasons for lowering the targets were Tanzania's inability to finance the expansion and the donors' unwillingness to support the development of new estates before efficient production had been achieved at the existing ones. Sudeco came up with new proposals based on a 'holding operation with a minimum necessary degree of rehabilitation' in order to prevent further deterioration and to maintain production levels (NEI, 1988). The subsequent Sudeco plans aimed at a total sugar output of 155,000 to 180,000 tonnes. Actual production levels during the 1980s were substantially lower than the estimated demand, the planned levels of output and potential output in terms of installed processing capacity. Therefore, assessing the performance of the Tanzanian sugar industry means replying to the question: why did the actual production levels remain behind planned cane output and available factory capacity, and how did underutilisation of available production capacity affect the financial and economic performance of the industry?

Cane Production

To identify the main factors which influenced the level of cane production, the estates and the outgrowers must be considered separately. In addition, two main aspects of the sub-optimal production have to be dealt with, namely the area under cultivation and productivity in terms of yield levels.

Estates
The inadequate utilisation of the available estate area has been an important factor responsible for the sub-optimal output levels. However, there is quite a big difference in this regard between the three main estates. Kilombero shows the highest rate of utilisation, followed by TPC. Achievements at Mtibwa were considerably lower, with the harvested area on average below 50 per cent of the total estate area during the first half of the 1980s. This percentage went up to 75 during the second half of the decade. At Mtibwa the problem was not only a question of planting part of the available area but also of harvesting the planted area. There are no exact figures for Kagera, but on this estate only a fraction of the area available was planted and harvested.

A second explanatory factor for the disappointing output during the 1980s was the low yield levels. These show strong fluctuations from one year to the next and a generally declining trend during the 1980s. Yield levels compare unfavourably with other eastern and southern African countries if account is taken of the proportion of land under irrigated cane, which is around two-thirds in Tanzania. The decreasing trend in yields in Tanzania during the 1980s also deviates from the almost world-wide increase in yield levels as a result of more intensive cultivation and an overall improvement in agronomic practices (Abbott, 1990). Furthermore, field trials in Tanzania indicated that the output per hectare might be increased considerably as yields were on average only 60 per cent of trial yields (see Figure 7.2).

In general, yield levels have been influenced unfavourably by three main factors. First, shortcomings in the irrigation system, which result in negligible differences between irrigated and rain-fed cane. In general, irrigation is applied to sandy soil and consequently it also functions as a safeguard against crop failures in dry periods. Second, the non-availability or shortage of inputs and equipment, especially those which had to be imported. This is related to Tanzania's problematic foreign exchange position and the inadequacies of the mechanisms for channelling foreign exchange to the sugar estates. Third, the salary structure and lack of incentives for estate staff, leading to deficiencies in management. Besides these structural problems, incidental factors had an unfavourable impact on yield levels in specific years: weather conditions (either excessive rains or periods of drought), a cholera epidemic and labour conflicts.

Outgrowers

As explained above, an important role was reserved for outgrowers in the initial plans for the expansion of the sugar industry. In line with Tanzania's rural development policy in the early 1970s, the outgrowers' contribution was organised chiefly through collective forms of production, namely the *ujamaa* villages. Participation of the outgrowers was planned around three of the four estates. For Kilombero, 35–40 per cent of total planned output had to originate from outgrowers, and for Kagera 40 per cent, whereas for Mtibwa a contribution of 50 per cent to total production was foreseen. The actual contribution was considerably lower for at least three reasons. First, the area planned was never realised, partly because the focus on outgrowers was scaled down substantially at a later stage, especially at Kagera. Second, the area under cane declined at Mtibwa and stagnated at Kilombero during most of the 1980s. This is strongly related to the failure of the collective production units, but also to the low prices paid to growers and to the lack of supporting services. Producer prices were especially low compared with returns for other crops such as cassava, maize, sorghum and paddy. If these crops were sold on the parallel market, returns to labour were two to four times higher in 1985/6 (NEI, 1988). Third, the yield levels among outgrowers fluctuated sharply but in general remained below the estates' yields because of their exclusive cultivation of rain-fed cane, the longer ratoon cycle of harvesting cane before replanting the fields and the rather poor crop husbandry practices.

Since 1990 the situation has been changing for the better. There has been a considerable price rise for sugar-cane, which exceeded the increase in production

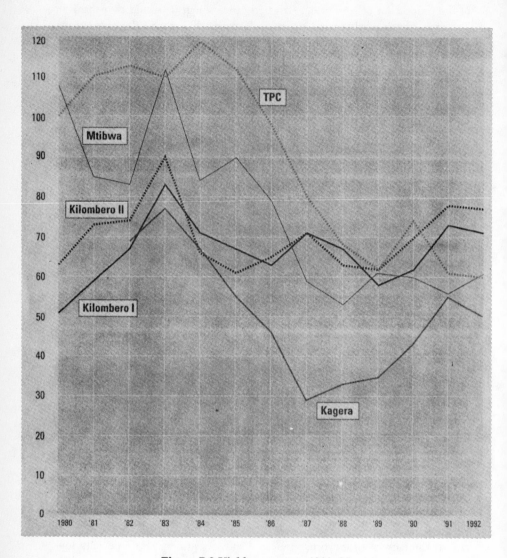

Figure 7.2 Yields per estate 1980–91

costs, so that gross margins have gone up. Moreover, communications between company management and outgrowers have greatly improved. In both the Kilombero and Mtibwa areas, the outgrowers have made preparations for establishing associations, representing all outgrowers in the area. Results of these changes are already noticeable: an increase in the number of outgrowers and in the area under new plantings of cane, and an improvement of estate services to the smallholders. In addition, a substantial growth in cane production has taken place in both the Kilombero and Mtibwa areas since 1990. Production increases are the result of both area expansion and higher yields. For Mtibwa the target of 50 per cent was almost achieved in 1993.

Utilisation of Factory Capacity

All factories suffered considerable interruptions to the production process during the 1980s. The percentage of hours lost varied from 40–45 per cent at TPC and Mtibwa to 20–35 per cent at Kilombero. On average, the relatively new Kilombero II factory showed the lowest percentage of hours lost. Even more important than the number of hours lost was the frequency of stoppages as a cost-increasing factor in sugar processing. The main causes of the sub-optimal use of the available capacity were threefold: mechanical breakdowns, the maintenance of machinery and lack of cane. For Mtibwa and TPC mechanical breakdowns and maintenance requirements were responsible for at least three-quarters of the hours lost. This means that the crucial factor here in low capacity utilisation on these estates was the inadequate supply of spare parts, in relation to both problematic access to sufficient foreign exchange and lack of finance. At Kilombero problems with cane supply played a much more important role, especially at the relatively new Kilombero II factory. The reasons behind the irregular supply of cane may have been the mechanical problems with transport equipment, poor weather conditions and the inadequate planning of cane deliveries. There was no tendency towards improvement of factory performance after the introduction of the ERP (see Figure 7.3). Only during the 1990/1 milling season did all four factories reduce factory downtime and three increase sugar extraction rates. The recent improvement in performance was closely related to the strengthening of the companies' financial position, which in turn was the result of higher ex-factory prices and better access to foreign exchange. This enabled the companies to acquire spare parts and to improve maintenance. In spite of this, downtime still varied between 16 per cent at Kilombero II to 40 per cent at TPC.

Financial Performance

The preceding analysis presents a rather gloomy picture of the performance of the Tanzanian sugar industry during the 1980s, with total production and yield levels substantially below potential ones and a processing utilisation rate at 50–60

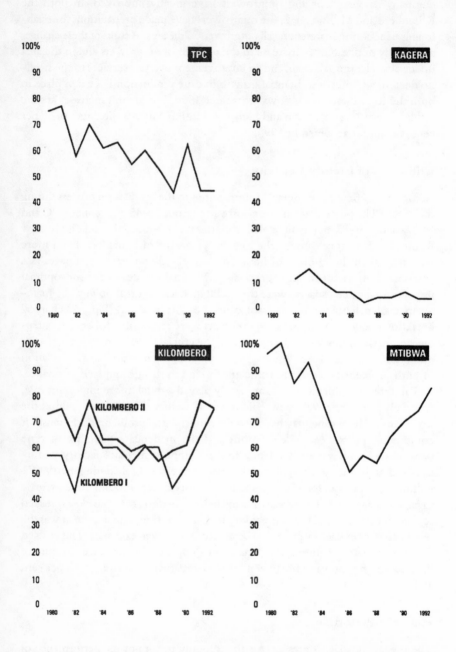

Figure 7.3 Utilisation of factory capacity on sugar estates 1980–92

per cent of installed capacity. This raises questions concerning the financial performance of the sugar industry. The structure of production costs for 1990/1 points to cultivation costs making up a substantial part of the total, varying from 50–60 per cent. Factory costs show far less variation. The high field costs at Kilombero are related to the considerable wage costs reflecting overemployment and relatively low labour productivity. Transportation costs also vary considerably between the three estates. Unfortunately, figures refer to one year only and, in fact, should be available for longer periods of time to identify trends. Ex-factory prices were below the actual cost price in several years during the 1980s. Total average production costs for the period 1980–91 were estimated at US$430 per tonne, including recurrent costs of US$350 and depreciation of US$80. For this period the ex-factory price was estimated at US$390 per tonne, indicating that total production costs were not fully covered. Since 1989 the profit margins have improved substantially. In 1991/2 an ex-factory price of almost US$450 per tonne had been approved whereas total production costs in that year amounted to slightly less than US$400 per tonne. With ex-factory prices fixed artificially below the actual cost of production, the estates experienced considerable losses for many years during the 1980s. The situation improved dramatically as a result of the increase in the ex-factory price and all companies except Kagera made profits in 1988/9 and 1989/90.

The underutilisation of installed capacity had an unfavourable impact on financial performance. Both the return on total assets and the return on capital remained well below the current interest rate of 30 per cent, in spite of recent improvements in the profit margins on sales and in the return on capital. These improvements were principally the results of higher ex-factory prices. This also makes clear that the low profitability in the past, which inhibited the building up of reserves for replacement investment, was a direct consequence of the artificially low prices set by the Tanzanian government.

Economic Performance

The economic analysis of the sugar industry evaluates the importance of the sector to the overall economy of Tanzania. Because of the substantial distortions in the economy during the 1980s, prices used in the financial analysis often did not reflect the real scarcity of production factors, goods and services. In the economic analyses, distortions are dealt with and financial prices are multiplied by conversion factors. In so doing, goods have first to be divided into traded and non-traded goods. Economic prices for traded goods are based on 'border prices'. For sugar, the cost/insurance/freight (cif) import price is its border price. Non-traded goods have to be broken down into their different imported and local components, each with a different conversion factor. In general, locally-produced goods are given in economic prices by means of a standard conversion factor, which is used to compare domestic goods correctly with international goods. Under normal conditions the official exchange rate could be used for this comparison, but if the official exchange rate is overvalued a shadow exchange rate has to be applied, which more accurately reflects the value of the currency. During the 1970s and 1980s, Tanzania had an overvalued exchange rate mainly because of a much higher domestic inflation rate than that in other countries (NEI, 1988). For an economic analysis of the sugar industry a standard conversion factor of 0.5 over the period 1980–91 has been applied to local costs, while imported items have been corrected for import duties and the opportunity cost of capital has been assumed to be 10 per cent. Under these conditions the economic costs of production amounted to US$320 per tonne over the period 1980–91. As sugar production in Tanzania is an import-substitution type of industry, the economic benefits of domestic sugar production can be measured by comparing the economic costs of production with the import parity price of sugar. The average world market price of sugar was US$250 per tonne over the period 1980–91, which equalled a cif price in Dar es Salaam of US$335. This means that, during the 1980s, the costs of production of the sugar industry were only marginally covered by economic benefits.

The use of the world market price for an assessment of the economic benefits of sugar production is complicated by the volatility of the sugar market, which results in sharp price fluctuations over time. For example, during the 1980s the world market price was below the US$250 mark for seven out of ten years. In 1990 the world market price had gone up to US$277 per tonne, which corresponds with a Dar es Salaam cif price of US$375. This means that, in 1990, the economic costs of production, estimated at US$400 per tonne (NEI, 1991), were not completely covered by economic benefits. It is clear that both the financial and economic rates of return were substantially lower than was expected at the time the expansion of the sugar industry was planned during the 1970s. The low productivity of the land in terms of yields per hectare and the underutilisation of available processing capacity were major causes of the disappointing rates of return on investment in the sugar industry. Another important causative factor was the EU's practice of dumping subsidised beet sugar on the world market, which not only contributed to the volatility but also influenced prices in a downward direction.

Netherlands Aid to the Sugar Sector

Characteristics of Aid Flow

The total Netherlands support to the sugar industry since the late 1960s was approximately Dfl260 million (US$130million). In addition, in 1988, a Dfln amount of 75 million was committed for the rehabilitation of a number of estates. The eventual Dutch contribution to the sector will therefore be around Dfl335 million over a period of more than 30 years. In general, Netherlands aid to the Tanzania sugar industry can be grouped under three broad categories: institutional support (including management assistance and training) commodity import support and investment activities. The distribution of funds over the three categories is given in Table 7.1.

Table 7.1: Composition of Netherlands Assistance to the Sugar Sector (in million guilders)

Type of aid	1970–79	1980–91	Total
Institutional support	42.1	63.4	105.5
Commodity import support (CIS)	–	51.7	51.7
Capital investment assistance	64.8	37.0	101.8
Total	106.9	152.1	259.0

The table illustrates the policy reorientation which was introduced at the beginning of the 1980s and whereby emphasis was put on improvement of the utilisation of existing production capacity ahead of expansion. In the period before 1980, about 60 per cent of all Netherlands aid was used for factory and estate expansion. During the 1980s the share of this type of investments decreased to about 25 per cent. The fact that, also during the latter decade, a significant proportion was still used for investment purposes indicates that this shift was a gradual and not an abrupt one. During the early 1980s investment-cum-rehabilitation was still an important expenditure category due to the continuation of construction–engineering type of works at Kagera and to a lesser extent at Kilombero.

During both periods institutional support played an important role in Netherlands development aid. In the 1970s the two main components of this type of assistance were the establishment of a National Sugar Institute (NSI) and management support to Mtibwa and Kilombero, with roughly equal shares in total aid within this category. In addition, a number of feasibility studies were financed by the Netherlands to investigate the potential for expansion of the sugar industry. During the 1980s, institutional development support again primarily consisted of management assistance to Mtibwa and Kilombero, with about two-thirds used for this purpose. For the NSI technical assistance was made available for management and training (course design and actual training); for Sudeco it comprised the topping-up of Indian middle-level personnel at the estates, the posting of a training co-ordinator at Sudeco headquarters and funds for training of Tanzanian staff abroad.

CIS for the sugar sector was made available from 1981 onwards, when the Netherlands contributed Dfl22 million to the agricultural export rehabilitation programme, earmarked for the import requirements of the four estates. The bulk of this was spent in 1982 (Dfl16 million), after which Netherlands CIS to the sugar sector fluctuated at around Dfl5 million per annum. In 1990 CIS to the sugar sector came to an almost complete standstill when foreign exchange became available via the OGL facility, while retention of moneys from the export of sugar were also used by the estates to meet part of their import requirements. Netherlands CIS was spent mainly on the purchase of machines, spare parts, transport equipment and agricultural inputs. Sudeco was responsible for procurement, but it was advised by the expatriate management team at the estate level on the identification of required commodities and the procurement procedures.

Major investment activities to expand production have been supported by the Netherlands over the period 1974–86. They were employed for the construction of a new factory at Kilombero in 1974–6 (Dfl36 million) and the overhaul of the existing factory, together with the rehabilitation of the irrigation system at the Msolwa section of the Kilombero estate between 1977 and 1979. This was followed by the construction of a weir to regulate the water availability for the factory and the irrigation system (Dfl18.5 million). A second major investment was made for the development of the Kagera sugar estate, for which Dfl3.7 million was committed. The project started in 1977 but came to an abrupt halt as a consequence of the Tanzania–Uganda war from 1978 to 1980. Activities were resumed after the war ended but when doubts were raised about the viability of the project the Netherlands withdrew further assistance in 1984 and reallocated some Dfl10 million to CIS. Finally, between 1982 and 1986, Netherlands aid supported the expansion of the factory capacity at Mtibwa (Dfl8.3 million).

Impact of Aid

Netherlands assistance to the sugar sector was primarily oriented towards increasing Tanzania's economic self-reliance, but the performance of the sugar sector, especially during the 1980s, provides a rather depressing picture. This applies also to the two companies which received ample support: neither Kilombero nor Mtibwa showed an upward trend in tonnes of cane crushed during the 1980s. The yields per hectare for both estates increased during the first half of the decade but stagnated thereafter, in spite of substantial investment in the improvement of the irrigation systems. Factory yields for the two Kilombero factories and the one in Mtibwa showed hardly any long-term improvement, and all three factories experienced stagnant or decreasing capacity utilisation.

The conclusion is that Netherlands assistance had only limited immediate effect with regard to sugar production. Yields remained far below the potential level and factory utilisation fluctuated around 60 per cent of installed capacity. Yet this percentage considerably exceeds the average for Tanzania's manufacturing industries. Considered in the light of its objectives, assistance did contribute to maintaining existing production capacity and the localisation of management, but did not lead to an effective use of this capacity. In addition, the results are rather disappointing when compared to the costs of the programme, namely about US$75 million during the 1980s, leaving aside the Tanzanian contribution to the sugar industry.

The effects were negatively influenced by Tanzania's highly unfavourable macro-economic situation, its sugar development policy and, in particular, by strong state intervention in production conditions and the low ex-factory prices. Taking into consideration the constraints operating in the country, Netherlands development assistance contributed to rehabilitating and maintaining production capacity and to a fairly successful holding operation, which prevented the total collapse of industry. The production performance of the sugar estates, especially that of Mtibwa and Kilombero, improved considerably after 1990. The main reasons for this were the policy changes emanating from the ERP, and in particular the better access to foreign exchange and the strong increase in ex-factory prices. Outgrowers' production, total quantities of cane crushed and factory capacity utilisation also rose sharply during the early 1990s. Netherlands assistance contributed substantially to the recent expansion of Tanzania's sugar production.

In determining the effects of Netherlands aid on the country's economy, one yardstick of particular importance is the impact of the sugar sector's development on the balance of payments. From a macro point of view, sugar production in Tanzania was considered primarily as an import-substitution activity. The main aim of developing the sugar industry was to reduce dependence on the import of sugar in meeting local demand. It appears that this objective has been achieved fairly successfully. At present Tanzania imports some 10–20 per cent of its consumption compared to 50 per cent in the early 1960s. About 10 per cent of local output is exported to the EU under the Lomé Convention Agreement. High priority is given to meeting the EU quota because of the very favourable price paid by the EU (about US$600 per tonne).

In establishing the net effects for Tanzania in terms of foreign exchange savings, the import of inputs must be taken into account, as they constitute an important part of the production costs of the sugar industry in Tanzania. It has been estimated that the total foreign exchange requirement for the sugar industry is US$210 per tonne. If compared to the import parity price of sugar cif in Dar es Salaam of US$335, the total net foreign exchange savings amounted to US$125 per tonne. The total foreign exchange savings due to domestic production amounted to about US$150 million over the period 1981–91. This figure is based on the assumption that lower domestic production would have been compensated for fully by increased imports. Such an increase in imports is doubtful, however, in view of Tanzania's problematic foreign exchange position. As a matter of fact, per capita sugar consumption dropped from approximately 10 kg at the beginning of the 1970s to 5 kg in the early 1990s. This illustrates that imports were not increased to maintain per capita consumption levels.

A second yardstick for measuring the economic impact of Netherlands assistance is its rentability, which is difficult to determine precisely. It has been assumed that, without this aid, annual sugar production would have been 50 per cent lower. This corresponds to data on capacity utilisation in the sugar industry (50–60 per cent) as compared to average overall capacity utilisation in Tanzanian manufacturing industry during the 1980s (25–30 per cent). Furthermore, development assistance is considered additional, which means that, without this aid, there would have been no support in the form of foreign exchange by other donors and only very little additional support by the Tanzanian government. In view of the withdrawal of the other two major donors to the sugar sector, the World Bank and Denmark, in the early 1980s and Tanzania's increasing scarcity of foreign exchange during the whole period, this assumption can be considered realistic. Total Netherlands assistance to Kilombero and Mtibwa over the period 1980–91 amounted to just over Dfl100 million. Given the assumptions mentioned above, this has resulted in about 400,000 tonnes of additional sugar production with a total value of about Dfl300 million (approximately US$150 million). The economic effect of this aid flow, which can be considered a continuous investment in the sugar industry, is clearly positive. Rentability rates in terms of net benefits as a percentage of Netherlands aid are 19 per cent for Kilombero, 14 per cent for Mtibwa and 17 per cent for both factories together. It may be concluded that these rates are very satisfactory, as they exceed the opportunity costs of capital.

A third yardstick to be taken into account is the spin-off effect on the country's general economic development. This contribution appears from the generation of extra government income through taxes, the improvement of the employment situation and the regional development effects in the areas surrounding the sugar estates.

The level of sales tax charged to the sugar industry by the government fluctuated significantly during the 1980s and varied between 30 and 70 per cent of the ex-factory price. Since the early 1990s the tax level has gradually been reduced to around 10–20 per cent. For the Tanzanian government, income from the sugar industry was substantial and amounted to about 10 per cent of total tax revenues for the 1980s. The sugar industry has therefore been an important source of income for the government and for the economic development of the country.

Netherlands aid also contributed to maintaining employment in the sugar industry. Assuming a decrease in capacity utilisation to 30–35 per cent without aid to the sector, it means that some 10,000 employees retained their jobs as a result of the above-average performance. This number becomes considerably higher if it is accepted that Netherlands aid prevented the total collapse of the industry.

The regional development effects of the sugar industry are clearly visible in the areas surrounding the estates. The expansion of the sugar industry has sparked off a process of regional economic development. It has stimulated the cultivation and sale of food crops and other commercial activities in the form of markets and shops, and the local population has obtained the benefits of hospitals, clinics and basic education facilities. Cash incomes in the area have encouraged the construction of better houses and, finally, communications in the area have been extended and improved, with transport services provided to neighbouring towns. Estates such as Kilombero and Mtibwa have become nuclei of development, as originally envisaged by the Tanzanian government. To sum up,

Netherlands aid to the sugar sector has clearly contributed to Tanzania's economic growth and self-reliance in sugar production.

Conclusion

The introduction of the ERP had important consequences for the sugar sector, with reforms since its inception including a liberalisation of price-setting, foreign exchange measures and institutional reforms. The ex-factory price of sugar increased more than tenfold between 1986 and 1992. Foreign exchange measures have resulted in improved accessibility for the sugar sector by allowing the industry to retain the foreign exchange earned through exports under the Lomé Convention and by establishing an OGL facility from which, in principle, every potential importer can purchase foreign currency. The structural adjustment policy also meant drastic changes for the parastatal sector. The position of the parastatal holding company Sudeco is under review and the companies have obtained greater autonomy, although they remain state-owned. Full privatisation of the sugar industry is not yet government policy, and sugar production on commercial terms to enhance efficiency is being pursued along lines such as ex-factory price increases, market liberalisation and measures to allow for a more effective personnel policy by the companies.

The effects of structural adjustment in the sugar sector have been manifest since the end of the 1980s, when output showed significant growth. In 1991/2, the capacity utilisation rates for Kilombero and Mtibwa averaged 75 per cent. Another positive effect of the price increases in relation to structural adjustment has been the sharply rising share of the outgrowers' contribution to total sugar-cane production since 1989. Finally, the profits of the sugar companies have gone up markedly since the increase in ex-factory prices, which allow for reservations for future investments. The first conclusion is, therefore, that economic liberalisation accompanying structural adjustment has had a favourable impact on the performance of the sugar sector.

The Netherlands support during the 1970s focused on investments for the expansion of sugar production which were made jointly with other donors. These investments did not, however, have the expected effect. The economic rates of return lagged considerably behind predictions and the Kagera estate is a complete failure. The factory has never operated at more than 10 per cent of its capacity and the company has experienced enormous losses. In retrospect, Netherlands participation in the Kilombero II factory must also be assessed unfavourably. A third example of unsatisfactory results is the investment in the Kilombero irrigation system. Yield-level differences between rain-fed and irrigated cane fields were insignificant and the costs incurred were not recovered.

During the 1980s the Netherlands changed its assistance policy from supporting the expansion of estates and processing capacity to supporting a holding operation aimed at a better utilisation of existing capacity, and from project-type support to a more comprehensive sector aid approach. Under the sectoral approach a combination of types of aid was provided: programme aid, project aid and technical assistance. In the policy dialogue between Tanzania and the Netherlands, the continuation of assistance was related to general economic reforms, such as liberalisation of price setting, retention of foreign exchange earned through exports and privatisation of the industry.

This approach has been quite successful. More specifically, factory capacity utilisation has been maintained at levels considerably higher than the national average. During the 1980s, Netherlands support to Kilombero and Mtibwa realised an average rate of return of 17 per cent. Positive results were also achieved in the localisation of personnel through local, in-service and overseas training.

The second conclusion is that the sectoral approach made a significant contribution to the reform process. The aid prevented the collapse of the Tanzanian sugar industry and provided a basis for the growth of production in the 1990s, which occurred under full Tanzanian management.

References

Abbott, G.C. (1990) *Sugar*. Routledge, London and New York.

Chambua, S.E. (1990) 'Choice of technique and underdevelopment: the case of the Sugar Development Corporation'. *Canadian Journal of African Studies*, 24, 1, pp. 17–35.

Cooksey, B., Kwayu, C. and Fowler, A. (1987) *Incentive Goods for Development in Tanzania: A Survey of the Demand Priorities among the Villages in Tanga and Mwanza Regions and Implications for Policy*. Consultants for Management of Development Programmes (CDP), Dar es Salaam.

Coulson, A. (ed.) (1979) *African Socialism in Practice: The Tanzanian Experience*. Russell Press, Nottingham.

Doriye, I. and Wuyts, M. (1993) *Fungibility and Sustainability: Import Support to Tanzania*. Swedish International Development Authority, Stockholm.

Inspectie Ontwikkelingsamenwerking te Velde (1992) *Sector Aid and Structural Adjustment: The Case of Sugar in Tanzania*. Operations Review Unit (IOV), Netherlands Development Co-operation, The Hague.

Maliyamkono, T.L. and Bagachwa, M.S.D. (1990) *The Second Economy in Tanzania*. Eastern and Southern Africa Universities Research Programme, Dar es Salaam and James Currey, London.

Netherlands Economic Institute (1988) *Feasibility Study of a Development Plan for the Sugar Industry in Tanzania*. Rotterdam.

Netherlands Economic Institute (1991) *The Sugar Industry in Tanzania: A Restructuring Study*. Rotterdam.

Rattsoe, J. (1992) *Structural Adjustment in Tanzania*. Ministry of Foreign Affairs, Oslo.

World Bank (1990) *World Bank/Tanzania Relations 1961–1987*. Washington, DC.

World Bank (1991) *Tanzania Economic Report: Towards Sustainable Development in the 1990s*. Washington, DC.

World Bank (1992) *Tanzania: Policy Framework Paper 1992/93–1994/95*. Washington, DC.

World Bank (1993) *Economic Situation and Status of Adjustment Programme*. Paper prepared for the consultative group meeting on Tanzania, Washington, DC.

CHAPTER 8

Structural Adjustment and Rural Development in Tanzania: The Case of Makete District

Milline Mbonile

Introduction

This chapter examines the impact of structural adjustment in the development of Makete district in south-west Tanzania. The difficult economic conditions imposed by the structural adjustment programme (SAP) adopted by the government at macro-level adversely affected the employment of migrants from the district, a former labour reserve. Generally, these reforms triggered a wave of return migrants whose contribution to rural development varies from one place to another. Although trade liberalisation promoted the growth of trade in major towns throughout Tanzania, the whole process aggravated the exploitation of more resources from remote areas such as Makete. Moreover, the introduction of a wide range of structural adjustment measures in the district has led to severe environmental degradation and development of a legacy of overdependence on international organisations in every aspect of life.

In general, Tanzania's post-independence 'Arusha' reforms affecting human settlements, from the smallest rural village to the primate city of Dar es Salaam, have generated much discussion on the role of governments in the structural transformation of society in the Third World. Since most of these reforms have been aimed at improving the living and environmental conditions of the people, they have been praised by many human settlement and development planners. Explicitly, these socialist policies aimed at transforming the rural society by discouraging overconcentration of population in a few urban centres by spreading the basic community infrastructure and non-agricultural employment to the countryside. Implicitly, they were intended to reduce the rural–urban gap and eliminate rural–urban migration by promoting a balanced distribution of economic activities (Kulaba, 1982, p. 16).

To implement this broad goal growth centres which could act as counter-magnets to discourage the fast growth of Dar es Salaam as the primate city were

136

introduced in 1969. In addition the decentralisation policy introduced in 1972 encouraged the development of infrastructure and social services in rural areas and small towns so that they could attract potential migrants and investors (Sawyers, 1989).

Despite the introduction of all these policies the decline of the rural economy in Tanzania since the 1970s has been dramatic. The major causes include drought in 1974 and 1979, the oil crisis of 1974, the villagisation programme which disrupted the established rural pattern of production between 1973 and 1976, the collapse of the East African Community in 1977, the Uganda War in 1979 and the abolition of co-operatives and local district councils by the government in 1976. In rural areas the vacuum caused by the abolition of co-operatives and local governments had a significant impact on the marketing of peasant crops and the maintenance of roads which were essential in transporting rural commodities. These important rural development institutions were replaced by bureaucratic crop authorities and central government. Furthermore, agricultural exports were adversely affected by government restrictions on imports and the low level of industrial output. These restrictions limited the quantity of agricultural inputs, such as fertilisers and farm tools, which could be imported into the country. During that period the agricultural sector also suffered from lack of transport as a result of fuel shortages and lack of spare parts (Maghimbi, 1992, p. 14).

The total stagnation of the economy in the 1980s forced the government to introduce a number of policies which could reverse this trend. In order to solicit foreign aid, which was essential to revive the economy, regional integrated development programmes (RIDEPs) were introduced. These divided the country into 20 planning units under the control of different foreign donors. This change isolated the government from participating directly in village development at the very moment when villages required a strong organisational base to transform peasant agriculture (Bryceson, 1988, p. 44). Other measures which addressed this problem included the National Economic Survival Programme (NESP) which was launched in 1981. Since this programme aimed at increasing national production and exports by using the existing economy it recognised the importance of agriculture as the backbone of the country. Another, the SAP, was launched between 1982 and 1985. It was concerned principally with pruning the central government budget by restructuring several public enterprises. In addition, it was this programme which restored co-operatives and local government functions and lifted import controls which increased the importation of agricultural inputs and minimised transport bottlenecks. It was also under this programme that the demands of the International Monetary Fund (IMF) were adopted. The change towards market-oriented economic policies compelled the government to remove subsidies on food and agricultural inputs, the first effect of which was an increase in the prices of consumer goods, which forced households to grow their own food and run other activities as a survival strategy (see Chapter 6). For those who

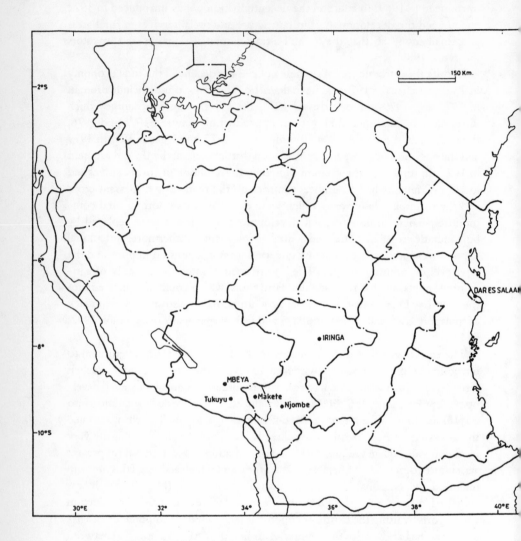

Figure 8.1 Locations of Makete Migration Survey areas

could not cope with such an increase in the cost of living the most immediate alternative was either return migration or starvation. The limited success of the SAP and the need for more foreign investment, coupled with positive results of trade liberalisation introduced in 1984, induced the government to launch the economic recovery programme (ERP) in 1986. Among the measures that the programme adopted which had direct impact on rural development were changes in the marketing of agricultural produce and further trade liberalisation (Campbell and Stein, 1992).

Makete Migration Survey

The empirical findings on which the present study is based derive from a household survey conducted in Makete district between July 1991 and April 1992. As shown in Figure 8.1, the rural part of the Makete Migration Survey (MMS) covered both villages and major trading centres. The sample of 100 agricultural households was obtained from Isapulano (Iwawa ward), Kilanji (Kipagalo ward), Iniho (Iniho ward) and Kinyika (Matamba ward) villages, which were selected at random from several villages in the respective wards. Samples of 82 business households and 78 waged employment households were selected from Makete, Matamba and Bulongwa trading centres. These major trading centres in Makete were selected after taking field inventories of all trading centres and grading them according to their administrative and commercial importance in the district. A few households from this category were interviewed in Isapulano and Iniho villages.

Migration and Rural Development

With regard to the wave of countermigration experienced after the introduction of SAPs, it can be said that, on most occasions, migrants return home not because of redundancy but for more complex reasons, which in turn influence the kind of impact they have in their home area (King *et al.*, 1983, p. 155). A critical examination of the period of first and last return migration of migrants in Makete shows a clear relationship between migration and economic stagnation in Tanzania which began late in the 1960s and escalated following the oil crisis of 1974. Generally, in MMS areas which depended on plantation labour and mining, most of the migration occurred before 1970. During this period the government took some measures to discourage labour migration to the plantations because it was believed to retard rural development in labour reserves (Table 8.1 and Figure 8.2). Above all, migration reflects the gradual decay of the plantation economy which was predominant during the colonial period (Lwoga, 1989, p. 340). At the same time labour migration to the mines in South Africa was boycotted by the government in 1963 to protest against that country's apartheid policy (Wilson, 1976; Sterkenburg and Luning, 1980, p. 188). According to Vandinege Sanga of Kilanji village, who was among the prominent migrants during this period:

> The Witwatersrand Native Labour Association Office in Tukuyu was closed immediately after independence and the few who managed to sneak through Chitipa in Malawi were later curtailed by further political hostility with Malawi. Also after the independence of Zambia in 1964, the employment in the mines was reserved for the Zambians. The last time I attempted to migrate to Zambia in 1965 I totally missed employment and I was forced to return forever. Locally, the gold mines in Chunya were less profitable at large-scale mining and so were closed in the early 1960s. I could not go to the plantations because they were paying smaller salaries than the mines.

Table 8.1: Return Migration by Period of First and Last Return Migration

Place	Period of First Migration				%	H/h
	<1960	1960–70	1971–80	1981–90+		
Isapulano	4.4	0.0	65.2	30.4	100	23
Bulongwa	5.7	20.0	25.7	48.6	100	35
Kilanji	65.4	23.1	3.9	7.6	100	26
Iniho	48.5	6.1	21.2	24.2	100	33
Matamba	5.9	29.4	23.5	41.2	100	17
Kinyika	40.0	20.0	13.3	26.7	100	15
Makete	9.7	16.1	29.0	45.2	100	62
H/h	**49**	**33**	**56**	**73**	–	**211**
	Period of Last Return Migration					
Isapulano	0.0	4.3	43.5	52.2	100	23
Bulongwa	2.9	2.9	20.0	74.3	100	35
Kilanji	19.2	34.6	19.2	27.0	100	26
Iniho	33.3	12.1	15.2	45.4	100	33
Matamba	5.9	0.0	5.9	88.2	100	17
Kinyika	20.0	20.0	6.7	53.3	100	15
Makete	4.8	4.8	17.7	52.7	100	62
H/h	**24**	**21**	**40**	**126**	–	**211**

Source: Makete Migration Survey, 1991/2.

An increase in private tobacco and maize smallholder farms in areas such as Ismani raised rural–rural migration to a certain extent between 1971 and 1980, mainly to Iringa region (Nindi, 1987, p. 93). Similarly, there was an increase in long-distance migration to Morogoro region due to the expansion of Kilombero and Mtibwa Sugar Plantations. Moreover, an overall change in housing conditions in rural areas promoted lumbering and building opportunities which increased migration to a few neighbouring regions such as Ruvuma (Lwoga, 1989, p. 189; Mayombo, 1990).

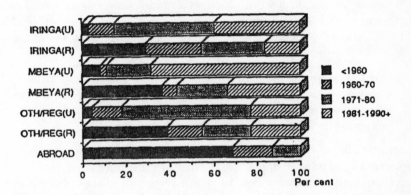

Figure 8.2 Returnees by direction in period of first migration

Since old traditions die hard, a few people still migrate to the plantations. A clandestine labour recruitment office in Nduramo (Lupalilo ward) operates occasionally. The few people interviewed were reluctant to reveal their destination because the term *manamba* (forced labourer) carries a social and political stigma. In addition, in the 1980s there was an upsurge of rural–rural migration to Mbeya region which was the result of reviving the Chunya Gold Mines under small-scale mining prospectors. Circular migration to these mines is expected to increase because the banks started to buy gold directly from these prospectors in 1992 as a structural adjustment measure (EIU, 1992, p. 13; *The Express*, 1993, p. 14). Furthermore, the construction of Mtera Dam in Iringa region and the creation of a large artificial lake attracts several fishermen.

On the other hand in trading centres the peak of first and return migration occurred in the 1980s, mainly as a result of the rapid growth of business after trade liberalisation in 1984 (Mbonile, 1993). This rise in the number of business households marked the beginning of a dramatic change in the direction of migration in the post-independence period in Tanzania. For the first time, rural–urban migration overtook rural–rural migration, which has been the dominant form of migration since the colonial period. When rural–urban migration is further disaggregated by period, it shows that before 1980 most migrants moved to towns within Iringa region and other distant regions. However, in the 1980s there was a total swing in favour of urban areas in Mbeya region followed by Iringa region. This rise in short-distance rural–urban migration completely overshadowed long-distance migration to other regions.

The main forces which brought about all these changes in the direction of migration are clearly revealed when the period of last return migration is examined. Undoubtedly the second peak of return migration of plantation and mining labourers which occurred in the 1980s is an aftermath of structural adjustment adopted in Tanzania during the same period. As in all developing countries, structural adjustment brought a striking change in all sectors of the economy which affected the overall employment of the population (Riddell, 1992). As stated by Rosemary Mlowezi of Kilanji village, who was among the few forced return migrants from Zambia:

> Due to structural adjustment in Zambia, the few miners from Makete who were still working in there were repatriated with nothing. Unfortunately, when my father attempted to strike another fortune in Chunya Gold Mines as a private prospector he was buried by falling mining sand.

In fact, this global change in employment opportunities was not confined to plantation and mine labourers alone. The harsh economic conditions in urban areas triggered a massive flow of return migration. The deepening of the economic crisis coupled with the removal of food subsidies subjected residents of large urban centres and long-distance migrants to food insecurity which in turn is the result of overdependence on purchased food (Bryceson, 1990, pp. 212–13; Maliyamkono and Bagachwa, 1990, pp. 123–6). When this rise in the cost of living combined with transport problems it compelled several migrant households to return to the area of origin or to neighbouring towns where it was easy to get land for cultivating food to supplement meagre incomes from wage employment or business. Those who could not manage to get land to cultivate their own food were either forced to rely on supplementary food from relatives in rural areas or to live on or below the poverty line. Positively, trade liberalisation promoted trade in major centres located along the Tanzania–Zambia Railway which acted as counter-magnets to long-distance migration (Gleave, 1992, p. 258; Holm, 1992, p. 241).

Overall it was relatively easy for most return migrants to settle in new areas because most of them were laid off by private and public enterprises. Therefore, they utilised their redundancy or retirement benefits to start their own businesses. Besides this, the availability of commodities after trade liberalisation enabled return migrants and others to establish businesses in small trading centres where there was less competition. Furthermore, MMS revealed that, during structural adjustment, the urban forces that were strong in attracting migrants were equally strong in encouraging return migration within those households which could not cope with the perpetual rise in the cost of living and other uncertainties about the future of the household (Mbonile, 1993).

Return migration had a considerable impact in the area of origin during the colonial period. However, migration as a contributor to change has generally declined in Africa during the post-independence period (Chilivumbo, 1985, p. 16). The same view appears to hold for international migration as well. King *et al.* (1985, p. 156) found that, in southern Italy, returnees came back with conservative ideas and limited ambitions. The only desire they had was to buy a plot of land, build themselves a new home and invest in small-scale enterprises. To a certain extent migration is still an agent of social change in Makete. The results of MMS indicate that both in villages and trading centres returnees have better houses than non-migrants. In general there are several factors which influence return migrants and other households to build modern houses in Makete. First, as a survival strategy, most households in trading centres are forced to construct modern houses for renting. At the other extreme, those who have less income are forced to build traditional houses to avoid rampant rent increases by landlords who are also struggling to survive in the harsh economic conditions. Second, the rise in producer prices promoted the construction of modern houses in several villages which have cash crops. Unfortunately the increases in the prices of building materials and transport costs due to macroeconomic changes have impeded the modernisation of houses in several areas. As expressed by the carpenter, Tulambona Ng'wavi, of Iniho village:

> The people of Makete would like to have modern houses as their neighbours the Wanyakyusa but transport and high prices after trade liberalisation retard them. Most of the people who build modern houses either carry corrugated iron sheets on the head from Tukuyu or pay exorbitant prices to hire motor vehicles from Mbeya and Njombe and a few get them from the co-operatives.

An in-depth study of the major sources of building materials revealed that the chance of getting building materials from co-operatives after their re-establishment in 1984 was very narrow because most of them have little capital and are riddled with corruption.

The influence of return migrants in the modernisation of Makete is not limited to housing only. In most *ujamaa* villages the leaders are return migrants. Severe economic conditions in the 1980s forced some educated people to return to their villages of origin where they were encouraged to compete for various leadership posts. In addition, most government departments in the district are staffed by return migrants. They are also leading in coffee production which was recently introduced to diversify the dependence of the district on a single cash crop, pyrethrum. As stated by Mzee Luvanda of Utengule village:

> I have been growing coffee since the 1950s when I came back from the tea plantations in Rungwe district but since it was not specified as a cash crop of this area I was growing it for my own consumption. That was until when the experts recommended it as a cash crop in the late 1980s when I stepped up its production and in the near future I will be getting a lot of money.

At a micro-level this overall impact of migration in the development of Makete differed by both type of employment of returnees at the area of destination and from one place to another. In villages such as Kilanji, where long-term migrants were made redundant due to old age, the impact was negative. A typical example is Mzee Zachariah Sanga of Kilanji village, who migrated to the tea plantations in Tanga in the 1950s while he was still young. When he was forced to return due to structural change in the tea plantations in the 1980s, his wife and children refused to return with him. On arrival in Kilanji village he had no close relatives. Consequently he was forced to depend on other return migrants who were helped by him to obtain employment when he was a tea plantation supervisor in Tanga. This situation was faced by several long-term return migrants who found that, due to the long period of absence, their traditional land was now occupied by other people. Moreover, in order to cope with rural life, they had to undergo traditional training and orientation. On the other hand, in villages such as Kinyika and trading centres where the majority of return migrants were young, their contribution to development was positive. Most of them were quick to adopt modern farming methods and to build modern houses, which are essential in the modernisation of the district. In villages such as Isapulano, the majority of returnees were engaged in lumbering and the little money they earned as migrants promoted polygamy and marriage instabilities. In villages such as Iniho and trading centres such as Bulongwa, where most returnees were employed as domestic servants, their contribution to the development of the district was negligible. The few returnees in Matamba trading centre who were engaged in private farming at the area of destination came with tractors, thus promoting modern farming. Those who were pursuing further education elsewhere, with greater higher education opportunities, raised the rural unemployment rate when they returned to Makete (Von Troil, 1992, p. 224). Those who were employed by relatives as shop assistants came back to Makete with some business skills and some capital which inspired them to establish businesses.

Although most older return migrants have no intention of migrating again because they believe that migration is no longer profitable, young returnees are prepared to migrate again if they accumulate enough capital to start business elsewhere. This desire to migrate after accumulating enough wealth in rural areas is motivated by the success of contemporary migrants in business in major urban centres. Since these migrant households invest heavily in terms of houses and *shambas* (farms) in urban areas, as a survival strategy in harsh economic conditions, the draining of both human and material resources from remote areas like Makete perpetuates rural-urban differentials. To add salt to the wound, most return migrants challenge the whole idea of building expensive houses in rural areas because it is uneconomical. When this is accompanied by dwindling remittances, caused by hard economic conditions, the overall impact of migration on the development of the district is negligible (Mbonile, 1993).

Land Reforms

Land Redistribution and Agricultural Reforms

Studies by Sutton (1978, p. 66) and Dixon (1990, p. 80) show that land reform frequently means little more than land redistribution. Although the villagisation programme referred to above had little impact on land redistribution in Tanzania as whole, the household shifts and house realignments affected housing development in rural areas (Bryceson, 1988, p. 42). In several villages in Makete, the movement of households within or to outside the village was accompanied by the destruction of modern houses (Table 8.2). The struggle to restore the old standard of housing is still going on in several villages due to hyper-inflation and astronomical rises in the price of building materials since trade liberalisation began. The expensive building materials forced some households to build with burnt bricks thatched with grass, while others reverted to traditional houses built with poles and thatching grass.

The most remarkable land reforms occurring during the period of structural adjustment are observed in agriculture. These changes, which can be construed as a *green revolution*, increased household agricultural production through greater use of hybrid seeds and fertilisers in the district (Rasmussen, 1986, pp. 192–4; Lawrence, 1988, p. 65). The most spectacular change in food production occurred with Irish potatoes, where old varieties like *loti* were replaced by several new varieties which include *alika*, *baraka*, *malawi*, *sasamua* and *kikondo*.

Table 8.2: Land Reforms in Surveyed Villages

Village	Distribution of Land by Villagisation					
	HGLP	*HLDP*	*HSV*	*HNAV*	*%*	*H/h*
Isapulano	10.5	5.7	78.9	5.3	100	19
Kilanji	3.3	0.0	93.4	3.3	100	30
Iniho	22.6	48.4	9.7	19.4	100	31
Kinyika	5.0	45.0	40.0	10.0	100	20
H/h	**11**	**25**	**54**	**10**	**–**	**100**

		Changes in Agriculture				
	Hybrid Seeds	*Chemical Fertilisers*	*Modern Tools*	*Soil Conservation*	*%*	*H/h*
Isapulano	47.4	26.3	15.8	10.5	100	19
Kilanji	46.7	3.3	46.7	3.3	100	30
Iniho	51.6	19.4	9.6	19.4	100	31
Kinyika	25.0	60.0	10.0	5.0	100	20
H/h	**44**	**24**	**22**	**10**	**–**	**100**

Notes: 1. HGLP = Household got land from other people. 2. HLDP = Household land distributed to other people. 3. HSV = Household shifted in the same village. 3. HNAV = Household not affected by villagisation programme.
Source: Makete Migration Survey, 1991/2.

The use of hybrid seeds is not confined to potatoes alone. The old varieties of wheat, the principal staple crop, like *kahesya* and *ngongile*, are being replaced by new varieties like *magunila* and *mabuge*. Similarly, a high-yielding variety of maize called *Bulongwa no. 19* was introduced and a quick-ripening variety of sweet potatoes called *dabaga* was introduced from Dabaga area in Iringa district. As stated by Komba, (1992, p. 80) and Eale *et al.* (1992, p. 20), the introduction of hybrids in cereals like wheat and maize presents a strong challenge to peasants in terms of disease and pest control. For example, the emergence of a pest known locally as *scania* has interfered with the traditional method of storing cereals in the barns with cobs or stocks. Furthermore, it is difficult to control such pests because the removal of subsidies from insecticides and other agricultural inputs has reduced the ability of most peasants to buy them. Generally the credit for the introduction of all these varieties of hybrids, bearing local names for easy diffusion of knowledge, goes to Uyole Agricultural Centre in Mbeya region which is assigned to carry out agricultural research in the Southern Highlands. However, all this research cannot succeed if there is no aid from international organisations like the Food and Agriculture Organisation (FAO), which fund these centres when the country is in economic crisis.

On the other hand, the household utilisation of modern fertilisers shows great variations by ward. In Matamba division, where there is significant land deterioration, most households use fertilisers intensively. By contrast, in villages like Kilanji, which have fertile, loamy soils, fertilisers are used only occasionally. The same trend is observed in the use of modern tools, where ploughs are confined mostly to Matamba division due to its low-lying topography. In other areas the only change in agricultural tools is in the use of a broad-based hand hoe called *rungwe*. Also most crops are planted with proper spacing and lines and in some areas ridges and terraces are used.

Another major development in agriculture influenced by structural change has been in animal husbandry. New breeds of cattle have been introduced in the district by using two externally funded projects. The first project, called Small Scale Dairy Development Project, partly funded by the government of Switzerland, began in 1989 in 32 villages. The project starts with training and improving pastures for almost a year before the dairy cattle are distributed to the respective households. During the survey, one cow was sold at a price of about Tsh32,000 while on dairy farms like Kitulo in Kitulo ward they were selling at about Tsh100,000. Running almost parallel to this project, the Lutheran Diocese of Southern Central Tanzania, based in Bulongwa, introduced another dairy cattle project funded by a grant from Lutheran churches in Germany. It involved transferring the first calf to another household to ensure a more widespread distribution of modern cattle among poor peasants. Both projects managed to construct several cattle dips which are used by livestock keepers. The introduction of high-quality bulls in several villages has led to an increase of crossbreeds which produce more milk and meat than local breeds.

More related to a change in cattle keeping is the introduction of donkeys which, together with wheelbarrows, are supposed to ease the local transport problem in the district. As part of Makete RIDEP this project imported donkeys from Usangu Plains which are developed and acclimatised at Mbela and Bulongwa breeding centres (ILO, 1990). According to Mr Mbwilo, the co-ordinator of Bulongwa Breeding Centre:

> The diffusion of the use of donkeys in transport is fast and more popular in wards like Matamba where they are used in transporting cash crops. Those households which understand the importance of this new technology buy donkeys from distant breeding centres like Bulongwa even by using different names for they earn a lot of money when other households hire them.

As in all projects which are imposed on peasants by external forces, these projects are facing several problems. As peasants' demand for cattle increased it outstripped the supply, and since the price of cattle was low, rich peasants and government officials bought large numbers at the expense of poor peasants. Moreover, when the cattle dips are handed over to the district council most of them are closed due to lack of funds. This is detrimental to modern cattle which are less resistant to tick diseases. The donkey and wheelbarrow project which is supposed to ease the burden of women in transporting firewood and water is in fact dominated by men who use them in other household activities like transporting cash crops. Thus, although the demand for wheelbarrows increased the use of wooden wheels recommended by the project, repairs have become more frequent and more expensive. This discourages both peasants and carpenters who opt for other more durable and profitable household activities such as the roofing of houses. Besides this, the diffusion of this new technology depends on the presence of cash crops and on topography. It is more widespread in Matamba division because donkeys are used in transporting pyrethrum and the low-lying topography allows donkeys to move very easily. Overall, the major problem of all these projects is overdependence on foreign investment, which threatens their survival once the foreign capital ceases.

Afforestation

Another area where structural adjustment influenced land use in Makete is in afforestation. Since firewood will remain the principal source of fuel for the majority of the people in Tanzania for several decades, serious attempts have been made to solve the problem of scarcity of firewood in the district (Nilsson, 1986, p. 160). The afforestation programme began even before the district was formed in 1979. It started with the distribution of black wattle, imported from Kibena Wattle Farm in Njombe district, to various households. Although the distribution of black wattle ceased a long time ago the project has been successful because these trees self-broadcast and at present provide firewood to several households. Despite this success, the project was abandoned in favour of exotic trees like cypress and pine, which were recommended by the RIDEP. These trees were introduced into the district in order to increase commercial timber production but, overall, this project is less successful because large areas of cypress trees have been devastated by an unidentified disease. Although pines produce timber it is difficult to market due to lack of transport in the district. This problem compels lumberers to migrate to other areas with better commercial and transport infrastructure. Furthermore, coniferous trees are not good for enhancing soil fertility and cannot be planted with other crops, a factor which aggravates land scarcity for agriculture. Nor can they regenerate once ravaged by fire, a common feature in the tropics. Besides the introduction of foreign species of trees, the conservation of natural forests in the Livingstone Mountains and other areas for soil and catchment area preservation is given high priority.

Despite all these efforts the problem of firewood is far from being resolved in Makete district. There are some villages in Matamba ward where the acute lack of firewood compelled them to solicit firewood aid from the Makete RIDEP. According to the district forest officer both afforestation and conservation of natural forests are facing several problems. The destruction of trees by fire in Ikuwo, Iniho, Ipelele, Kitulo, Lupila and Mang'oto wards is very common. The destruction is more intense in areas with high in-migration of population from urban areas and other neighbouring districts. These migrants are searching for virgin land for growing potatoes and other crops to satisfy the demand for food in urban areas. Driven by both profit motive and survival strategy these migrants slash and burn every piece of virgin land available, leading to a big loss of natural vegetation cover and exacerbating the problems of soil erosion and floods in low-lying districts like Kyela. The increase in potato demand also adversely affects the production of the main cash crop, pyrethrum, which is subject to international markets characterised by fluctuating primary product prices.

Improvement of Socio-economic Infrastructure

Water Supply

In 1971 Tanzania embarked on an ambitious goal of providing safe water within easy access to all rural households by 1991 (Therkildsen, 1986, p. 293). In Makete this goal has been achieved in only a few areas or villages, because the provision of this essential service to the rural population lies solely in the hands of the Danish International Development Agency (DANIDA), which, under the RIDEPs, is assigned to develop water supply in the Southern Highlands. If the efforts of DANIDA are not supplemented by the local authorities and other organisations, the aim of supplying water to every household in Makete will not be fulfilled for many decades. The delay in the development of a clean water supply means that villages such as Isapulano are still dependent on the traditional rural sources of water such as rivers and wells (Table 8.3). In wards like Iniho and Bulongwa, this goal was fulfilled only recently, following the construction of Bulongwa Water Supply Complex. The project is supposed to extend to Ijoka, Mahulu and Kilanji villages in Kipagalo ward where, during the survey, the construction was in the final stages. Negotiations were still going on to extend the water supply to Utengule village, which was not originally in DANIDA's plan as it had an established water supply installed by the Lutheran Mission. This project failed due to poor initial planning by the Mission. In Ipelele, Lupalilo, Lupila, Mang'oto, Matamba, Mlondwe and Ukwama wards the clean water supply was installed several years ago with the help of DANIDA and private initiative from the proprietor of Makete Bus Services, Yohana Mnange Sanga, especially in Ukwama ward.

Due primarily to inadequate local input, this project also has numerous internal and external problems which undermine the control of water by the local population. Internally, even in areas where the piped water supply is available, there are some households which still use traditional water supplies. This is because the fixing of minimum distances from one piped water station to another places some households too far away from the station. Other households are prohibited from using the clean water supply because they disobeyed strict regulations on the use of water set up by DANIDA and implemented by the villagers. Further, since the control of the water supply rests with the villagers who provided labour, there are few households that have a piped water supply. Only in Matamba and Makete trading centres is an attempt to install a piped water supply inside the houses being made because of their better prospects of developing into major towns. Externally, the future of this project appears bleak once DANIDA leaves. A clear indication of this is shown by the number of closures of piped water stations in wards like Ipelele and Mlondwe where piped water was installed several years ago.

Table 8.3: Household Water Supply by Place of Residence

Place	Type of Water Supply				%	H/h
	Piped Water in H/h	Public Piped Water	Wells	Rivers		
Isapulano	0.0	0.0	0.0	100.0	100	30
Bulongwa	0.0	91.9	8.1	0.0	100	37
Kilanji	0.0	0.0	46.7	53.3	100	30
Iniho	0.0	100.0	0.0	0.0	100	38
Matamba	21.4	75.0	3.6	0.0	100	28
Kinyika	0.0	100.0	0.0	0.0	100	20
Makete	5.2	85.7	5.2	3.9	100	77
H/h	**10**	**179**	**22**	**49**	**-**	**260**

Source: Makete Migration Survey, 1991/2.

Transport

For any agropolitan rural development programme to succeed, intervention in rural transport is essential (Friedmann, 1988; ILO, 1990). Lack of reliable transport is the most acute problem in Makete, as clearly stated by Bishop Solomon Swalo, who was among the first people to raise this problem at international level:

> All most meaningful and productive operations in the district are done during the dry season. Unfortunately, the district has rainfall for almost ten months in a year which leaves only two months for all transactions to be done which is impossible for any institution which would like to serve the community effectively.

It was this concern which inspired the Lutheran Diocese of South Central Tanzania to send a request for aid to improve transport in Makete to the World Council of Churches in Geneva. The Council contacted the government of Switzerland which agreed to fund the project provided it was under the auspices of the government of Tanzania. Eventually, after a long period of negotiation, the Makete integrated rural transport project was initiated in 1986. The project was funded by the Swiss Development Corporation but, as in most externally-funded projects, the basic planning and implementation was left in the hands of the International Labour Organisation, which was appointed as the consultant. As in all integrated programmes, one of its main objectives is to assist Makete district to set up sustainable interventions in transport that would result in improvement of basic social and economic services of the community, including water supply, firewood, agricultural and marketing facilities and social services (ILO, 1988, 1990).

To implement this major objective the project recommended self-help participation by the community along with the use of local materials in the manufacture of low-cost means of transport. As stated above, the latter included donkeys and wheelbarrows. In addition the project intervened directly to improve roads and footpaths. As a result there has been some improvement of major outlets in the district, enabling a bus to reach Makete trading centre even in December. After that, rain becomes more intense and leaves the district almost cut off from the rest of the country.

Despite all its good intentions, this project also has several problems. First, since it is funded by an international organisation, it employed several experts who are paid a high proportion of aid as salaries and allowances. Second, the demand of the people of Makete is to improve trunk roads which can link them with major trading centres. Contrary to this demand, more funds are being used to improve footpaths which, in rural areas, change regularly. Third, intensive research is being conducted on escarpment tram transport in Livingstone Mountains which is similar to countries like Norway and Switzerland. However, it is totally unrealistic to contemplate adopting this advanced type of transport in a district like Makete, which does not even have electricity. Fourth, and even worse since the project falls under the government, it was caught up in regional politics. The contract to improve major roads in Makete was given to the Mwananchi Transport Services, which runs passenger bus services and does not even have a construction subsidiary. As a result a large proportion of roads and bridges made of softwood collapsed immediately the contractor disappeared to Iringa town.

Besides external aid for transport, the district council motivated the people to contribute to buy a bus which was supposed to travel between Makete trading centre and Njombe town. However, during the survey the bus was not operating because it is controlled by the district executive director, who collects the fares. A mere change of these officers led to the bus being out of operation for more than six months. Added to this, the rise in prices of spare parts after trade liberalisation put all hope of reviving the bus out of reach for a long period.

Milling Machines

Another area where the Makete RIDEP is supposed to intervene is in the improvement of milling machines in order to replace grinding stones (ILO, 1990). The importance of hand-milling machines to households in Makete can be traced back to the 1950s, when parents were demanding part of the bride price to be paid in luxury goods. According to Mwisebege Sanga of Kilanji village, parents during that time said that: 'My daughter was singing and grinding in my house which meant the bridegroom was obliged to pay a gramophone and hand-milling machines as part of the bride price.'

It was this high demand for luxury goods by return migrants at that time which encouraged most households in Makete to purchase hand-milling machines. Other households also managed to purchase them because the world market price of pyrethrum was high. When those good days ended after the oil crisis in 1974 most grinding machines ceased to operate due to lack of spare parts. Afterwards an attempt by missions to install motor-milling machines almost collapsed due to lack of spare parts and fuel and the problem was only partially solved by buying them from the Small Industries Development Organisation workshops established in most regional capitals. However, these spare parts are less durable and few businessmen are prepared to stock them in large quantities due to lack of capital. The major setback to the project occurred when the machine for making spare parts for the milling machines was stolen from Makete trading centre.

Health and Nutrition

The decentralisation and rural development policy adopted in Tanzania in the late 1960s led to a rapid expansion of health infrastructure in order to combat sickness, malnutrition and infectious diseases (Kamuzora, 1986, p. 30). Relative to population size Makete district is not deprived of essential health services, and is only surpassed by districts such as Rungwe in Mbeya region and Moshi in Kilimanjaro region, which were favoured in the allocation of social services during the colonial period (Mbonile, 1993, p. 253).

However, despite this improvement, structural adjustment affected the development of health services in the district in several ways. First, the decline of medical aid from developed countries to the Third World during the 1980s imposed a severe strain on both government and non-governmental organisations' (NGOs) health services (Thebaud, 1986, p. 43). This problem is more acute in a district like Makete where health services depend on missionary aid. Locally the two large hospitals (Ikonda and Bulongwa) and several dispensaries owned by missions charge the patients for medical services, but the high price of imported medicine prevents the majority of peasants from receiving even the most basic health care. At the national level the cost has led to several health centres having no medical stock, and because of this most health centres depend on the Essential Drug Programme, where a fixed number of drugs to be distributed is predetermined by donor countries. As a result these drugs are exhausted before the end of the month, leaving the centres with no medicine until another allocation arrives.

Second, as stated by the district medical officer and the medical officer in Bulongwa Lutheran Hospital, malnutrition and ill health are still prevalent in Makete district, because of the daily working schedule of the mother rather than food scarcity. As a result of the recession most mothers are multi-occupational and spend more time making ends meet than feeding their children properly (Cornia *et al.*, 1987, p. 94; Holm, Chapter 6). To a certain extent the problem is magnified by the outmigration of males, which intensified after trade liberalisation: ultimately the women and old people remaining in rural areas cultivate less food to feed their children. Third, the harsh economic conditions imposed by structural adjustment compel the government to raise the salaries of medical workers more often. However, due to overdependence on foreign aid and the low earning capacities of these hospitals, the missions are not able to adjust these salaries in time. As a result they lose medical experts at an alarming rate to other institutions with better salary structures. Fourth, the problem of transport, cited above, inhibits the procurement and distribution of medicines.

Generally, in areas such as Bulongwa trading centre and Iniho village, where the majority of return migrants found marginal jobs such as domestic service, there was a rapid increase in premarital birth and promiscuity. Above all, a few cases of Acquired Immune Deficiency Syndrome (AIDS) reported at Ikonda Roman Catholic and Bulongwa Lutheran Hospitals are those of return migrants. After losing any hope of survival in urban areas, most AIDS victims return to rural areas to die and so indirectly disrupt the household activities of relatives who are supposed to care for them for a long time, arrange for their funerals and finally take care of orphans (Barnett and Blaikie, 1992).

Education

Tanzania is among the few countries in Africa which attempted to reorient their education systems so that the majority of the people could have access to this important social service. This move started with the introduction of education for self-reliance in 1967 and culminated with universal primary education (UPE) in 1977. This broad-based educational pyramid limits the role of higher education to the provision of skilled personnel needed to manage national development (Block, 1988, pp. 110–13). It is this education policy which enabled almost all 96 villages in Makete district to have at least one primary school. Despite the introduction of UPE in the district almost one-third of children aged 7–14 never attend any school. This problem became more critical after trade liberalisation because some children opted out of formal education, including secondary education, to go into business. In the 1980s the district managed to open up Itamba, Lupalilo, Lupila and Makwauta private secondary schools but it is only Itamba and Mwakauta which have no enrolment problems. According to the district education officer and the Director of Makete Trust Fund, Mr C. Mahenge, the total enrolment of Forms I–IV in Lupalilo Secondary School was only 101 students while in Lupila Secondary School the total enrolment of Forms I–III was 38 pupils. Two major reasons were given to explain the low enrolment in these schools, both of which are in wards from which most business households in Makete district originate. The regulation of the Ministry of Education encouraging all schools built in rural areas to have an agricultural bias therefore grossly underestimated the desire of the people in these wards for business. Second, most successful business households in major urban areas educate their children and relatives in urban areas, despite the fact that they contribute heavily to the construction of schools in Makete. This paradox prompted the Makete Development Association based in Dar es Salaam to appoint a retired education officer, Mr Michael Sanga, to investigate the whole educational problem in Makete (Mbonile, 1993, p. 258).

Supplementary Occupations

During the period of recession and SAP, both rural and urban households are obliged to engage in supplementary occupations (Maliyamkono and Bagachwa, 1990, p. 119). These include the manufacture of local crafts, brewing of local beer and petty trade (Collier *et al.*, 1986, p. 65). Most households in Makete have supplementary occupations in order to boost their monetary income or enhance their level of subsistence (Table 8.4). Nevertheless there are remarkable differences in the type of supplementary occupations between villages and trading centres. In villages the supplementary occupations are disproportionately dominated by petty business, such as the selling of local beer, which enables households to earn a little cash to buy essential commodities like kerosene and salt.

They also sell local bread, known as *ntutemeke,* to extol the name of the local member of parliament. The main local crafts include decorated bamboo baskets on which are inscribed good religious messages or names of owners and *fidilu* made of special water lilies. On the other hand, in trading centres the main supplementary occupation is agriculture. The people grow food crops, a small proportion of which is sold to supplement whatever meagre monetary income they earn from business and waged employment. The land for growing these crops is bought or hired from the villagers near the trading centres. None the less, some households have no supplementary occupation because, as in major urban centres, land near the trading centres is very expensive. This drive to sell land for profit is eroding the most fundamental African tradition of retaining land, which belongs to the whole clan. In addition, the proportion of the population with supplementary occupations is higher in trading centres which largely depend on external supplies of commodities.

Table 8.4: Household Participation in Supplementary Occupations

| Place | Type of Supplementary Occupations | | | | | | |
	Agriculture	Business	Part-time job	Multi-occupation	None	%	H/h
Isapulano	40.0	43.3	0.0	3.3	13.4	100	30
Bulongwa	75.7	5.4	2.7	16.2	0.0	100	37
Kilanji	0.0	53.3	0.0	0.0	46.7	100	30
Iniho	18.4	31.6	7.9	0.0	42.1	100	38
Matamba	85.7	3.6	0.0	3.6	7.1	100	28
Kinyika	0.0	45.0	20.0	5.0	30.0	100	20
Makete	75.3	6.5	2.6	5.2	10.4	100	77
H/h	**129**	**58**	**10**	**13**	**50**	**–**	**260**
	Member of Household Participation in Supplementary Occupation*						
Isapulano	42.3	26.9	30.8	0.0	0.0	100	26
Bulongwa	54.1	35.1	10.8	0.0	0.0	100	37
Kilanji	0.0	12.5	87.5	0.0	0.0	100	16
Iniho	33.3	4.8	61.9	0.0	0.0	100	21
Matamba	69.2	19.2	11.6	0.0	0.0	100	26
Kinyika	0.0	64.3	35.7	0.0	0.0	100	14
Makete	78.3	14.3	4.3	0.0	2.9	100	69
H/h	**110**	**47**	**50**	**0**	**2**	**–**	**209**

Note: * Households with no supplementary occupations omitted.
Source: Makete Migration Survey, 1991/2.

The participation of members of the household in supplementary occupations depends on the type of occupation involved. In trading centres where the dominant supplementary occupation is agriculture the whole household is involved. As such, the division of labour among members of the household tends to follow local farming traditions. In petty trade, especially when it involves the selling of local beer and bread, the role of women is significant. There are some households which manage to hire casual labour in supplementary occupations, especially lumbering and quarrying, which require some experience. Although very few households keep proper records of their expenditure, the contribution of supplementary occupation to the household income ranges from 10 per cent to more than 50 per cent. Most households (99 per cent) underlined the fact that they participate in supplementary occupations as a survival strategy under the harsh economic conditions (*hali ngumu* or *hali halisi*) imposed by structural adjustment.

Conclusion

This study has examined the impact of structural adjustment on rural development in Makete and concludes that the SAP had both positive and negative impacts on the development of the district. The adoption of structural adjustment at the macro-level triggered a significant flow of return migrants to the district but their impact on its development differed by the type of returnee and from one place to another. In areas where most of the returnees were employed in marginal jobs and returned in their old age their impact on rural development was negative or negligible. However, in areas where most returnees were young and came back with some basic skills, their contribution to rural development was positive. Last but not least, the establishment of business in major trading centres by return migrants represents a great contribution to rural development in a former labour reserve such as Makete. This still does not offset the fact that, with trade liberalisation, most contemporary migrants from Makete invest heavily in major urban centres, especially in the south-west of Tanzania, as a result of which the district loses both material and human resources. This problem is aggravated by an overall decline in remittances due to the hard economic conditions imposed by structural adjustment.

The astronomical rise in prices of building materials after trade liberalisation halted the modernisation of houses in Makete. The reintroduction of greater powers for co-operatives and local governments has proved a heavy burden to peasants. Since they were re-established without skilled management and capital, both institutions are riddled with corruption and lack funds, so retarding the development of the district.

Remarkable strides have been made in revolutionising agriculture. Nevertheless the removal of subsidies on agricultural inputs has dealt a devastating blow to agriculture because the price has increased more than fivefold. This change has been detrimental to rural development because it came just at the time when the farmers began to realise the importance of these inputs.

The introduction of exotic trees solved neither the problem of firewood nor of the supply of timber for marketing. Instead, it increased environmental degradation and outmigration from the district. The survival strategy adopted by urban residents to invade virgin lands in neighbouring districts in order to produce food for consumption and commercial purposes is thwarting all soil and forest conservation measures there.

Improvements in household clean water supplies are offset by overdependence on foreign aid. It is very doubtful whether this programme will survive when DANIDA leaves the country or stops giving aid. Transport is still the most critical problem in Makete district. However, the various methods which are used to solve this problem do not satisfy the main aspirations of the local population, who need better links with major transport centres. Lack of spare parts and fuel hinders the introduction and revival of both motor and hand milling machines.

The harsh economic conditions imposed by structural adjustment have compelled even rural households to take on supplementary occupations. This struggle for survival by households, coupled with heavy outmigration of males after trade liberalisation, has serious repercussions for health development in the district. Health development is also undermined by the government wage retrenchment policy which causes the district to lose medical personnel to other areas offering better pay. The overall overdependence on the Essential Drug Programme leaves the rural population without any medical care for several days per month. Frankly, trade liberalisation has retarded educational development in Makete. Since the majority of the people in Makete view business as a short cut to prosperity, many opt out of formal education and this problem is most serious in wards from which the majority of business households in Makete originate.

References

Barnett T. and Blaikie, P. (1992) *AIDS in Africa: Its Present and Future Impact.* Belhaven, London.

Block, L. (1988) 'Political process and education'. In M. Hodd (ed.) *Tanzania after Nyerere.* Pinter, London.

Bryceson, D.F. (1988) 'Household, hoe and nation: development policies of the Nyerere era'. In M. Hodd (ed.) *Tanzania after Nyerere.* Pinter, London.

Bryceson, D.F. (1990) *Food Insecurity and the Social Division of Labour in Tanzania 1919–1985.* Macmillan, London.

Campbell, H. and Stein, H. (eds) (1992) *Tanzania and the IMF: The Dynamics of Liberalisation.* Westview Press, Boulder, Colorado.

Chilivumbo, A. (1985) *Migration and Uneven Rural Development in Africa: The Case of Zambia.* University Press of America, New York/London.

Collier, P., Radwan, S. and Wangwe, S. (1986) *Labour and Poverty in Rural Tanzania*. Clarendon Press, Oxford.

Cornia, G.A., Jolly, R. and Stewart, F. (eds) (1987) *Adjustment with a Human Face: Protecting and Promoting Growth*. Clarendon Press, Oxford.

Dixon, C. (1990) *Rural Development in the Third World*. Routledge, London.

Eale, G.J., Duncan, A. and Lawson, A. (1992) *Environmental Change and Response by Small-holder Farmers: Some Evidence from Tanzania*. Food Study Group paper based on research carried out in collaboration with Sokoine University of Agriculture, Tanzania.

Economist Intelligence Unit, The (1992) *Mozambique and Tanzania Quarterly Report*, 2, p. 13.

Express (1992) 'Business and economy', 31 December–6 January 1993, p. 14.

Friedmann, J. (1988) *Life Space and Economic Space*. Transactions Books, New Brunswick, NJ.

Gleave, M.B. (1992) 'The Dar es Salaam transport corridor'. *African Affairs*, 91, 363, pp. 249–68.

Holm, M. (1992) 'Survival strategy of migrants to Makambako: an intermediate town in Tanzania'. In J. Baker and P.O. Pedersen (eds) *The Rural–Urban Interface in Africa: Expansion and Adaptation*. The Scandinavian Institute of African Studies, Uppsala.

International Labour Organization (1988) *Makete Integrated Rural Transport Project*. Geneva.

International Labour Organization (1990) *Makete Integrated Rural Transport Project II: Low cost-transport (a) Socio-economic Report*. Geneva.

Kamuzora, P. (1986) 'Redefining occupational health for Tanzania'. *Review of African Political Economy*, no. 36, pp. 30–4.

King, R., Mortimer, J., Strachan, A. and Viganola, M. (1985) 'Back to Bernalda: the dynamics of return migration to a south Italian agro-town'. In G.A. Van der Knaap and P.E. White (eds) *Contemporary Studies of Migration*. International Symposia Series. Geo Books, Norwich.

Komba, A. (1992) 'Technological factors in peasant production in Tanzania: three decades of learning by doing'. In P.G. Forster and S. Maghimbi (eds) *The Tanzanian Peasantry: Economy in Crisis*. Avebury, Aldershot.

Kulaba, S.M. (1982) 'Rural settlement policies in Tanzania'. *Habitat International*, 16, 1/2, pp. 15–29.

Lawrence, P. (1988) 'The political economy of the green revolution in Africa'. *Review of African Political Economy*, 42, pp. 59–75.

Lwoga, C.M.F. (1989) 'From long-term to seasonal labour migration in Iringa region, Tanzania: a legacy of colonial forced labour system'. In A. Zegeye and S. Ishemo (eds) *Forced Labour and Migration: Patterns of Movement within Africa*. Hans Zell, London.

Maghimbi, S. (1992) 'The decline of the economy of the mountain zones of Tanzania: a case study of Mwanga district (North Pare)'. In P.G. Forster and

S. Maghimbi (eds) *The Tanzanian Peasantry: economy in crisis*. Avebury, Aldershot.

Maliyamkono, T.L. and Bagachwa, M.S.D. (1990) *The Second Economy in Tanzania*. James Currey, London.

Mayombo, R.P. (1990) 'Economic structural changes and population movements in Kilombero Valley'. Unpublished MA Dissertation, University of Dar es Salaam.

Mbonile, M.J. (1993) 'Migration and structural change in Tanzania: the case of Makete district'. Unpublished PhD thesis, University of Liverpool.

Nilsson, P. (1986) 'Wood: the other energy crisis'. In J. Boesen, K.J. Havnevik, J. Koponen and R. Odgaard (eds) *Tanzania: Crisis and Struggle for Survival*. Scandinavian Institute of African Studies, Uppsala.

Nindi, B.C. (1987) 'Labour and capital and settler economy in colonial Tanganyika'. *Journal of Eastern African Research and Development*, 17, pp. 90–6.

Rasmussen, T. (1986) 'The green revolution in the Southern Highlands'. In J. Boesen, K.J. Havnevik, J. Koponen and R. Odgaard (eds) *Tanzania: Crisis and Struggle for Survival*. Scandinavian Institute of African Studies, Uppsala.

Riddell, J.B. (1992) 'Things fall apart again: structural adjustment in sub-Saharan Africa'. *Journal of Modern African Studies*, 30, 1, pp. 53–68.

Sawyers, L. (1989) 'Urban primacy in Tanzania'. *Economic Development and Cultural Change*, 1, pp. 843–59.

Sterkenburg, J.J. and Luning, H.A (1980) 'Population growth and economic growth in Tanzania: a case study of the Rungwe district'. In L. Bondestam and S. Bergstrom (eds) *Poverty and Population Control*. Academic Press, London.

Sutton, K. (1978) 'Reform of agrarian structures in the Third World'. In A.B. Mountjoy (ed.) *The Third World: Problems and Perspectives*. Macmillan Education, London, pp. 64–75.

Thebaud, A. (1986) 'Aid games'. *Review of African Political Economy*, no. 36, pp. 43–50.

Therkildsen, O. (1986) 'State, donors and villagers in rural water management'. In J. Boesen, J. Havnevik, J. Koponen and R. Odgaard (eds) *Tanzania: Crisis and Struggle for Survival*. Scandinavian Institute of African Studies, Uppsala.

Von Troil, M. (1992) 'Looking for better life in town: the case of Tanzania'. In J. Baker and P.O. Pedersen (eds) *The Rural–Urban Interface in Africa: Expansion and Adaptation*. Scandinavian Institute of African Studies, Uppsala.

Wilson, F. (1976) 'International migration in southern Africa'. *International Migration Review*, 4, pp. 451–88.

CHAPTER 9

Structural Adjustment Programmes and Peasant Responses in Tanzania

Claude G. Mung'ong'o and Vesa-Matti Loiske

Introduction

The history of many African countries over the last two decades or so has been one of civil strife, economic crises, environmental degradation and poverty. Empirical evidence to correlate these factors has not been wanting. Studies carried out in various African countries have clearly demonstrated that poverty often tends to be associated with environmentally-sensitive and low-potential areas. One study, for example, estimates that 51 per cent of the 'poorest of the poor' are found in such areas in Africa (Leonard, 1989). Another points out that an African map of 'absolute poverty' tends to coincide with that of the deforested areas of the continent forming a 'Crescent of Hunger' stretching from Senegal in the west to Somalia in the east (Kates, 1990).

Although lack of access to resources and/or inequitable distribution of land and other amenities that could potentially improve livelihoods are often alluded to in these studies, overpopulation of both humans and livestock are strongly emphasised to be the prime causes of, and impediments to, the alleviation of poverty. The United Nations estimates for 1991 show that about two-thirds of sub-Saharan Africa's population is susceptible to 'absolute poverty' because of rapid population growth and low agricultural productivity (Durning, 1989; UN, 1991). The general scenario painted by these studies is of Africa as a continent in a state of socio-economic and ecological collapse. The crumbling economies, recurrent drought and famines, mounting external debts and so forth are cited as indicators of this collapse.

To this multifaceted crisis numerous donor agencies – both bilateral and multilateral – have responded variously to 'alleviate' the pangs of poverty in the continent. Foreign aid to help address the environmental problems (perceived in the west as catastrophic) in many African countries has come to form a major proportion of the budgets of all major donor agencies. The logic behind this preferential budgeting has been based on the Brundtlandian assumption that poverty

159

was the cause of the socio-economic and environmental problems experienced in the South today.

Financial institutions like the International Monetary Fund (IMF) and World Bank have come up with structural adjustment and recovery programmes for the national economies (see Chapters 1, 2 and 3). Meanwhile the bilateral organisations have, in most cases, operated at regional or district levels in the countries concerned. Reminiscent of the behaviour of multinational corporations in Third World countries, these organisations have often formed institutions that work parallel to state institutions. Thus the administration of foreign aid has become the largest industry in Africa in recent years involving large amounts of money and expertise (Aseffa, 1991).

The case of Tanzania is interesting in that, unlike many other African countries, it had consciously charted out a unique socio-political programme aimed at extricating its people from the problems it has come to suffer in the last two decades. The Arusha Declaration of 1967 was formulated as a comprehensive programme to carry the country to self-reliant socio-economic growth and development. However, Tanzania could not escape the very predicament it had intended to avoid. Ironically, the country has ended up being one of the most crisis-prone countries in the south (cf. Chachage, 1992).

This chapter attempts to analyse the effects of the structural adjustment programmes (SAPs) in that country. The aim is to try especially to provide a view of what has been happening at the local societal level as a result of these programmes. The chapter is divided into four sections. Following this introduction, in Section Two the effects of the SAPs on four different communities are analysed in an attempt to provide a glimpse of the resultant processes that have been taking place in many social groups. The cases are taken from the pastoralist Maasai of Loliondo and Kiteto districts, and from the Barabaig of Hanang district. A fourth case study comes from an agro-pastoral village, Giting, in Hanang district (Figure 9.1). The choice of these social groups was determined mainly by the availability of relevant material on the issues under discussion. However, the fact that these groups have historically been on the losing end in many economic development programmes, as well as being blamed for environmental destruction in their home areas, adds urgently to their choice. Section Three identifies the general trends of these effects and discusses the implications of the responses to the well-being of the people concerned and the country as a whole. The final section offers some concluding remarks.

The Macro-economic Adjustment Programmes

Generally, the SAPs in Tanzania are now formally divisible into three main phases. These are the National Economic Survival Programme, the SAP and the Economic Recovery Programme (ERP).

Figure 9.1 Administrative divisions in Tanzania indicating study areas

The National Economic Survival Programme (1981–1982)
This was a programme devised by the Tanzanian state itself in an effort to revive agricultural and other non-traditional exports in the wake of the breakdown in negotiations with the IMF. It was also meant to increase industrial output for the same purpose, while reducing public expenditure. The aim was to raise, by the end of the programme, a targeted amount equivalent to US$903.5 million. The targets were, however, unrealistic and the result was that both crop production and industrial output fell (Mbelle, 1982, p. 73).

The Structural Adjustment Programme (1982–1985)
Perhaps due to the frustrations born of the failure of NESP, this programme was much more comprehensive and encompassed a greater part of the national economy. The policies adopted included the partial devaluation of the shilling, the partial liberalisation of internal and external trade and partial liberalisation of agriculture, especially through the formulation of the national agricultural policy which, for the first time, allowed private ownership of land. Emphasis was put on further reductions in government spending and rationalisation of foreign exchange use (Campbell, 1988, p. 5; Chachage, 1992, p. 5).

The Economic Recovery Programme (1986–onwards)
This has been a continuation of the SAP, and has involved further structural adjustment efforts in the economy as a whole and in the general socio-political life of the nation. The policies involved have included the rehabilitation of infrastructure, increasing producer prices, decontrolling co-operatives, the privatisation of land ownership and the restoration of the internal and external balance of payments through prudent fiscal policies. Other policies have involved the removal of all subsidies on agricultural inputs and urban food supply, reintroduction of direct taxation and further cuts in social services expenditure (Mbelle, 1988, p. 34; Chachage, 1992, p. 7). At the socio-political level the programme has involved the decontrolling of the political space by opening up to multi-partyism as the best form of democratic governance.

Although all three programmes may appear to have been homegrown, one should not forget the fact that the programmes were basically a reaction to the pressures enforced by various international financial institutions. This is evidenced, for example, by the parallel increase in external assistance to the country from US$287 million in 1985 to US$680 million at the beginning of the ERP – which was incidentally also the time Tanzania accepted all the IMF conditionalities (Chachage, 1992, p. 6).

Reports from the planning departments of the Tanzanian government indicate that the economy has experienced real growth for the duration of these programmes. The annual report of the Bank of Tanzania for 1991 actually pegged this growth at 4 per cent. Other knowledgeable observers of the Tanzanian socio-political scene, however, believe that these programmes have only benefited local and international private capital at the expense of the less-endowed social groups in the country (cf. Chachage, 1992).

The Case Studies

The Ngorongoro Maasai

Ngorongoro district is one of the border districts in northern Tanzania. Its area of 14,000 square kilometres is the home of the pastoralist Maasai. By accident of nature and history it is also the home of a multitude of wildlife that roams the Ngorongoro Conservation Area, the Serengeti National Park, and the Loliondo Game Controlled Area (Figure 9.2). The first two have been designated a world heritage area where human activity such as cultivation is discouraged. In the Loliondo Game Controlled Area some controlled hunting and grazing are allowed.

Studies of pastoralist ecology in the Ngorongoro area (cf. Århem, 1984, 1985; Homewood and Rogers, 1987; Ndagala, 1982, 1990; Parkipuny, 1977, 1979, 1983) indicate that pastoralists, livestock and wildlife have co-existed in the area in a symbiotic relationship for more than 2,000 years. It has also been clearly established that pastoralist grazing and burning activities and the absence of settled agriculture have helped to shape the area's currently highly valued landscape.

Furthermore, the studies show that although livestock numbers have been fluctuating for the last 20 years, according to the varied incidences of disease and drought, the figures show no overall trend towards absolute increase. Wildlife populations, on the other hand, are shown to have undergone a dramatic increase, despite uncontrolled hunting, during the same period as disease interaction between cattle and wildlife populations favour the latter.

The revered wildlife
Despite these facts, the Ngorongoro Conservation Authority, backed by the government, would like to see more than 50,000 pastoralists and their livestock moved out of the conservation areas on the grounds that they degrade the environment by overgrazing and generally threaten the existence of wildlife by poaching. This disregards the well-known fact that wildlife meat is taboo to the Maasai, except in circumstances of acute shortage of food; and even then only eland meat is allowed (Serengeti Regional Conservation Strategy (SRCS), 1992, p. D5). Furthermore, the Wildlife Department has not come across any Maasai who are poachers. The problem with the Maasai in the conservation areas has much more to do with land use conflicts than poaching.

The struggle between the state and the indigenous Maasai for the Ngorongoro dry season grazing reserves dates back to colonial times. By 1953, the Maasai Council of Elders had been negotiating with the government to reconsider the

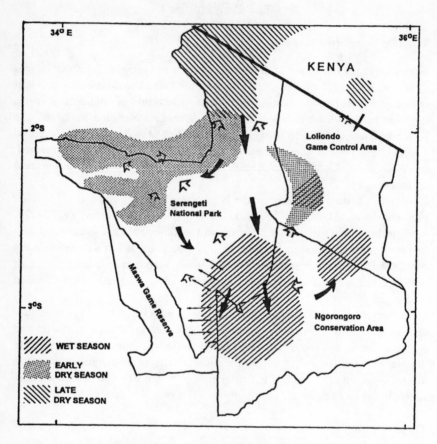

Figure 9.2 The wildebeest migration routes (1986–9) in the Serengeti-Loliondo-Ngorongoro conservation areas

Notes:
1. Serengeti Wildebeest Migration Routes observed from 1986 to 1989.
2. Major wet season, early dry and late dry season wildebeest distributions are shown by three different shading patterns. Also indicated are the principal directions of movement broken down as follows: Open arrows indicate the northward and solid arrows the southward migration. Double-headed arrows show areas where important movements occur during short dry periods within the wet season.

restrictions put on the Maasai in using the Ngorongoro reserves. The Council even argued for some compensation for the loss of the pastures and for livestock killed by predators. Originating from a supposedly conservative and backward people, none of these proposals was ever taken seriously. With the concerted efforts by the state towards the generation of as much foreign exchange as possible, tourism has been placed very high on the SAP agenda. Aided by a strong international conservation lobby, wildlife conservation has become something of a revered activity in the country as a whole.

Thus, apart from the valuable grazing lands lost to settler farms in Arusha and Monduli during the 1940s and 1950s, the Maasai have had to lose the essential dry season pastures as well – in this case to the Ngorongoro Conservation Authority. On the low-lying grazing areas, large tracts of pasture are also lost to the vastly increased overflow of wildebeest which cause a malignant cartarrhal fever in livestock (Figure 9.2). The restrictions on the use of fire as a pasture development method have rendered a large part of the remaining pastures susceptible to increased incidence of an inedible grass, *Eleusine jaegeri*, and tick-borne diseases. Moreover, over the last ten years or so, 30–40 per cent of the best grazing lands have become unsafe due to the rampant rustling by well-armed gangs (Enghoff, 1990, p. 103), who have found a profitable cattle market in neighbouring Kenya.

Cropping the grazing lands
Meanwhile, with the privatisation of land tenure in Loliondo district, a move made possible by the SAP-related liberalisation policies of the 1980s, more and more land is being alienated to large-scale farming (Enghoff, 1990, p. 104; SRCS, 1992, pp. 8–9). The force behind this move is the stilted logic that abounds among many bureaucrats and international funding agencies that pastoralism is a backward form of land use that should either be 'developed' towards a western-style ranching system or give way to settled agriculture.

The result has been an overcrowding of people and animals on the remaining grazing lands leading to serious loss of livestock for a considerable number of *bomas* (kraals) due to shortage of pastures, watering facilities and disease. They are becoming more dependent on grain for their livelihood than ever before. With the liberalisation of trade in recent years, grain has become very expensive for the ordinary *bomas*, not only in Loliondo district but in the whole of Arusha region. By September 1992, for example, a bag of maize cost approximately Tsh10,000. An average *boma* would need about 30 such bags to survive through a single year. This means that such a *boma* had to sell at least ten head of cattle each year just to be able to buy grain. Meanwhile, cattle markets that originally served as trade links between the Loliondo district pastoralists and their agricultural neighbours have ceased to exist due to the widespread rustling. Generally the threat from rustlers has made the formal exchange of goods at the local level very difficult indeed.

Survival by migration

For a long time, a very close relationship has existed between the Loliondo Maasai and those of the Maasai–Mara district in neighbouring Kenya. In times of trouble in one country, the affected Maasai have often migrated across the border to get solace from their kith and kin in the neighbouring country. In fact, these intra-ethnic relations have been so well established that it is very difficult to chart the population movements either way across the border in any one year. In any case, the district officials in Loliondo believe that there has been a major movement of people and livestock from Loliondo into neighbouring Kenya in recent years as a result of increased cattle rustling, decreasing pastures and famine.

Survival by small-scale cultivation

However, there are also those who lack the resources to enable them to migrate. These are the *bomas* that have had to take up small-scale cultivation as a survival strategy. The comparatively rich among them manage this by hiring tractors from outsiders who come to crop in the area and by employing labour from their agricultural neighbours. Maasai people are not utilised as day labourers on the large-scale farms. For the majority of not-so-well-off pastoralists, survival is sought from very crude cultivation methods that can hardly produce anything in their type of environment.

Hence the overall impact of this process of land alienation and concerted marginalisation has been general impoverishment of the pastoralist Maasai, who form 90 per cent of the population of Loliondo district. Moreover, these developments have also precipitated extensive erosion both by increased crowding of cattle and through unconscious or deliberate mining of the soils. Ironically it is the Maasai who are being accused of having initiated these problems.

The changes in land tenure and use have, on the other hand, greatly affected the workload and possibly the health of the women. Among the Maasai, women are responsible for building the residential huts – the *manyatta* – and the provision of the general reproductive functions of society. However, with the change in dietary composition, the women are now also responsible for the provision of grain in the *bomas,* apart from the normal processing of milk and its products. Therefore, in *bomas* where some agriculture has to be practised, it is also the responsibility of the women to cultivate, weed, harvest, process and store the grain (Talle, 1990).

Indigenous people's organisation

Lacking an effective socio-economic power base from which to fight for their rights, the Maasai have, until very recently, failed to articulate their demands at the political level. However, during the last few years, the Maasai pastoralists of Loliondo district have started organising themselves under a local non-governmental organisation (NGO) called Korongoro Integrated Pastoralist Organisation and Conservation (KIPOC). The aim is to establish a forum to fight for pastoralist rights and offer an alternative participatory approach to nature conservation, in the Ngorongoro area in particular and in Maasailand in general (Parkipuny, 1983; SRCS, 1991, p. 12). Given the present liberalisation of the political space in Tanzania under multipartyism, it is hoped that this NGO will manage to articulate the pastoralist interests at both the micro- and macro-levels of political life in the country.

The Naberera Maasai

Historical evidence shows that the Maasai of this southernmost part of Maasailand had been using the land for pastoralism for the last two thousand years or so. In the process they developed a transhumant system of pasture utilisation that was governed by the changing patterns of the seasons (Fosbrooke, 1954; Århem, 1984, 1985).

Advent of large-scale farming
For many years its remoteness from the urban centres of Arusha and Moshi and its relatively drier climate successfully kept it away from the attention of land-hungry agriculturalists, land developers and the state. Recently, however, this situation has changed. Fuelled by the government's move to privatise land in the country in the wake of the SAPs advocated and financed by the IMF and World Bank, many developers have found Naberera an excellent agricultural frontier.

By February 1991, for example, some 7,200 ha (18,000 acres) had been parcelled out to private developers under long-term leaseholds. According to the Maasai elders we consulted, the process was finalised at the regional level in Arusha and at the national level in Dar es Salaam without even involving the indigenous people of the area. To the government's bureaucratic eyes, these vast tracts were apparently idle land to be parcelled out for 'productive' use.

Defence by parcellisation
The Maasai reacted by seeking leaseholds of 99 ha – the maximum a household could own – for each *boma*. In this struggle they were led by a committed member of parliament for the Kiteto constituency with the help of some progressive Maasai people living in Arusha and Dar es Salaam. Since no really big money was initially involved in the 'scramble' for the Naberera farmlands the Maasai won their petition. Thus by mid-1991 the best part of the 25,000 square kilometres or so of Naberera was 'legally' in the hands of private developers and the local Maasai pastoralists (National Environment Management Council (NEMC), 1992).

But in order to continue owning land in Tanzania one has to show that one is putting that land to productive use. This is not a problem to the developers as they have to make a profit as quickly as possible and so vast lands had, by March 1991, been opened up using the most modern bulldozer land-clearing methods, tractor farming and disc-ploughing technology. Bean-seed monocropping for export was the prevalent cropping pattern, but no soil conservation measures of any kind were seen to be applied in these fields.

For a pastoralist *boma* to cultivate 99 ha is, however, another matter altogether. Rich Maasai *bomas* manage by hiring labour from agriculturalist ethnic groups and tractors from the nearby private developers, paying them in cattle or cash. The not-so-rich *bomas* solve this problem by sharecropping with the neighbouring rich Maasai *bomas* or some of the developers. Hence the cropping pattern and the agricultural practices applied here are typical of frontier agriculture: large-scale monocropping with few, if any, soil conservation measures. Just as among the Maasai community of Loliondo district, these changes in tenure and use of land have here adversely affected the health and workload of the women and their children. Meanwhile, due to lack of resources, the relatively poor *bomas* can hardly maintain a grip on the land that by law is supposed to be theirs.

Destocking by starvation and disease

The process of change in land tenure and use described above had originally been expected by the Maasai to safeguard their all-important grazing lands. The outcome has, however, been very different. The virtual enclosure of cultivated plots and large-scale farms has, in effect, led to diminished grazing lands, as movement of livestock to distant lands has also been largely impeded. The remaining pastures are, therefore, apparently being overgrazed and degraded and the not-so-rich Maasai *bomas* are already said to be losing more and more livestock due to shortage of pastures.

This problem has, in fact, accentuated an already existing bad situation for all pastoralists, not only in Maasailand but elsewhere in the country. The reduction of government expenditure resulting from the SAP-oriented policies discussed above has also greatly reduced the government's capacity and political will to provide the extension services, dipping facilities and veterinary medicines necessary for sustainable livestock keeping in such politically marginal areas as Naberera. Hence, although individual pastoralists are struggling to obtain some of the medicines sold on the open market at exorbitant prices, Maasai elders are positive that the incidence of disease among their herds is approaching epidemic proportions.

The incipient problem of degradation

Land degradation through soil erosion is still an incipient problem in many parts of Naberera, but if the present land use patterns are left to take their toll it will only be a matter of time before it becomes a major problem (Rapp, 1987). The environmental problem has further been exacerbated by the recent discovery of precious stone deposits in some parts of Naberera. As a result there has been a great rush by prospectors, speculators and associated groups of people to the area, virtually turning the deposit areas like Kambi-ya-Ndovu into a moonscape-like environment.

The Barabaig of Hanang

The Barabaig are a pastoralist people who live in Hanang district, northern Tanzania. This society has been the subject of many studies (cf. Kjaerby, 1979; Klima, 1970; Lane, 1990; Tomikawa, 1979; Watson, 1953). All these studies show that, until the early 1970s the Barabaig community, even if squeezed by agriculturalists, had been living in and adapted to the ecological system around Hanang Mountain. They had developed a complex transhumant system of resource management relevant to the semi-arid conditions of the area.

Appropriation of land by sedentarisation
In 1978 the villagisation programme, in which the Barabaig had initially been 'overlooked', was implemented in the area. New villages for the resettlement of the Barabaig were chosen by state functionaries, and 'development' plans were drawn up by 'experts' and endorsed by the state authorities. Barabaig involvement in these plans was actually 'bought' by promises of new infrastructure such as water supply for the Barabaig *bomas*.

The confinement of the pastoral Barabaig to permanent villages, however, opened up vast areas to agriculturalist ethnic groups and large-scale farming interests. The social services that were introduced as a development package into the area in the early 1980s attracted members of other communities which had originally avoided the harsh Barabaig environment. Gradually the lands that had up to then been used solely as pastures were opened up and virtually alienated for agricultural development. Livestock keeping was pushed into marginal lands such as the tsetse-infested Mang'ati Plains.

Between 1981 and 1985, a state corporation with international finance from Canada managed to alienate some 40,000 ha of an important Barabaig traditional grazing area for the extension of its wheat farms. Though a legal battle ensued, with the pastoralists being defended by a Legal Aid Committee of the University of Dar es Salaam, they lost on a technicality: their villages had no leaseholds to the alienated lands before the state corporation occupied them (Shivji and Tenga, 1985).

Survival by migration
The extension of agricultural interests in Barabaig lands has meant that the traditional grazing patterns are no longer tenable in this semi-arid area. That is why, by 1991, almost 50 per cent of the Barabaig pastoralists had moved out of the area in search of better pastures in Iringa and Mbeya regions in the south-west. Some are even said to have reached the international border with Zambia.

Those remaining in the land of the Barabaig have to make do with temporarily moving their animals into the tsetse-infested Mang'ati Plains during the dry season. This option is, however, open only to the pastoralists with larger herds who can afford to sell at least one head of cattle in 20 to buy veterinary medicine before entering the tsetse fly belts and to compensate farmers for passing the herds through their *shambas* (farms). The poor are thus left with virtually no option but to overgraze and degrade the diminished pastures within the confines of their homesteads. The result is, of course, poor livestock health and degradation of the pasture lands.

Survival by shifting cultivation

Those who could not migrate, strive to survive from the production of their livestock, but like the Ngorongoro Maasai they can no longer exist entirely on a pastoral diet. Only those few *bomas* with comparatively large herds can be assured of receiving at least half of their food requirements from livestock products. Grain remains important to a majority of the Barabaig *bomas*. Until very recently maize has been obtained through exchange or sale of livestock to their agro-pastoral neighbours – the Iraqw to the north and the Rangi to the south. However, with the liberalisation of trade in the last few years, most of the grain finds its way to better markets in the urban areas. Some of it is even reported smuggled abroad, where it fetches a better price. Hence the not-so-well-to-do Barabaig *bomas* have had to resort to growing their own grains through shifting cultivation with the help of communal labour. However, the crude methods of cultivation applied in this semi-arid environment cannot guarantee enough food for the whole year. Many of these *bomas* are, therefore, virtually starving for the greater part of the year.

Attempts at people's organisation

Interethnic discussions between the Barabaig and their Maasai pastoralist counterparts have been taking place for some time. The aim of the discussions was the formation of a joint forum for voicing the pastoralists' grievances and articulating their interests at the political level. By 1991 it was agreed that a branch of the Maasai NGO, KIPOC, should be opened in Katesh, the district headquarters of the Barabaig, to act as an interim institution while the two groups were searching for a better alternative. However, in an obvious effort to safeguard Tanzanian state interests and Canadian international capital in the form of wheat schemes, the KIPOC branch office in Katesh was immediately closed by the state security agents.

Giting Village

Giting village is located in Hanang district on the north-eastern slope of Mount Hanang. The area surrounding the mountain was inhabited by the pastoralist Barabaig up to the beginning of this century when the Iraqw, an agro-pastoral group from the Mbulu Highlands, migrated into the area and slowly pushed out the Barabaig. By the end of the 1920s the Iraqw dominated the area. In the beginning most of the Iraqw living in the village concentrated on agro-pastoral production, but as the village became incorporated into the colonial market economy, agriculture came to dominate production. A few big landowners utilised the lower-lying areas for cash crop production. By the 1960s the village had grown into a 'rich' agricultural village supplying maize and wheat to Arusha – the regional centre – and beyond.

The events described below have all happened during the SAP period. Some of them are more easy to connect to the SAP policy while others just coincide in time. It is, however, the general ideological changes in the community that have allowed these events to happen.

Land reform

Increased cropping changed land use and when the villagisation programme was launched in 1974 all areas fit for cultivation were fairly evenly distributed among the inhabitants. Most households received a 1.6 ha (four acre) cultivation plot and a 0.4 ha (one acre) household plot. Some land was also allocated for communal use, with a village *shamba* of 200 ha (500 acres) set aside to cater for investments in communal development. Plots for a school, dispensary and commercial centre were also demarcated.

After the villagisation programme a genuine effort was made by the village government to develop the village. Communal investments included a school, dispensary, cattle dip, milling machine, tractor, lorry, a village go-down, butchery and shop. These investments, however, came under serious threat from a few rich farmers who, from the very beginning, believed that the communal investments had taken business from their own shops, tractors, milling machines and transport.

There was, as a result, a continuous struggle between this group of people and the rest of the village over the control of these resources. The village government managed to maintain control for the benefit of the majority in the village but by the late 1980s things had changed drastically. In the following paragraphs we provide a few glimpses of events that have occurred in the village during the last few years of SAPs.

Sharecropping

Before the implementation of the SAPs rich farmers could increase their land-holdings by sharecropping or renting land. The former was more common. The village has a specific kind of sharecropping system, in that the landowner is a resource-weak party who depends on the sharecropper, who is resource rich, for land preparation and ploughing services, including the supply of inputs. The most typical arrangement is that the sharecropper, who has the capacity to plough, receives three-quarters of the sharecropped land for own cultivation as payment for ploughing. A more appropriate term for this type of arrangement would be 'land sharing' rather than 'sharecropping', as the crop is not actually shared.

One interesting point here is that the sharecropper was traditionally given the responsibility for assuring the survival of the landowner's family for the duration of the cropping season in question. Such survival assurance was often achieved through the provision of day-labouring opportunities or by giving them loans in cash or kind. In the process, the landowner became increasingly indebted to and often completely dependent on the sharecropper for his household's livelihood.

During the last few years this traditional survival strategy for the poor has changed considerably. The resource-rich farmers are now increasingly hiring labour from outside the village, in areas like Singida, where the labour cost is low. According to the resource-rich farmers, it is no longer possible to guarantee the survival of a whole family or two by sharecropping 1.2 ha (three acres). Instead, encouraged by a weakened village administration, the resource-rich farmers today invade grazing areas and cultivate them. The poor peasants, who earlier relied on the rich farmers, are today marginalised even in the limited labour market of the village.

Cropping the grazing lands
The increased cropping of the grazing areas has had a tremendous effect on the peasants who try to maintain an agro-pastoral mode of production. The most common reason for out-migration from the village today is lack of grazing. Those who keep a considerable number of livestock have to find pastures outside the village. They therefore either establish satellite dwellings in other villages and keep the cultivation plot and a part of the household in Giting, or they move completely to areas with better grazing opportunities.

In the process the rich farmers are left with ample opportunities to increase their cultivation onto the better parts of the grazing areas. Nevertheless, located as they are on sloping land or on land with very shallow soil, the grazing areas are not suitable for sustainable agriculture, besides which the fields are purposely soil mined for a few years without any effort to maintain soil fertility. The result is an increased rate of soil erosion and other forms of land degradation.

The shift to more commodified farming has also changed the cropping pattern in the village. Traditionally the common system was to intercrop beans and maize but today monocropping of maize is almost universal. This has negative impacts not only on soil maintenance but also on the crops, which are reported to have become more vulnerable to new crop diseases in recent years. These crop diseases are spreading fast, even into the traditionally intercropped areas. Those with resources can afford to buy pesticides and their farms are therefore less affected. For the resource poor the outbreak of a major crop disease can mean absolute starvation for the whole year.

Sale of land
On the other hand, the renting of land is less common among individually owned plots and is more often practised on communal landholdings such as the village *shamba*. Sale of land is, however, more common today than before, despite there being no established market, and land trading is often done at an individual level between poor and rich households. Often the poor household sells its landholdings to settle some kind of debt or satisfy some social obligation. A tragic example

of this is told in Giting, where a rich farmer attempted to buy 1.6 ha (four acres) of land from an alcoholic for one drum of home-brewed beer. Although this sale was finally stopped following an intervention by the resident Catholic priest, similar kinds of events are increasing daily in the village as the landless group slowly but surely increases in number.

Land laws and corrupt courts

Insecurity of land tenure not only increases due to ineffectiveness of the land laws but also due to inefficient and corrupt courts. In 1989, for example, the village government decided to redistribute land on account of increased landlessness among the youth and also to set aside some areas for roads to make the fields accessible by tractors and oxen. Some new areas were allocated for cropping while part of the old cropping area was, as a result of the road project, reduced for about forty of the landowning households. These households had been promised compensation in the new cropping area by the village government but the compensation never materialised and the households decided to go to court.

The court decided that the village had no legal right to allocate land and as such the forty households should just accept the hard fact that they had lost their land. A few protested to the party leadership who formed a sort of court of last appeal but the households were not listened to. Instead the ward secretary, who is responsible for redistributing the land and who has the right to confine 'troublemakers', detained them for nine days, following which they were asked if they were prepared to drop the case. Several of the protesters who maintained that they would pursue the case were repeatedly confined until they 'saw the wisdom' of dropping the case.

The village government decided to distribute the new cultivable land to those who were already registered as households in the village and who, in addition, could pay a 'registration fee' to be placed on the waiting list. The landless youth who initiated the redistribution process hence failed to get cultivation plots, while the richest existing households in Giting received an additional 0.2–0.5 ha of 'coffee or pyrethrum plots' on the well-watered slopes close to the mountain.

In another case, ten of the rich households in the village were taken to court by the village government to answer charges of 'invading' areas set aside for grazing. The court case dragged on for about a year. Finally, the village lost the case on the technical point that it had no legal mandate to allocate land for any specific use. This judgement had a profound impact on the whole land tenure system in the village, with the few farmers who had controlled large tracts of land before the villagisation programme land reform starting proceedings in the court to regain their pre-villagisation lands.

The court has not yet made any judgements in these cases. However, in other villages in the region rich farmers have managed to regain their former lands, and it is possible to speculate what will happen if the rich farmers in Giting win their cases. One of the big landowners, for example, had 200 ha before the villagisation programme land reforms, which means that more than 100 families will be evicted from their land if only this one former landowner gets his land back. This court case may result in a major catastrophe for many households in Giting.

Communal resources: the piped water system
Giting has had a piped water system since 1985. The system serviced the school, the dispensary and a few livestock watering points. In 1989 two well-off farmers were connected to the system without the consent of the village government and both built two big water tanks on their household plots. Water had been scarce before it was connected to the two households but their added consumption decreased the rate of supply in other parts of the village. This annoyed many people in the village, some of whom are reported to have sabotaged the water pipe, and today access to piped water is haphazard.

Communal resources: the village shop
A village shop was established in the 1970s to provide the people of Giting with agricultural inputs and other necessary commodities. The shop had previously been privately owned. The village shop sold at officially controlled prices until it was closed in the late 1980s for a variety of reasons; but several new shops have since been established in Giting. Prices are considerably higher here than in shops in other nearby villages and many people are growing increasingly indebted to the shopowners.

Communal resources: the village go-down
A go-down was built in the village in 1984 and was used by the village co-operative to store the cash crops sold to it and awaiting transportation. After some time the caretakers of the go-down refused to buy some of the poor peasants' crops on the pretext that they were of poor quality. However, when such crops were sold to a rich peasant at less than half the price and taken to the go-down, these same crops got the price for best quality. This process not only considerably decreased the income opportunities of the poorest group of peasants in the village but also made the unfortunate peasants lose faith in the official local institutions.

Communal resources: the lorry and the tractor
The village bought a lorry at the beginning of the 1980s to transport crops to distant markets where prices are higher. Two persons in the village government were responsible for the maintenance of the lorry and the buying and selling of the crops. Because of its comparatively low charges, the village lorry took much of the business from the two privately-owned lorries in the village and a maintenance fund was established for the lorry out of the profits.

At the beginning of the 1990s, however, the lorry had a major breakdown that needed a substantial amount of money to repair. When the two-person committee decided to draw from the maintenance fund to repair the lorry the money was not there and no one in the village government could be held accountable for its disappearance. Indeed, some well-placed people in the village leadership seemed to prefer the issue to be forgotten. The lorry has been idle ever since and the profitable business that gave the village so much income and eased the villagers' communications problems with the outside world is now monopolised by the two private lorry owners.

The village tractor was bought to help cultivate the village *shamba* and also to serve as a machine pool for the village. Until the late 1980s this provided the village with a good income. Many of the peasants in the village also got their own fields ploughed with the village tractor, which was cheaper to rent than the private ones. Just as with the lorry, a separate maintenance fund had been set aside for the tractor. However, when this fund was needed in 1989 to finance a major breakdown the money was nowhere to be found. The tractor was at a standstill until the 1992 cultivation season, during which period the village *shamba* was not cropped and the village finances deteriorated. In the 1992 cultivation season a small part of the village field was cropped following orders from the regional commissioner in Arusha.

Power by manipulation and intimidation
From the late 1970s until 1986, when the village made all the communal investments we have discussed above, the village government was led by its secretary. Over the years, however, the rich quarter of the village grew to dislike his methods of running the village. Slowly the village government was infiltrated by representatives working under the influence of the rich peasants, and by 1986 these people had formed a majority. From that moment the secretary started experiencing direct opposition in meetings and was actually accused of many crimes, the most severe being the murder of a villager in 1987.

The initiative to accuse him of murder was taken by a few rich villagers in Giting. The court did not find any evidence to convict him and he was released from jail after two weeks. Those who accused him did not, however, give up and mounted a spirited campaign to get rid of him. Finally, in 1989, with the help of some corrupt party official at the district level, they managed to get him transferred to another village eleven kilometres away. He was succeeded in Giting by a village secretary to their liking, and within two years the whole structure of communal investments so laboriously erected was in a shambles.

Leadership accountability: some micro- and macro-issues
On the initiative of a party official, a subscription of money was undertaken in Giting ward in 1992. The money collected, Tsh4.5million, was meant for investment in a bus and the idea was well received by the inhabitants of the ward. The problem of public transport is severe in the whole ward as the private bus lines charge high fares. The party official did not, however, purchase the bus, but diverted the money into some other use. In early 1972 he had promised the villagers he would return the money but very few believed him. The matter was reported to the district party headquarters, but even after an investigation the party official did not face any punishment from the party branch.

Following complaints from the villagers, the regional commissioner for Arusha visited Giting in 1992. The disgruntled villagers decided to air all their complaints, including, for example, the erosion of communal investments, the problem of land losses during the redistribution of land in 1989, the corrupt village government and the cultivation of grazing areas. As a result of his meeting with the villagers the regional commissioner ordered, among other things, that the village rehabilitate its communal resources and crop the village *shamba*. He also nullified the redistribution of land of 1989 and initiated an investigation into the irregularities involving the village finances.

The party branch at the district level performed the investigation, which resulted in the village chairman being dismissed and the village secretary transferred to another village. All the members of the land committee in the village government were also dismissed while the investigation was carried out. The tractor was repaired and part of the village *shamba* was cropped. However, due to pressures from the rich within the village, the dismissed officials had not been replaced by the end of the year.

The Impact of SAPs and Peasant Responses: A Discussion

The impact of SAPs at the local level is often difficult to assess. The policy formulations are made at the national and international levels while implementation occurs at many different levels of society. When actual implementation reaches the local level the policies are often so modified from their initial content that it is hard to perceive them as part of the original policy. The temporal correlation is, therefore, often the only link available between the SAPs and their effects at the local level. Furthermore, when talking about local agricultural, pastoral or agro-pastoral societies, the effects of the SAPs will, of necessity, vary according to how connected the society in question is to the nation state.

One of the most obvious effects of SAPs at the national level has been the further incapacitation of an already ineffective state, especially at the local level. In marginal areas, for example, where state-imposed services (e.g. schools, dispensaries, extension services) and market involvement were non-existent or weak before the implementation of the SAPs, the effects may not even be traceable. However in other areas, such as in cash crop producing agricultural areas or in areas with 'surplus' land, in this case Maasailand, the SAPs may bring about considerable changes. From the foregoing case studies, for example, it is possible to discern a generalised pattern of changes and people's response that could be typical of many Tanzanian rural communities operating under SAP-oriented socio-economic policies.

Shift in Ideology and Welfare Structures

The most striking change of the SAP at all levels in society has been the general shift in ideology. Traditionally, every community in the country had its rules and regulations that controlled access to resources. Although in communities like the Maasai and Barabaig these are largely still functional, in many others they appear to have been rendered ineffective. The nation-building efforts of the late 1960s and early 1970s, culminating in the highly publicised *ujamaa* ideology, had in many places replaced this communal resource use with state-controlled communal systems. Even among such largely traditional communities as the Maasai and the Barabaig, their rules were in many respects incapable of regulating the use of such important common resources as land and water, long before the advent of the SAPs.

With the SAPs, however, the *ujamaa* ideology itself has been replaced at the national level. The government now espouses private capital and prescribes limits to public spending, currency valuation rates, employment growth etc. At the local level it has been replaced by an ideology that celebrates privatisation of resources and the supremacy of the entrepreneur.

As a result, many ways of acquiring additional resources and wealth that were formerly considered morally unjust are now not only considered socially acceptable, but are increasingly being supported by the authorities as legitimate means of capital accumulation. As the case studies clearly demonstrate, phenomena such as land renting, sharecropping and land grabbing have increased and have further disempowered the poorest part of the population.

Communal resources like schools, piped water systems, go-downs, animal dips, village shops, village tractors and lorries, that were once communal investments in the villages and accessible to all households and *bomas*, are increasingly being taken over by the local elite who have turned into local entrepreneurs, or they are simply left unmaintained. As the Giting case study clearly illustrates, the poor people now have to rely more on 'market forces' without competition, since the capital owners form a numerically small and socially well-integrated group. They have to buy these services, often at inflated prices, from the entrepreneurs who have taken over, or just try to manage without them. The commodification of the communal resources has simply further increased the vulnerability of a majority of the population to absolute poverty and poor health.

In the Tanzanian context it may be argued that the local welfare structure never worked properly anyway, due to the inability of the state to maintain the structures built during the 1960s and 1970s. This is a valid point in the sense that the welfare structures were limited and often also favoured the already well off. It is also valid in the sense that many of the goods and services that were in short supply before the SAPs are now available even in the remotest part of the country – for those who can afford to pay the informal rates now routinely being charged by underpaid government staff. The point here, however, is that the limited former communal welfare services, with all their shortcomings, were still vitally important for the survival of a majority of the rural population, who at present belong to the marginalised households and *bomas* because they can hardly afford these goods and services. The cuts in wages for government officials such as teachers, health workers and others have converted services that formerly were provided without any cost into an informal black market, which further limits access to these service opportunities for poor people.

Changes in Land Tenure

A major change in resource use and control at the local level that derives directly from the shift in ideology due to the SAPs is the tenure and use of land. The Village Act of 1975 gave the village authorities the power to allocate land for use within the village. Although the Act was used as land law from 1975 to the mid-1980s, it was never legally binding because some of the preconditions for its validity were usually not fulfilled.

The villages were, for example, supposed to have a leasehold given by the state before they could legally allocate land within the villages. One of the conditions for obtaining such a leasehold was to have the village mapped and, due to a lack of resources, the mapping process could only be conducted in a very limited number of villages. As a result, the Village Act has been used for all those years as a 'party directive' without legal validity in many villages.

In pastoralist areas like Maasailand and the land of the Barabaig, the SAPs have conveniently provided an ideological justification for a simmering prejudice among many government bureaucrats, namely that grazing lands are essentially idle lands. Hence there is little concern at the national level when these lands are grabbed permanently by speculators.

However, a more serious effect of this whole process is that the marginalisation of livestock keeping also virtually separates two otherwise interrelated production systems. In many of these highly variable semi-arid areas, livestock keeping is often engaged in as a precaution against bad years. In some agro-pastoral communities, e.g. the Rangi of Kondoa and the Iraqw of Mbulu Highlands, the two systems have actually been integrated. Livestock provide traction power and manure for agriculture while the latter supplies crop residues for post-harvest grazing during the dry season. Hence the separation that is taking place now between the two production systems in places like Giting not only threatens the future development of livestock keeping but also, in the final analysis, threatens future possibilities of using manure and thus establishing a more sustainable agriculture.

Change in Power Relations

Most cash crop producing societies were socially and economically stratified well before the introduction of the SAPs. This was also true of the hierarchical societies like the Maasai and the Barabaig. Before the SAP the power relations between the weakest part of the population and the 'progressive' farmers or traditional elders were often a combination of traditional and 'modern' ways of exploitation. Furthermore, the often egalitarian traditions were further enhanced and modernised by similar thoughts stemming from the *ujamaa* experiment of the 1970s.

In the Village Act of 1975, for example, co-operation between peasants was stressed. The basic idea was that, as accumulation for development was performed communally, all households and *bomas* should have adequate resources to sustain themselves. In this way communal resources formed an important part of the social network that protected the poorest part of the population from economic and social marginalisation. This corresponds with the traditional relations between the elite and the poor that were often patron–client relations based on the traditional 'patriarchies', whereby the well-being of the poor depended on the goodwill of the elite. Such goodwill was not, however, an individual decision made by the elite. It was socially defined and regulated.

The introduction of the SAPs and the drift towards capitalist relations of production have weakened the logic of communal co-operation and the traditional patriarchal bonds in these societies. As a result the elites have strengthened their relative power at the local level at the expense of the most economically and socially vulnerable groups. Among the Maasai communities discussed above, for example, age and gender formed the basis of all social differentiation. The oldest male members of these communities formed the elite of society and were thus socially responsible for the welfare of all the members of their communities. These traditions have been changing since colonial times but with today's general state of helplessness at the local level this group of people is increasingly being aligned with, and more responsive to, the interests of the economically powerful groups from outside the community and the state.

The severe social differentiation at the local level has actually been accentuated by the increasing privatisation and virtual commercialisation of resources such as land. These processes have attracted outside entrepreneurs whose interests in most cases conflict with the traditional concern with resource conservation and equitable access. These people are often from groups with powerful links to the state and are in many cases supported by state-enforced legislation. Hence it is virtually impossible for the people at the local level to have a say in the exploitation of their resources.

The penetration of external entrepreneurs does not only intensify the existing social differentiation. As illustrated by the Maasai and Barabaig cases, this encroachment marginalises the not so well off social groups and leads to unsustainable human and livestock densities in fragile areas where both moral and environmental degradation are absolute.

Possibility for Local Resistance?

At the political level the alliances forged between the local elite, the entrepreneurs and the state on the one hand, and between the state and international financial institutions on the other, seem to have had the effect of bolstering the status quo, thus denying a majority of the poorer populations their rights to democratic representation and participation. The case of the Giting peasants is revealing in that, by concerted effort, they managed to take their grievances to the regional commissioner in Arusha, although that action did not solve their problems. By the end of 1992 the village was still without a chairman and secretary. Any attempt to replace the dismissed chairman was strongly 'discouraged' by the rich peasants hoping that, if the vacuum persisted, the district authorities would allow them to continue as before. Whether multipartyism will enhance the power of the poor remains to be seen.

It is encouraging to see that the Maasai of Loliondo district are currently organising themselves outside the normal channels of political activity in the form of an NGO – KIPOC. It is also true, however, that the Barabaig attempt to have a branch of this very organisation established in Katesh was frustrated by the state. It would appear, in this respect, that a community's ability to organise itself and articulate its interests depends largely on the kind of toes that can be trodden on as a result of its activities. In their worst form, therefore, the alliances between the entrepreneurs and the state have had the overall effect of frustrating many communities' initiatives and their capacity to organise and mobilise local resources for self-development and self-reliant problem solving.

Conclusion

In general, the case studies cited above show that, apart from being a relative concept, poverty is not a historically-determined condition. The studies clearly demonstrate that poverty is a condition resulting from a process of deprivation. The condition that the Barabaig of Hanang, the Maasai of Loliondo district and a large section of people such as the Giting villagers currently find themselves in is the pauperisation of the rural communities described by Chambers (1983), with induced marginality, powerlessness and vulnerability in social and political terms.

Furthermore, these studies illustrate that, although the problems of poverty and hunger are local and very place-specific events, their occurrence is, more often than not, related to socio-political events taking place in far-off places. To understand these relationships one needs a careful analysis of the politico-economic forces at play locally and the relationship of these to the state policies and related international interests.

In our case studies, for example, these interests are articulated through the usurping of resource-related decision-making powers by the state – a situation that has created a problem of assurance among pastoralists and agro-pastoralists alike – leading to serious ambiguities over who has legal access to rangelands and other resources at the local level. This has resulted, as we have already seen, in severe social differentiation among otherwise fairly egalitarian communities.

Hence many of the relatively poor families find it increasingly difficult to mobilise resources for sustainable livelihoods and economic improvement.

The general effect of all this for the country as a whole has been increasing dependence on external aid and expertise and, of course, borrowing. It has also increased the country's vulnerability to ecological perturbations, hunger and pestilence. The socio-ecological crises we are witnessing in Tanzania and the rest of the Third World today are, therefore, no more than mere *symptoms* of a much more serious crisis at the socio-political level. It is actually a crisis of legitimacy for the national elite itself. Unfortunately though, the self-styled international economic policing institutions like the IMF and World Bank, and the national elites themselves that struggle to maintain control of state power and resources, seem to like to believe that the symptom is the disease.

Hence the diagnoses and prescriptions currently made by these agencies actually rest on an ideological perception that assumes that the poor people are poor because they misuse resources, especially by keeping large herds of cattle and having large families, and by practising poor cultivation methods. Naturally this type of problem conceptualisation does not allow one to penetrate the dynamics of the human–environment interrelationships in Third World environments (cf. Hardin, 1968; Watts, 1985). Instead it leads to specious and sometimes insulting generalisations and, of course, the application of ill-conceived solutions such as have been illustrated in the case studies analysed above.

The discussion above clearly demonstrates that problems of poverty in most Third World countries are basically political problems resulting from a process of deprivation and marginalisation of a majority of the population from resources essential to development. The solution to these problems should thus not be sought in average economic growth; rather it should be sought at the political level through the empowerment of people at the grassroots by encouraging and helping them to organise and articulate their needs in the political arena. They should also be helped to mobilise and utilise their local resources to the maximum for the benefit of the communities themselves rather than for that of outside interest groups and international capital. External institutions should only be present to give moral support to such local efforts and open access to external resources and information where and when these are in short supply.

References

Århem, K. (1984) *From Subsistence to Poverty: The Demise of a Pastoral Economy in Tanzania*. Dept of Cultural Anthropology, University of Uppsala, Uppsala.

Århem, K. (1985) *The Maasai and the State*. International Workgroup for Indigenous Affairs, Copenhagen.

Aseffa, S. (1991) 'Enhancing food access in Africa; the Botswana experience'. *Studies in Comparative International Development*, 26, 3, pp. 59–83.

Campbell, H. (1988) 'Tanzania and the World Bank's urban shelter project: ideology and international finance'. *Review of African Political Economy*, no. 42, pp. 5–18.

Chachage, C.S.L. (1992) Agriculture and structural adjustment in Tanzania. Paper presented at a workshop on The State, Structural Adjustment and Changing Social and Political Relations in Africa, Scandinavian Institute of African Studies, Uppsala, 19–21 May.

Chambers, R. (1983) *Rural Development: Putting the Last First*. Longman, New York.

Durning, A.B. (1989) Poverty and environment: reversing the downward spiral. Worldwatch Paper 92, Worldwatch Institute, Washington, DC.

Enghoff, M. (1990) 'Wildlife conservation, ecological strategies and pastoral communities: a contribution to the understanding of parks and people in East Africa'. *Nomadic Peoples*, nos. 25–7, pp. 93–105.

Fosbrooke, H. (1954) Maasai history in relation to tsetse fly. Arusha. Mimeo.

Hardin, G. (1968) 'The tragedy of the Commons'. *Science*, 162, pp. 1243–8.

Homewood, K.M. and Rogers, W.A. (1987) 'Pastoralism, conservation and the overgrazing controversy'. In D. Anderson and R. Grove (eds) *Conservation in Africa*. Cambridge University Press, Cambridge.

Kates, R.W. (1990) Hunger, poverty and the human environment. Center for Advanced Study of International Development, Michigan State University. Mimeo.

Kjaerby, F. (1979) The development of agropastoralism among the Barabaig in Hanang district. Bureau for Resource Assessment and Land Use Planning Research Paper no. 56, University of Dar es Salaam.

Klima, G.J. (1970) *The Barabaig: East African Herdsmen*. Holt, Rinehart & Winston, New York.

Lane, C. (1990) Barabaig natural resource management: sustainable land use under threat of destruction. UN Research Institute for Social Development Discussion Paper no. 12.

Leonard, H.J. (ed.) (1989) *Environment and the Poor: Development Strategies for a Common Agenda*. Overseas Development Council, Washington, DC.

Mbelle, A.V.Y. (1982) Capacity utilization under foreign exchange constraint: the case of selected industrial linkages in Tanzania. Unpublished MA Dissertation, University of Dar es Salaam.

Mbelle, A.V.Y. (1988) *Foreign Exchange and Industrial Development; A Study of Tanzania*. PhD Thesis, Gothenburg University.

Mung'ong'o, C.G. (1990) Environmental conservation as a social process: the case of HADO Project in Kondoa district, Tanzania. Unpublished MA Dissertation, University of Dar es Salaam.

Mung'ong'o, C.G. (Forthcoming) *Socioecological Processes and the Land Question in the Kondoa Irangi Hills of Central Tanzania*. PhD Thesis, Stockholm University.

Ndagala, D. (1982) 'Operation Imparnati: the sedentarization of the pastoral Maasai in Tanzania'. *Nomadic Peoples*, 10, pp. 28–39.

Ndagala, D. (1990) 'Pastoralists and the state in Tanzania'. *Nomadic Peoples*, nos 25–7, pp. 51–64.

National Environment Management Council (1992) *Mapping for Monitoring of Desertification in Naberera Area (Southern Maasailand)*. Dar es Salaam.

Parkipuny, M.L. (1977) The alienation of pastoralists in post-Arusha Declaration Tanzania. University of Dar es Salaam. Mimeo.

Parkipuny, M.L. (1979) 'Some crucial aspects of the Maasai predicament'. In A. Coulson (ed.) *African Socialism in Practice, the Tanzanian Experience*. Spokesman, Nottingham.

Parkipuny, M.L. (1983) Maasai struggle for home right in the land of Ngorongoro Crater. Paper presented at the Symposium on the Anthropology of Human Rights, 11th International Union of Anthropological and Ethnological Sciences Congress.

Rapp, A. (1987) 'Desertification'. In K.J. Gregory and D.E. Walling (eds) *Human Activity and Environmental Processes*. Wiley & Sons, New York.

Serengeti Regional Conservation Strategy (1992) Project co-ordination unit and district support programme. Project proposal. Wildlife Division, Ministry of Natural Resources and Tourism, Dar es Salaam.

Shivji, I.G. and Tenga, R. (1985) Ujamaa in court: reports on an acid test for peasant rights in Tanzania. *Africa Events*, 1, 12, pp. 18–20.

Talle, A. (1990) 'Ways of milk and meat among the Maasai: gender identity and food resources in a pastoral economy'. In G. Palsson (ed.) *From Water to World Making: African Models and Arid Lands*. Scandinavian Institute of African Studies, Uppsala.

Tomikawa, M. (1979) 'The migrations and intertribal relations of the pastoral Datoga'. In *Warfare among East African Herders*. National Museum of Ethnology, Osaka.

United Nations (1991) *World Population Monitoring*. UN Dept of International Economic and Social Affairs, New York.

Watson, G.M. (1953) 'The Tatoga of Tanganyika'. *Tanganyika Notes and Records*, 34, pp. 35–56.

Watts, M.J. (1985) 'Social theory and environmental degradation'. In Y. Gradus (ed.) *Desert Development*. Blackwell, New York.

PART FOUR

Sub–Saharan Africa in Comparative Perspective

Structural Adjustment and Government Consumption: Sub-Saharan Africa and Industrialised Countries Compared

Indra Wahab

Introduction

The conception of the role of government in the economy underwent a remarkable change in about 1980. It became the generally accepted philosophy in the developed countries that the role of government should diminish in order to permit market forces to regulate the economy to a greater extent. Interest payment on the national debt, generally in local currency, became such a burden that it restricted the possibilities of government policies, unless they switched to a restrictive fiscal policy in order to restore budgetary equilibrium.

Whereas these restrictions were adopted voluntarily by developed countries, they were imposed on developing countries. The national debts of these countries, as distinct from the developed countries, were mostly expressed in foreign currencies. Adjustment policies for reducing foreign debt and/or meeting debt service requirements generate not only fiscal, but also balance-of-payments problems. In order to alleviate the latter, stand-by credits from the International Monetary Fund (IMF) are required. The IMF is willing to provide such credits only if certain conditions are met. The recipient country must draw up a 'proper' adjustment policy set out in a letter of intent to obtain the IMF seal of approval. The approval of the IMF was in turn a precondition for getting new loans from the World Bank and commercial banks and for getting official development assistance from developed countries.

It is legitimate to speculate whether reducing the role of the government in a developing country leads to a more efficient market economy. In this chapter, a more specific question is raised: have the policies adopted by the sub-Saharan African (SSA) countries resulted in reducing government expenditure and eliminating budget deficits? In addition, the consequences of the policies pursued for the economies of those countries are reviewed.

Following this introduction, Section Two provides some observations on the data used, the methods of calculation applied, the definition of government consumption and the sample of SSA countries. In Section Three the changes in the share of government consumption in the GDP of the selected countries will be considered. Section Four discusses changes in other macro-economic variables and the final section assesses to what extent the policy pursued has contributed to the stated objectives.

Data, Calculation Method and Sample

Empirical studies on developing countries, especially in SSA, tend to be restricted either by lack of data or by the fact that data are 'out of date' by the time they become available. What little there is, is often not very reliable. This also applies to data on foreign trade. According to Yeats (1990), trade statistics of SSA countries cannot be relied on, not even to indicate the level, composition, direction and trends in their trade. The doubtful validity of the available data implies that any conclusion based on these data requires very careful interpretation.

Most of the data for the present study have been drawn from IMF publications (IMF, 1991, 1992 and various). IMF data are relatively reliable and are consistently estimated; therefore country data are comparable to a certain extent. Initially data for all the SSA countries on government consumption, private consumption and GDP, all in constant prices, were collected.[1] The definition of government consumption used is in accordance with *A System of National Accounts* of the United Nations:

> The value of goods and services produced for their own use on current account, that is the value of their gross output *less* the sum of the value of their commodity and non-commodity sales and the value of their own-account capital formation which is not segregated as an industry. The value of their gross output is equal to the sum of the value of their intermediate consumption of goods and services, compensation of employees, consumption of fixed capital and indirect taxes. (UN, 1969, p. 233)

Where countries consider ancillary agencies and/or unincorporated government enterprises selling to the general public to be both operating on commercial

1. For the analysis in this study, data on GNP of national income would have been more appropriate, but due to lack of data GDP figures have been taken. The GDP measures the total final output of goods and services produced by the country's economy, regardless of its allocation between domestic and foreign output claimed by residents of a country. GNP comprises GDP plus factor incomes accruing to residents from abroad, less the income earned in the domestic economy accruing to persons abroad. In general, for developing countries GNP is lower than GDP.

principles and charging prices that reflect market values, these entities are treated on a net basis. The distinction between ancillary and/or unincorporated agencies and other government enterprises is very difficult to specify precisely. Whether state enterprises are included or excluded determines to a large extent the *absolute* level of government consumption and may lead to incomparability of the absolute expenditure levels in a cross-country analysis (UN, 1991, p. xiii). The present study, however, aims at reviewing *changes* in government consumption and the incomparability referred to might not therefore be that relevant. It is more important to stress that losses incurred by state-owned enterprises – be they incorporated or not, and often considered *the* heavy burden on government budgets – are included in the data on government consumption. This is because, according to the definition in the system of national accounts, the unincorporated agencies are treated on a *net* basis.

Data on government consumption and GDP in constant prices have been collected for the period 1970 until the most recent year available, and the share of government consumption in GDP has been calculated. In order to determine whether there is a significant change in the share of government consumption the period has been subdivided into two intervals: 1970–early 1980s, and the early 1980s–the most recent year available. It is assumed that at the beginning of the 1980s a break occurred between a period of an annually *increasing* share of government consumption and an annually *decreasing* share of government consumption in GDP. For 27 of the more than 40 SSA countries, 'sufficient' data are available.[2] In this study, sufficient means a minimum of five observations in order to derive a trend. Next, there is a change in the share of government consumption if the calculated annual changes of the two sub-periods differ at a level of significance of 1 per cent. Further, if the calculated annual change of a sub-period does not vary significantly from zero, the share of government consumption is considered to be constant during that sub-period. Finally it must be mentioned that in those cases where the available data end before 1991, the share of government consumption has been extrapolated to the end of the period.

Share of Government Consumption

The Sample of 27 SSA Countries and Eight developed countries[3]

There is no 'optimal' share of government consumption in GDP. What the duties of a government ought to be depends on various factors of an institutional, political,

2. The 27 SSA countries in the sample are: Benin, Botswana, Burkina Faso, Burundi, Cameroon, Congo, Côte d'Ivoire, Ethiopia, Ghana, Kenya, Lesotho, Liberia, Madagascar, Malawi, Mauritius, Niger, Nigeria, Rwanda, Senegal, Seychelles, Sierra Leone, Swaziland, Tanzania, Togo, Zaïre, Zambia, Zimbabwe.
3. The eight DCs in the sample are: Belgium, France, Germany, Italy, Japan, Netherlands, United Kingdom, United States of America.

historical and cultural nature. These factors determine to a large extent what individuals of a country expect from their government, but they also influence the levels (intensities) of government services. Data from eight developed countries (DCs) have been collected in order to obtain a 'benchmark' for the share of government consumption in GDP.

In the early 1970s the average share of government consumption for the eight DCs was approximately 15 per cent. During the 1970s government consumption grew faster than GDP and the share of government consumption increased by about 0.25 percentage points per year. In 1981 this share reached a peak value of 17.5 per cent. During the 1980s the share decreased by nearly 0.18 percentage points and, by 1992, the share of government consumption was only slightly higher than in the early 1970s, at 15.6 per cent.

For 1970 the average value of the share for the 27 SSA countries was approximately 13.6 per cent. During the 1970s this share increased by approximately 0.37 percentage points per annum, reaching a maximum value in 1982 of about 18 per cent. During the 1980s an annual decrease of approximately 0.26 points occurred and, by 1992, the value of the government share decreased to about 15.2 per cent.

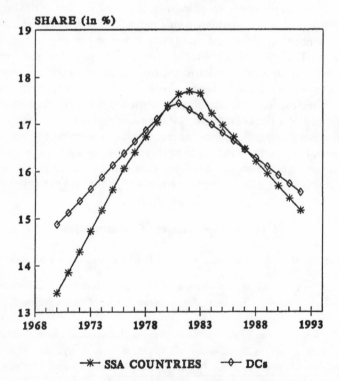

Figure 10.1 Share of government consumption
(27 SSA & eight developed countries)

The levels of and changes in the share of government consumption for the two samples are highly comparable (see Figure 10.1). The two patterns of government consumption share have strong resemblances: both graphs look like an 'inverted V'. The only difference is that the average annual increases during the 1970s and the decreases during the 1980s were larger for SSA countries than for DCs. Hence, the 'inverted V' of the SSA countries looks somewhat more pointed than that of the DCs.

The above figures may lead one to conclude that the share of government consumption in SSA countries is not noticeably higher than that in the DCs. On the one hand, annual increases were higher, but on the other annual decreases were also higher. It seems therefore that, in relative terms, policies aimed at reducing the share of governments' consumption in GDP were more successful in the SSA countries than in the DCs.

The Sample of 20 SSA Countries and Six DCs

The above analysis is based on the (unweighted) average of 27 SSA countries and eight DCs. It may be questioned whether the 'inverted V' is representative for all the individual countries that make up the two samples. For the DC sample, two countries – Italy and the US – show no significant break between the two sub-periods.

For Italy, the share of government consumption increases during both periods, by 0.1 per cent per annum. As during the first period the average annual change does not vary significantly from zero, the share is more or less constant (approximately 14.5 per cent). During the second period the annual increase differs significantly from zero and the calculated share increases to 16 per cent at the end of the period.

For the US, the share decreases during both periods, by 0.1 and 0.2 percentage points respectively. Those sub-period averages both vary significantly from zero, but the difference between the average annual changes of the two periods is not significant. Therefore the share of government consumption decreases continuously during the whole period: from 18 per cent in 1970 to 15 per cent in 1992. As there is no 'inverted V' for those two DCs, the sample of the DCs is reduced to a sample of six countries: Belgium, France, Germany, Netherlands, United Kingdom and Japan, which all show an 'inverted V'.

For seven of the 27 sampled SSA countries, the pattern of government consumption fails to conform to the 'inverted V'. In three countries (Cameroon, Ghana and Niger) a break occurs, but a break the opposite way round: a decrease during the 1970s and an increase during the 1980s. For four other countries (Ethiopia, Zimbabwe, Seychelles and Mauritius) the break between the two sub-periods is not significant. For Ethiopia and Zimbabwe the share increases continuously in both periods. In the Seychelles the share increases in the first period and remains constant during the second and in Mauritius the share is constant during the first period and decreases during the second. But, as stated, the average changes during the first period do not differ significantly from those during the second. So the sample of the SSA countries is reduced from 27 to 20 countries.

For the limited samples of six DCs and 20 SSA countries, the results can be summarised as follows. In 1970, the first year of observation, the average share of government consumption was 14.4 per cent for the six DCs and 14.2 per cent for the 20 SSA countries. The annual increases of the government consumption share during the first period were 0.39 and 0.35 percentage points respectively. Both samples reach their maximum values in 1981: 18.2 per cent for the six DCs and 18.5 per cent for the 20 SSA countries. During the second period the averages decrease by 0.23 for the DCs and by 0.45 points for the SSA countries. In 1992 the shares of government consumption are down to 15.5 per cent for the six DCs and to 13.6 per cent for the 20 SSA countries (see Figure 10.2).

It would appear that the average pattern of government consumption in both groups of countries is highly comparable and that the exclusion of two DCs and seven SSA countries makes no real difference to the average pattern: both

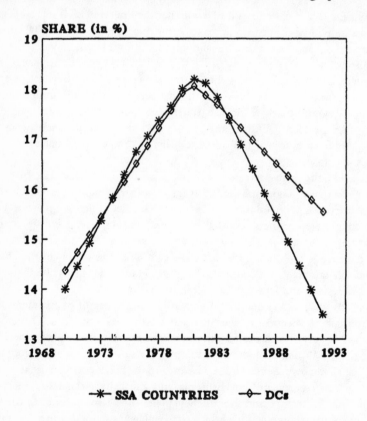

**Figure 10.2 Share of government consumption
(20 SSA & six developed countries)**

remain an 'inverted V' and the shape for the SSA countries is again a bit more pointed than for the DCs. One can therefore repeat the conclusion formulated above that, at first sight, the policies aimed at reducing the share of government consumption are more successful in the SSA countries than in the DCs. The reduction in SSA countries during the second sub-period was nearly twice as large as the reduction in the DCs (0.45 and 0.23 per cent respectively).

The similarity in the relative shares of government consumption is merely apparent: there is a big difference in reality. In the DCs a *relative* reduction in government expenditure occurred, but in the SSA countries this reduction was *absolute*. In the DCs the reduction of the government consumption share took place in a period during which the growth of GDP exceeded population growth to such an extent that – notwithstanding the diminishing share of government consumption – government consumption per head increased. During the 1980s GDP growth averaged 2.8 per cent and the population growth 0.3 per cent per annum. As the reduction of the government share by 1.4 per cent was smaller

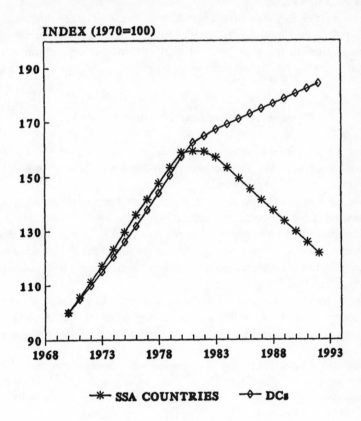

Figure 10.3 Index of government consumption
(20 SSA & six developed countries)

than the growth of GDP per head, government consumption per head actually *increased* by approximately 1.1 per cent annually.[4]

For the SSA countries the situation during the 1980s was quite different. They suffered from stagnating economies: average GDP growth (3.5 per cent) only marginally exceeded average population growth (3.3 per cent). Given the reduction of government consumption share of 2.8 per cent per annum, this meant that government consumption per head decreased by 2.6 per cent per year. The pattern of government consumption per head in the SSA countries proves to be dramatically different. This can be visualised by indexing government consumption per head for both groups of countries (base year 1970=100) (see Figure 10.3). The index for both samples increased during the first period and by 1981 the indexes were estimated to be 162 and 159 respectively. During the 1980s the index for the DCs continued to grow – albeit at a slower rate – to 184 in 1992. However, for the SSA countries the index *decreased* to 122. These results appear to permit the conclusion that government consumption per head in the DCs in 1992 was approximately 14 per cent *higher* compared to 1981, whereas for the SSA countries it was 25 per cent *lower*. According to Stewart (1987, p. 33), the situation for the SSA countries could be even more grim. She estimated that, in the years 1980–4, real government expenditure in those African countries which adopted the IMF programme was more than halved.

Changes in Other Macro-economic Variables

Has the steep decline in government consumption per head resulted in a more balanced budget for the SSA countries? Probably not. There is evidence that government deficits have increased, not decreased. For the years 1975–9, the average government deficit as a percentage of total revenues (including grants) is estimated at 5.4 per cent. For the first half of the 1980s the deficit increased to approximately 6.2 per cent.[5] This implies that the decrease in government revenues must have exceeded the decrease in government expenditure. The objective of lowering government deficits by reducing government expenditures was therefore not successful.

What could be the causes of the sharp reduction in government revenues? One argument is the sharp fall of commodity prices during the 1980s. The reasoning of the argument is as follows. As opposed to developed countries, taxes

4. The figure of the annual decrease of the share of government consumption differs from the figure mentioned earlier. In order to make the annual changes of various variables comparable they have been transformed to indices with base year 1970=100.
5. The countries included in this sample differ from our sample of 27 and 20 SSA countries. For country coverage see United Nations Development Programme/World Bank (1992).

on international trade and transactions form a major source of government revenues in developing countries. While those tax revenues are negligibly small for the six DCs (only 0.03 per cent of total government revenues), for the SSA countries their contribution is quite substantial, on average 35 per cent. A number of countries are much more dependent on international trade than the average figure indicates. In general, one could say that the less developed an economy the more important levies on exports and imports are as a source of government revenues. Eleven countries raised more than 50 per cent of their tax revenues from international trade, while 18 countries raised between 25 and 50 per cent of their revenues in this way (Gersovits and Paxson, 1990, pp. 38–9).

Of those tax revenues, approximately 80 per cent are derived from imports and only 20 per cent from exports. Although tax revenues on imports are much more important as a source of government revenues than export tax, there is a connection between the two. A decline in export revenues does not merely lead to lower tax revenues on exports, but it reduces the capacity to import as well, because of foreign exchange constraints. As a consequence, tax revenues from imports will be lower when export revenues decrease. Lower export revenues lead to lower export tax revenues which in turn induce lower imports and lower import tax revenues. The decrease in imports has a negative effect on the domestic industry and on the export sector. Both sectors depend for their production activities on imported materials. Therefore, it is more appropriate to consider all tax revenues from international trade instead of only export tax.

The price level of the export products, coupled with their volume, determines the total export revenue. Hence it is an important factor for government revenue. Taxes are usually levied as a fixed share of the value of exports (*ad valorem*). Most developing countries, the SSA countries in particular, are basically commodity exporters. Commodity prices have been very depressed during the last decade and a half. After the 1979–82 recession the world economy began to expand again but commodity price recovery did not follow. Comparing the weighted commodity price index of 33 commodities, excluding energy, with the unit value index of manufactured exports to the developing countries from the Group of Five industrial countries, the commodity terms of trade deteriorated by more than 4.5 per cent per year between 1980 and 1993. The index for 1980 was 122 and estimated at 66 for 1992 (World Bank, 1992). This is a historically low level, even lower than during the great depression of the 1930s. The annual losses in export earnings attributable to the deterioration in the commodity terms of trade were not only larger in comparison to those during the depression years but the duration of persistently depressed prices has been longer. In the 1930s, after approximately four years of falling prices, they began to recover. But now, throughout the 1980s and the mid-1990s, the prices have fallen or remained stagnant, with the exception of two rather short-lived periods of price recovery (Maizels, 1992, p. 12).

The fall in commodity prices is caused by a stagnating or even declining demand, surprisingly at a time of world economic expansion. This apparent contradiction is not the result of the gradual change-over of the economic structure of developed countries from manufacturing to services, but to rapid changes in technology. There is no firm evidence for an ongoing worldwide *deindustriali-sation* process but evidence does exist for a *dematerialising* process. According to our estimates, commodity demand will decrease by 0.4 per cent per annum, given a constant growth rate of manufacturing. For the mid-1980s a 4–5 per cent man-ufacturing growth rate still proved to be sufficient to sustain a constant or a very slight increase of commodity demand. In the mid-1990s such growth rates seem no longer able to maintain commodity demand (Wahab, 1990, p. 703). Hence the price prospects are still not very promising. The World Bank is constantly adjusting its estimates of the price index of the 33 commodities, excluding energy, for the years 2000 and 2005, downwards (compare the various editions of the World Bank's *Price Prospects for Major Commodities* 1989, 1991, 1992).

The sharp fall in commodity prices cannot be ascribed only to stagnating demand. The fall has been aggravated by expanding supply. The supply increase is the outcome of net investments made during the second half of the 1970s, a period of relatively remunerative commodity prices. The negative effects of a price drop on revenues will be reduced if volumes are larger. But the SSA countries have not increased the volume of their exports. On the contrary, the average growth rate of the export volume during the years 1982–8 was approximately –2.6 per cent per year. So, during the 1980s, the SSA countries were hit by a negative combination of falling prices and lower volumes.

What can be said about the consequences of the low export prices and export revenues on the imports of the SSA countries? During the 1980s the capacity to import of the SSA countries – deflating the current export revenues by the unit value of manufacturing exports of the Group of Five countries to developing countries – deteriorated by approximately 8.8 per cent per year. Nigeria was hit particularly hard, due to the collapse of oil prices. The estimate of the decrease of the SSA countries, excluding Nigeria, was less dramatic: approximately –4.5 per cent annually.

However, the unit value of African imports is increasing at a slower pace than the unit value of manufactures exported by the Group of Five countries to developing countries. Estimating the deterioration in the capacity to import by using the unit value of African imports as a deflator for the export revenues in current values, the decrease is nearly –4 per cent per annum during the 1980s. For the SSA countries, Nigeria excluded, the capacity to import remains more or less stable; i.e. the estimated average annual change does not deviate signifi-cantly from zero. So it appears to be legitimate to conclude that, in spite of lower volumes and lower prices, the deterioration of the export revenues is apparently not that negative: the capacity to import appears not to be affected at all. Whether one could regard this as a positive sign without any qualification is doubtful. It could mean that the composition of the basket of imported goods consists predominantly of products whose prices lag behind or remain equal in comparison to the price changes of the products exported by the SSA countries.

This is the case for products in the food and energy categories. If this reasoning is correct, it would imply that Africa, due to falling export revenues, is forced to import consumption goods merely to survive and the SSA countries are not in a position to import manufactured goods for replacement, not to mention imports for net investments.

The observation based on the difference in the changes in the capacity to import, that Africa is importing increasingly more food and less capital goods, is in line with the general opinion that Africa's agriculture is declining and that Africa is not expanding its volume of exports. The decline of Africa's agriculture is not solely a phenomenon of the 1980s. According to Timmer, for example, the productivity of land as well as labour has been deteriorating since 1973 (Timmer, 1988, p. 309). Agriculture, the backbone of Africa's economy, was stagnating before the 1980s, the decade of adjustment policies. In a stagnating or contracting economy, the tax sources from both international trade and domestic production will decline. If, in such a situation, governments are forced to reduce their expenditure, the contracting forces will merely be intensified. In a shrinking economy, therefore, decreased government expenditure, leading to increased rather than reduced government deficits, is not that unexpected an outcome.

What are the effects of a shrinking economy on the share of private consumption in GDP? The aim of a reduction of government consumption is, next to a reduction of the budget deficit, the reduction of total consumption in order to increase savings, which will lead to growing investments. Although this reasoning might generally be correct in an expanding economy, it does not apply to the SSA countries. For the years 1975–9, gross national savings of the SSA countries are estimated to be 15.4 per cent, for the years 1980–5 the figure stands at 9.8 per cent and from 1986 till the beginning of the 1990s it declined further to 7.7 per cent. For the SSA countries, excluding Nigeria, the estimates are 10.0, 8.3 and 7.4 per cent respectively (UNDP/World Bank, 1992). During the second half of the 1970s, SSA investments were estimated to be approximately 28 per cent of GDP and for the years 1983–8 the figure is 19 per cent. For 14 of the 20 SSA countries the share of investments in GDP has decreased by an (unweighted) average of approximately 1.1 percentage points per annum. This indicates that the reduction of government consumption has not led to a decrease of national consumption and a concomitant increase in national savings. In other words, the effects of a reduction of government consumption have been annulled by an increase in private consumption.

In a shrinking economy an increase in the share of private consumption is not unexpected. It is in line with – or at least not contrary to – the Duesenberry hypothesis, according to which there is a time lag for consumption to adjust to changed income. If income is increasing/decreasing, the increase/decrease in consumption will be relatively smaller. One might therefore expect a decrease of savings if income decreases. There is evidence that this occurred in the SSA countries. For 23 countries, the relationship between a change in the growth rate of income per head (GDP$_{cap}$) and a change in the share of private consumption (CONS$_{pr}$) has been calculated. For the 1980s the relationship works out as follows:

$$CONS_{pr} = -0.42068 - 0.37054 * GDP_{cap}$$
$$(5.556) \qquad (R^2 = 0.607)$$

From this relationship one could deduce tentatively that, given a negative GDP per head growth rate of 2 per cent, the consumption share tends to increase by 0.3 percentage points per year (Figure 10.4).

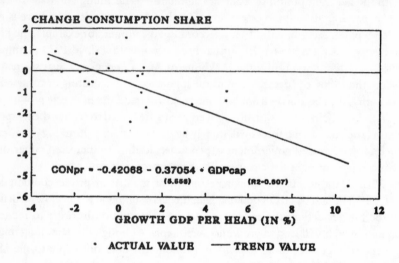

Figure 10.4 Growth of GDP per capita and consumption (22 SSA countries)

The final questions – and probably the most important – are: on which items of expenditure have the governments carried out the biggest cuts, and has the burden been placed on the most vulnerable social groups? Hicks and Kubisch (1984) are of the opinion that, in general, the tendency of government policy is to cut relatively more from projects in production and infrastructure with medium- or long-term gestation periods and less in respect of social sector projects, with the administration and defence sector occupying an in-between position. They conclude: 'That the social sectors do not appear to be highly vulnerable to expenditure reductions in terms of austerity is a novel finding of this study, but one requiring further examination with more complete data' (Hicks and Kubisch, 1984, p. 39).

Their conclusion, even though prudently formulated, stands in marked contrast to the findings of other studies. The UNICEF and WIDER[6] projects

6. WIDER is the World Institute for Development Economics Research, which was established by the United Nations University as its first research and training centre in 1984 and started work in Helsinki in 1985.

document reductions in government outreach and social service activities, increased or reduced rates of decrease in observed indices of malnutrition and public ill health (Taylor, 1988). In *Africa Recovery* (1992), a study of the Alexis de Tocqueville Institute is quoted. This study has identified a relation between the adjustment programmes and the expenditure cut in the social sector. In two-thirds of the 42 IMF programmes reviewed, the budget of the social sector has been reduced, especially for education and health.

The IMF reply is that, given the magnitude of the macro-economic shocks suffered by poor countries, their citizens were bound to suffer: 'The cost of adjustment, therefore, must be seen in perspective. In the short run, these costs are unavoidable sacrifices that accompany the correction of an unsustainable situation' (quoted in Tseng, 1984, p. 5).

Furthermore, the opinion that the burden of the adjustment policy is borne especially by the most vulnerable groups could be disproved by the observation that, even in 'normal' times, the lowest income groups are not reached by government programmes. Mansuri (1990), referring to a joint study of the Overseas Development Institute and the International Fund for Agricultural Development on agricultural development in five SSA countries, stated: 'The studies found that in many instances these (agricultural) services were of little value to most small-scale farmers before the expenditure cuts and so the adverse effects were minimal' (Mansuri, 1990, p. 420).

According to Sahn (1992), too, there is little evidence that the adjustment jeopardises the welfare of the poor in the SSA countries, with the exception of a few middle-income countries such as Côte d'Ivoire and Cameroon (Sahn, 1992, p. 4).

We may therefore conclude that a disproportionate burden of the adjustment programme is not necessarily borne by the most vulnerable groups in society, but by the lower strata of the middle groups: redundant employees, wage freezes for minor government employees, and cuts in food subsidies, reductions in educational and health services for the lower middle-income urban groups. The reduction in expenditure on the physical and social infrastructure will lead to a further deterioration of the growth potentials of the SSA countries. In other words, the overall most vulnerable groups are not necessarily the same as the groups most vulnerable to structural adjustment.

Summary and Conclusions

The question raised in this chapter is whether government expenditures have been reduced. The answer is affirmative. The share of government expenditure in GDP has been reduced, as in the DCs. Contrary to the DCs, however, the reduction was not only relative but also absolute. On average, government expenditure per head declined by 25 per cent, but the effects of this have been wiped out by an even sharper decrease in government revenues. This was initially caused by the low prices for the commodities exported. The external shock had negative consequences for the imports and therefore for the whole economy. As income per head stagnated or even decreased, private consumption increased relatively and savings and investment levels reached new lows. After a decade of austerity the state of the macro-economic variables does not hold out much promise. This does not imply, however, that the deterioration of the macro-economic variables can be ascribed directly to the adjustment programmes, the recommendations of which were focused on contraction of the economy. The combination of an already deteriorating agriculture and the external shock of a prolonged period of low commodity prices and the reduction of government expenditures lead to such an overkill of contracting forces that the structure of the economies of the SSA countries and their growth potential are at stake. As for the second half of the 1990s, a substantial price recovery is not expected; a continuation of the austerity programmes will probably lead to a further deterioration in the economies of SSA countries.

This picture may be too bleak. The observation by Yeats (1990) springs to mind: for the SSA countries trade statistics cannot be relied on, not even to indicate the level, composition, direction and trends of African trade. This thought would appear applicable for other macro-economic variables as well: probably those variables do not reflect the 'real' economy of the SSA countries. The industrial sector is deteriorating, but activities in the informal sector seem to hold out more promise. These activities, not included in official statistics, could have such widespread effects that the 1990s might turn out to be less grim than one would fear on the basis of official, but far from reliable, statistics.

References

Africa Recovery (1992) 'Assessing Adjustment's Social Impact', 6, 2.

Gersovits, M. and Paxson, C.H. (1990) *The Economies of Africa and the Prices of Their Exports*. Princeton Studies in International Finance no. 68. Princeton University, Princeton, NJ.

Hicks, N. and Kubisch, A. (1984) 'Cutting government expenditures in LDCs'. *Finance and Development*, 27, 3, pp. 37–9.

International Monetary Fund (1991) *Government Finance Statistics Yearbook 1991*, XV. Washington, DC.

International Monetary Fund (1992) *International Financial Statistics Yearbook 1992*, XLV. Washington, DC.

International Monetary Fund (various issues) *International Financial Statistics*. Washington, DC.

Maizels, A. (1992) *Commodities in Crisis: The Commodity Crisis of the 1980s and the Political Economy of International Commodity Policies*. Clarendon Press, Oxford.

Mansuri, B. (1990) 'Reflections on development aid policies'. In F. Stewart, H. Thomas and T. de Wilde (eds) *The Other Policy*. Intermediate Technology Publications, London, pp. 419–23.

Sahn, D.E. (1992) 'Adjustment is not responsible for poverty in Sub-Saharan Africa'. *European Association of Development Research and Training Institutes Newsletter*, 2, pp. 4–5.

Stewart, F. (1987) 'Should conditionality change?' In K.J. Havnevik (ed.) *The IMF and the World Bank in Africa: Conditionality, Impact and Alternatives*. Seminar proceedings no. 18. Scandinavian Institute of African Studies, Uppsala, pp. 29–46.

Taylor, L. (1988) *Varieties of Stabilization Experience: Towards Sensible Macroeconomics in the Third World*. Clarendon Press, Oxford.

Timmer, C.P. (1988) 'The agricultural transformation'. In H. Chenery and T.N. Srinavasan (eds) *Handbook of Development Economics. Volume 1*. North Holland, Amsterdam, pp. 275–331.

Tseng, W. (1984) 'The effects of adjustment'. *Finance and Development*, 21, 4, pp. 2–5.

United Nations Development Programme/World Bank (1992) *African Development Indicators*. Washington, DC.

United Nations (1969) *A System of National Accounts*. Studies in methods. Series F, no. 2. rev. 3. New York.

United Nations (1991) *National Accounts Statistics: Main Aggregates and Detailed Tables, 1989. Part I*. New York.

Wahab, I. (1990) 'De prijsval van grondstoffen' (The fall of commodity prices). *Economisch Statistische Berichten*, 75, 3768, pp. 700–3.

World Bank (1989, 1991, 1992) *Price Prospects for Major Primary Commodities: 1990–2005*. Including *Quarterly Review of Commodity Markets*. Washington, DC.

Yeats, A.J. (1990) 'On the accuracy of economic observation: do sub-Saharan statistics mean anything?' *The World Bank Economic Review*, 4, 2, pp. 135–56.

CHAPTER 11

Structural Adjustment in Comparative Perspective: Lessons from Pacific Asia[1]

Chris Dixon

Introduction

The general picture of sub-Saharan Africa (SSA) presented in this book is one of increasing poverty, relative levels of debt and marginalisation within the global economy. Already weak economies have been subjected to a variety of structural adjustment and liberalisation programmes. There is little evidence to suggest that the imposition of structural adjustment and the adoption of associated 'neo-liberal' policies have generated economic growth or increased stability outside of very limited sectors. Indeed, for the majority of the populations and national economies the situation has deteriorated. In many cases structural adjustment appears to have 'locked' economies into a downward spiral. Similarly, in terms of balancing external accounts, the most that can be said is that structural adjustment has reduced the rate at which the level of indebtedness has increased.

The international agencies have been, in general, extremely critical of the 'limited', 'partial' or 'slow' implementation of structural adjustment in SSA. In addition, even those countries which have most fully implemented agency policies, at the cost of considerable economic and political disruption and declining living standards for large sections of the population, have been told that either the programmes have not been far-reaching enough or that this is a necessary part of the protracted transition towards economic stability and long-term economic growth.

The above situation contrasts strongly with the generally accepted views of Pacific Asia. Here structural adjustment programmes (SAPs) and related policies are presented as having been instrumental in promoting rapid export-oriented economic growth, reducing the burdens of debt, inflation, excess state expenditure and balance-of-payments deficits. In Pacific Asia, unlike SSA, it is asserted that economies have undergone rapid and far-reaching reforms and governments

1. This chapter deals only with the main pro-capitalist developing economies of the region, that is, the Asian newly industrialising countries of Hong Kong, Singapore, South Korea and Taiwan, and the ASEAN Four – Indonesia, Malaysia, Philippines and Thailand.

have adopted 'correct' neo-liberal developmental policies. These views have been most forcibly presented with respect to Thailand. The rapid growth and structural change that the kingdom's economy has experienced since 1985 have been directly attributed to 'successful' structural adjustment (World Bank, 1990). For the international agencies the key question is why structural adjustment has succeeded in Pacific Asia while failing to do so elsewhere (International Monetary Fund (IMF), 1990, p. 13). The aims of this chapter are twofold: first, to review the validity of these views of Pacific Asia in general and Thailand in particular, and, second, to consider what lessons the Pacific Asian experience has for SSA.

The Less-developed Pacific Asian Economies in Perspective

Pacific Asia is rapidly emerging as a dynamic and increasingly integrated regional grouping within the global economy (Dixon and Drakakis-Smith, 1993). The region's less-developed economies comprise three distinctive groups, the NICs (newly industrialising countries) of Hong Kong, Singapore, South Korea and Taiwan, the ASEAN (Association of South East Asian Nations) Four, namely Indonesia, Malaysia, the Philippines and Thailand, and the socialist group, comprising Cambodia, China, Laos, Myanmar, North Korea and Vietnam. It is on the first two groups that this chapter concentrates, for it is these economies that have been widely described as successful cases of development and adjustment to changing internal and external conditions.

The generally high rates of growth and structural change that these economies have experienced (Tables 11.1, 11.2, 11.3 and 11.4) have blinded observers to both the special circumstances that have been attendant on their development and its consequences. This has resulted in general assertions that the Pacific Asian experience is directly applicable to other less-developed countries, notably those of SSA.

Table 11.1: Average Annual Rate of Growth of GDP, 1963–90

	1960 –69	1970 –79	1980	1981	1982	1983	1984	1985	1986	1987	1988	1989	1990	1991
ASEAN FOUR														
Indonesia	3.5	7.6	9.6	7.6	5.4	3.3	5.3	1.6	2.0	2.5	5.7	6.2	7.0	7.0
Malaysia	6.5	7.6	8.0	6.5	4.9	3.8	5.9	−1.5	0.0	3.0	7.4	8.5	10.0	8.6
Philippines	5.1	6.3	5.4	3.0	3.5	−1.4	−1.4	−4.0	1.0	5.7	4.5	3.6	2.5	0.0
Thailand	8.2	7.2	4.9	7.6	6.0	5.8	5.5	3.5	4.5	8.4	11.0	10.8	10.0	7.9
THE ASIAN NICS														
Hong Kong	10.0	9.3	9.8	10.4	4.3	5.2	6.0	0.8	6.0	13.6	7.3	2.5	2.3	3.9
Singapore	8.8	8.8	10.2	9.9	3.7	7.9	8.0	−2.9	2.0	8.8	11.0	9.2	8.9	6.7
South Korea	8.5	9.5	−6.7	7.1	3.5	9.5	7.5	5.1	10.0	11.1	12.2	7.4	8.9	8.4
Taiwan	9.2	8.0	7.2	5.5	5.0	7.5	11.0	5.1	10.8	11.7	7.0	7.1	5.2	7.0
OECD	5.1	3.3	1.4	1.2	−0.2	2.7	4.9	3.6	2.8	3.5	4.5	3.5	2.5	3.6
Low- and middle-income countries	4.8	2.1	2.1	0.5	2.3	3.7	4.5	3.7	3.3	3.9	3.7	3.0	1.9	2.2
Sub-Saharan Africa	4.6*	3.0	3.2	0.7	2.7	0.0	0.2	3.4	3.6	0.9	4.4	3.1	1.1	2.5

Note: * 1965–73.
Source: World Bank, *World Tables*. Washington, DC, various issues.

Table 11.2: Annual Average Rate of Growth of Merchandise Exports (Value)

	1970–9	1980	1981	1982	1983	1984	1985	1986	1987	1988	1989	1990	1991
THE ASEAN FOUR													
Indonesia	12.9	−2.0	−6.1	−4.7	19.2	0.0	0.4	13.0	−0.3	5.6	8.4	−3.5	24.5
Malaysia	5.7	−0.8	1.4	15.2	15.4	13.7	3.2	7.2	9.7	9.0	13.7	18.1	13.9
Philippines	7.7	15.5	8.0	−2.5	−3.1	5.8	−6.3	3.4	3.4	9.2	13.9	7.7	4.7
Thailand	8.4	10.6	20.8	19.4	−8.8	23.1	5.5	11.6	22.6	21.0	24.0	12.4	18.8
THE ASIAN NICS													
Hong Kong	19.4	30.1	23.9	3.3	22.3	27.3	3.6	19.2	37.0	32.0	12.8	14.8	4.4
Singapore	26.0	30.0	7.3	0.0	3.8	10.8	−2.3	−4.4	25.0	31.7	10.1	13.8	8.9
South Korea	25.9	10.0	19.2	7.1	14.6	18.2	6.3	16.4	25.8	13.3	−3.9	4.8	9.8
Taiwan	30.1	22.9	16.5	4.2	14.0	20.0	1.6	23.2	13.3	1.5	0.9	3.1	13.2
OECD	2.3	1.4	1.2	−0.2	2.7	4.9	3.6	2.8	3.5	4.5	12.6	4.3	2.6
Sub-Saharan Africa	5.7	−0.3	−17.7	−9.2	−4.6	8.9	8.4	1.2	0.7	−0.2	−2.8	7.1	11.8

Source: World Bank, *World Tables*. Washington, DC, various issues; World Bank, *African Development Indicators*. Washington, DC, various issues.

Table 11.3: Changing Structure of Production: Manufacturing Production as a Percentage of GDP

	1970–9	1980	1981	1982	1983	1984	1985	1986	1987	1988	1989	1990	1991
THE ASEAN FOUR													
Indonesia	9.2	11.6	10.8	12.9	12.7	14.5	15.8	16.3	17.2	18.2	18.5	19.3	21.0
Malaysia	20.0	19.6	19.2	19.2	19.5	20.3	19.7	20.9	22.4	24.4	25.2	26.6	27.3
Philippines	24.9	24.4	24.6	24.4	13.9	25.4	24.6	24.5	24.5	25.0	25.9	24.8	26.0
Thailand	19.7	19.6	20.1	19.5	19.1	19.8	20.1	21.8	22.6	23.2	23.9	24.7	27.0
THE ASIAN NICS													
Hong Kong	n.a.	22.2	22.0	19.5	21.3	22.3	20.3	21.0	20.5	19.1	17.5	18.0	17.0
Singapore	27.7	29.1	28.5	25.0	24.3	24.6	23.6	26.4	28.3	30.0	29.4	29.1	29.0
South Korea	24.6	29.2	29.9	29.2	29.9	32.1	30.3	31.7	32.2	32.5	31.8	29.2	28.0
Taiwan	36.2	34.0	33.7	33.4	34.2	36.5	36.6	39.5	39.4	37.8	35.2	33.6	33.6

Source: World Bank, *World Tables*. Washington, DC, various issues; Republic of China, *Industry of Free China*, Taipei, various issues.

Table 11.4: Manufactured Exports as a Percentage of the Value of Total Exports

	1965 −73	1973 −80	1980	1981	1982	1983	1984	1985	1986	1987	1988	1989	1990
THE ASEAN FOUR													
Indonesia	1.0	5.4	2.4	3.3	3.9	7.7	10.8	13.2	19.4	25.0	29.7	32.0	35.5
Malaysia	6.6	15.5	19.0	20.1	23.1	25.0	26.7	26.0	37.3	39.5	43.9	43.9	43.9
Philippines	6.9	24.3	36.8	44.7	49.6	50.0	55.1	56.8	57.1	61.8	60.5	61.8	61.2
Thailand	12.7	24.5	28.1	27.3	27.7	31.7	34.1	38.9	44.4	52.5	54.8	54.8	64.3
THE ASIAN NICS													
Hong Kong	90.2	91.6	96.5	96.9	96.7	96.1	96.7	96.4	96.9	96.8	96.5	96.3	95.8
Singapore	14.4	37.1	53.9	56.9	56.9	56.7	57.3	58.4	65.4	71.2	74.3	73.0	72.8
South Korea	68.0	84.3	90.0	90.5	91.3	91.0	91.3	91.4	92.0	92.4	92.4	93.0	93.6
Taiwan	75.0	88.4	97.2	97.3	97.6	93.5	94.9	93.9	94.2	94.5	95.4	95.8	96.2

Source: World Bank, *World Tables*. Washington, DC, various issues; Republic of China, *Industry of Free China*, Taipei, various issues.

Table 11.5: Pacific Asia in Perspective 1991

	GNP per capita US$	Life expectancy at birth	Infant Mortality per 1000 births	Population Growth annual average 1980–91
THE ASEAN FOUR				
Indonesia	620	60	74	1.8
Malaysia	2,520	71	15	2.6
Philippines	730	65	41	2.4
Thailand	1,420	68	27	1.9
THE ASIAN NICS				
Hong Kong	13,430	78	7	1.2
Singapore	14,210	74	6	1.7
South Korea	6,330	77	16	1.1
Taiwan	7,623	n.a.	n.a.	1.1
Low-income economies	350	62	71	2.0
Middle-income economies	2,040	66	51	2.1
Sub-Saharan Africa	350	51	107	3.1

Source: World Bank (1993) *World Development Reports 1993*. Washington, DC; Republic of China, *Industry of Free China*, Taipei, various issues.

The distinctiveness of the NICs and the ASEAN Four is apparent from the key indictors contained in Table 11.5. However, behind these figures lie patterns of development and positions within the global economy that set all these countries apart from the Third World in general and SSA in particular. More significantly, it must be remembered that two of the NICs, Singapore and Hong Kong, are city states that were developed during the colonial period as major international transshipment and strategic centres with high degrees of nodality. Similarly, Taiwan and South Korea experienced Japanese colonisation which laid the basis for modern industrial development and gave them semi-peripheral characteristics *vis-à-vis* South East Asia and China (Cummings, 1987, pp. 51–9). Further, during the 1950s and 1960s, Taiwan and South Korea came to occupy key positions in American global and regional strategy. In consequence, they received considerable volumes of aid from the US and the international agencies. Between 1951 and 1965 the US supplied Taiwan with US$1.5 billion of economic aid. This was equivalent to 95 per cent of the country's cumulative trade deficit (Cummings, 1987, p. 67). American aid to South Korea was even more generous, between 1948 and 1978 it amounted to US$6.5 billion. Effectively, during this period, 80 per cent of Korean imports were paid for by the US. In total American aid to South Korea exceeded that received by the whole of SSA in the same period (Cummings, 1987, p. 67).

The ASEAN Four are, at first sight, much more typical of developing countries than the NICs, both in terms of their history and socio-economic structures. However, they are all remarkably well endowed with a wide range of strategic primary products and, like the NICs, came to occupy key positions in American global and regional strategy. In consequence, they also received disproportionate American and international agency aid. American economic and military assistance was particularly important in Thailand during the 1960s, in Indonesia during the late 1960s and early 1970s and in the Philippines almost continuously since the 1950s. In Thailand, while the level of assistance was nowhere near that enjoyed by South Korea, it was targeted on key infrastructural 'bottlenecks' and consequently had an impact out of all proportion to its volume (Caldwell, 1974, pp. 63 and 69).

The members of the ASEAN Four and NIC groups have all experienced long-term political and economic stability. Despite insurgency movements, major regional tensions and wars, Pacific Asia has been characterised by remarkably long-lasting regimes. Only in Thailand have governments been short-lived and *coups d'état* endemic. Even here, the impermanence of regimes had little apparent impact on the long-term pattern of growth. Perhaps only in the Philippines since the early 1980s has political instability been a major barrier to economic growth. In general, stability has been reinforced and in part determined by the region's significance to global geopolitics. Thus a favourable climate for foreign investment and transnational activity was maintained. Where perceptions of instability discouraged investors, aid, particularly from the US, provided an important supplement or on occasions almost a complete substitute.

Since the late 1960s, the roles of the US as a major source of finance and trading partner have been replaced by Japan. The rapid growth and integration of the less-developed Pacific Asian economies have become closely associated with the emergence of Japan as a key component in the global economy. Indeed, for the NICs and the ASEAN Four, proximity to, and long-term relationships with, Japan have been critical to their economic development.

The Pacific Asian region has been characterised by three successive and continuing waves of industrial development, involving Japan after World War II, the NICs during the 1960s and 1970s, and the ASEAN Four, particularly Malaysia and Thailand, since the early 1980s. These developments have brought economic dynamism and increasing integration without any formal institutional arrangements.

Since the early 1980s, the appreciation of currencies, rising production costs, the reduction in the absorption capacity of the US for the region's exports and increased reliance on domestic markets have pressurised Japan and the NICs to relocate into the region's low-cost economies. This process accelerated from 1986, following the exchange rate realignments that followed from the 1985 Plaza Agreement. The result has been a critical interdependence between trade and investment flows, which are giving rise to marked regional divisions of labour, most clearly between the ASEAN four and the NICs. This has been a major factor in the acceleration of growth and structural change.

The dynamism of the NICs and the ASEAN Four has tended to blind observers to the less desirable consequences of rapid economic growth and structural change (Forbes, 1993; Henderson, 1993). However, it is all too apparent that growth has had considerable human and environmental costs.

The rapid increase of per capita GDP, particularly in the NICs, has diverted attention away from the persistence of poverty and inequality. Indeed, it has become almost unfashionable to mention these in a Pacific Asian context. The World Bank (1993a) has made very optimistic claims concerning the decline in poverty in the region (Table 11.6), suggesting that 'South Korea and Malaysia have almost eradicated poverty, which virtually disappeared in the past ten years in Taiwan, Hong Kong and Singapore' (cited in *Far Eastern Economic Review*, 18 February 1993, p. 66). However, the World Bank data also reveal that declines in the incidence of poverty have not always been matched by a fall in the numbers living in poverty. This is particularly apparent in Thailand and the Philippines, where the number of absolute poor has shown little change since 1970 (Table 11.6).

Table 11.6: Incidence of Absolute Poverty* in Pacific Asia

	Incidence (%)			Number (millions)		
	1970	1980	1990	1970	1980	1990
Indonesia	60	29	15	70	42	27
Malaysia	18	9	2	2	1	0.4
Philippines	35	30	21	14	13	14
South Korea	23	10	5	7	4	2
Thailand	26	17	16	9.5	8	9

Note: * Absolute poverty is defined by the World Bank as a level of income that only allows subsistence amounts of food and other necessities.
Source: World Bank (1993a) *The East Asian Miracle Economies*. Washington, DC.

While data are far from comprehensive or reliable, a number of individual studies, including ones produced by national governments and earlier World Bank reports, cast serious doubt on the validity of the World Bank's 1993 claims. In the Philippines, earlier World Bank studies (1980a and 1988) reported that the percentage of families living in poverty rose from 43.3 in 1964 to 44 in 1975 and 52 in 1985. In addition, the 1988 study concluded that real wages had dropped constantly since 1960. Canlas *et al.* (1988) cite a study by a private research organisation (IBON Database Philippines) which concluded that in 1983, 71 per cent of the population were living in poverty. More recently, Montemayor (1993) suggested that 'half of the population do not have access to basic needs such as adequate food, clothing and shelter'. All this is a far cry from the World Bank's (1993a) estimate of only 21 per cent.

Whilst it is generally agreed that some reduction in poverty has occurred (Booth, 1993), the overall impact of growth on inequality has not been as widespread as the World Bank would have us believe. As Forbes (1993, p. 54) has remarked, 'despite the modern facade of much of Asia, there remains a grinding poverty in both urban and rural areas'. This is clearly evident from Table 11.7, where UNDP data indicate that the proportions of total population in poverty remain quite high and that the distribution of wealth as measured by gini coefficients or shares of national income correlate poorly with levels of GNP.

Table 11.7: Income Distribution and Poverty

	Income Share (Lowest 40%)	Ratio (Highest 20% to Lowest 40%)	Gini Coefficient	Population living below the poverty line (%) Total	Rural
Hong Kong	16.2	8.7	0.45	n.a.	n.a.
Singapore	15.0	9.6	0.42	n.a.	n.a.
Taiwan	20.0	8.0	n.a.	n.a.	n.a.
Indonesia	21.2	4.7	0.31	39	44
Malaysia	13.9	11.1	0.48	27	38
Philippines	15.2	8.7	0.45	58	64
South Korea	17.0	n.a.	0.36	16	11
Thailand	15.0	n.a.	0.47	30	34

Source: United Nations Development Programme (1991) *Human Development Report 1991*. Oxford University Press, New York.

Rapid economic growth and structural change have had serious environmental consequences throughout the region. Taiwan and South Korea are amongst the most polluted countries in the world (Bello and Rosenfield, 1992). Since the early 1980s, increased public concern and the imposition of more stringent regulations have resulted in many noxious processes being relocated from the NICs to ASEAN low labour-cost locations (Burnett, 1992, pp. 228–9; Fornader, 1991). Thailand, for example, has been a recipient of a considerable volume of East Asian 'pollution exports' since the early 1980s. McDowell (1989, p. 327), in particular, cites Japanese textile plants which discharge 'harmful acetate dyes' and 'Asahi's mercury-discharging soda ash plants which have been relocated on the Chao Phraya River'.

Even less attention has focused on the question of human rights and the limited development of civil society in Pacific Asia. In a comprehensive attempt to produce an index of human suffering, the Population Crisis Commission (1992) assembled data on many aspects related to the quality of life, amongst which were civil rights and human freedom. Almost without exception, the Pacific Asian nations were in the lowest third of world nations with respect to these data. Thus Pacific Asia's late industrialisation appears to be associated with even later development of democracy and human rights.

However, the economic crises of the 1980s and the transition of power, or its prospects, in a number of long-standing regimes is bringing these issues to the fore. In South Korea, for example, there have been repeated clashes since 1987 between workers and the forces of the state. As one trade union leader said of Korean industrialisation, 'there is nothing in it for us' (cited in Bello and Rosenfield, 1992, p. 1). Moreover, Hsiao (1992) has noted with respect to Taiwan that the emergence of a middle class has strengthened the demand for more liberal democratic freedoms and posed new challenges of political adjustment for the government. Indeed, elsewhere in the region much of the political turmoil of recent years has been the consequence of urban middle-class pressure for reform, *viz* the overthrow of the Marcos regime or the pro-democracy movements in Hong Kong and Thailand. To date these types of events have had little impact on economic growth, or the image of the region as highly suitable for foreign investment and transnational activity. However, it may well be that pressure for representation and welfare arrangements may come to disrupt many of the region's economies in the near future.

The advocates of the Pacific Asian 'model' of late industrialisation have tended to draw as much of a veil over the consequences of the region's recent rapid development as over the very special circumstances attendant upon it. Similarly, the international agencies, in asking why structural adjustment has succeeded in Pacific Asia and failed in so many other places, have consistently ignored the radically different circumstances that prevail. It cannot be stressed strongly enough that the Pacific Asian 'success cases' are a very small and highly selected group. Broad comparisons of these eight countries with the immensely varied group of over 40 comprising SSA would appear to be of limited meaning; this has not inhibited the international agencies from repeatedly drawing policy conclusions from such comparisons.[2]

Pacific Asia and the International Economy

Since the early 1970s the global economy has been subject to recurrent major crises. However, the impact of these crises has varied enormously both in intensity and timing. During the 1970s the less-developed economies of Pacific Asia maintained remarkably high and consistent growth rates (Table 11.1). These tended to divert attention away from deepseated contradictions of the various

2. A more appropriate comparison would be between the Pacific Asian group and the nine sub-Saharan African economies whose 1991 per capita GDP was at or above that of Indonesia (Table 11.5). In terms of income, the wealthier SSA economies compare favourably with the ASEAN four. However, only Botswana and South Africa have levels of life expectancy and infant mortality approaching those of the ASEAN group. Similarly, over the last 20 years, only Botswana, Gabon and Lesotho have approached the Pacific Asian rates of economic growth.

development processes operating in the region. The high rates of growth in many cases obscured the escalation of overseas debt, inflation, budget deficits, adverse trade balances and increasing dependence on a limited range of developed world markets (Tables 11.7, 11.8, 11.9 and 11.10). In Indonesia, Malaysia and Singapore oil exports did much to offset the impact of the international recession. It was only in Thailand and the Philippines, both heavily dependent on energy imports and the export of a limited range of non-oil primary products, that recurrent crises became a focus of concern to governments and the international agencies. In both of these states a series of measures was implemented, many at the behest of the Asian Development Bank (ADB), the World Bank and IMF. None proved to be more than short-term palliatives. In the case of the Philippines the overall economic situation deteriorated throughout the 1970s, with the country achieving by far the lowest rate of growth in the region (Table 11.1). In contrast Thailand, despite political upheaval and recurrent balance-of-payments crises, maintained remarkably high rates of growth (Table 11.1).[3]

Table 11.8: Indicators of Indebtedness

	External Debt as a Percentage of GNP				Debt Service as a Percentage of Export Earnings			
	1975	1980	1986	1991	1975	1980	1986	1991
THE ASEAN FOUR								
Indonesia	35.6	27.9	58.5	66.4	7.5	7.9	29.3	32.7
Malaysia	19.6	21.9	76.3	47.6	3.3	2.5	13.7	8.3
Philippines	17.7	48.4	93.6	70.2	7.4	7.2	18.3	23.2
Thailand	9.2	25.1	44.7	30.0	2.4	5.0	16.7	13.1
THE ASIAN NICS								
Hong Kong	0.2	3.3	n.a.	n.a.	★★	★★	n.a.	n.a.
Singapore	11.8	10.2	11.8	n.a.	3.8	4.3	2.3	n.a.
South Korea	9.7	13.7	13.6	14.4	11.6	12.2	16.7	7.1
Taiwan	n.a.	2.8	8.8	n.a.	n.a.	5.8	7.9	n.a.
Sub-Saharan Africa	41.9	98.2	227.9	340.8	5.5	10.9	28.3	20.5

Note: ★★ Less than 0.1.
Source: World Bank, *World Tables*. Washington, DC, various issues; World Bank, *World Debt Tables*. Washington, DC, various issues.

3. In part the explanation for this lies in Thailand's lower degree of integration into the global economy (Dixon, 1991a, p. 20).

Table 11.9: Current Account Balance as a Percentage of GDP

	1965–73	1973–8	1980	1981	1982	1983	1984	1985	1986	1987	1988	1989	1990
THE ASEAN FOUR													
Indonesia	20.5	16.7	−3.6	−0.9	−5.8	−7.5	−2.2	−2.2	−5.1	−3.0	−1.8	−1.4	−2.3
Malaysia	9.5	11.8	−1.3	−10.0	−13.5	−11.7	−5.0	−2.1	−0.6	8.1	5.0	−0.8	−4.1
Philippines	−15.9	−10.6	−5.1	−5.8	−5.8	−8.4	−8.7	−4.8	−0.7	2.4	−1.9	−1.7	−4.1
Thailand	−19.7	−9.9	−3.5	−6.9	−7.7	−3.1	−7.6	−5.4	−4.4	0.2	−1.0	−3.1	3.8
THE ASIAN NICS													
Hong Kong	−24.2	−19.4	−4.6	−5.5	−3.6	2.0	4.5	5.6	4.1	6.2	5.1	8.0	5.0
Singapore	−14.8	−10.8	−13.1	−10.2	−8.4	−3.6	−2.1	0.0	1.7	−0.8	3.6	9.0	7.1
South Korea	−17.7	−10.6	−5.4	−8.6	−6.8	−3.6	−2.0	−1.5	−1.0	4.3	7.5	8.2	2.4
Taiwan	−10.8	−5.8	−2.2	1.1	4.6	8.5	14.9	14.8	18.1	16.0	8.2	7.7	6.9

Source: World Bank, *World Tables*. Washington, DC, various issues.

Table 11.10: Government Expenditure as a Percentage of GDP

	1970–9	1980	1981	1982	1983	1984	1985	1986	1987	1988	1989	1990
THE ASEAN FOUR												
Indonesia	18.5	23.1	24.1	20.5	20.3	18.3	21.1	23.0	20.2	19.3	18.6	18.9
Malaysia	28.8	29.6	38.4	36.1	31.2	27.6	29.0	21.5	29.8	27.2	28.6	29.7
Philippines	14.8	13.4	13.8	12.9	12.2	11.1	11.2	13.5	15.8	16.1	18.0	23.5
Thailand	18.0	19.1	19.7	21.1	20.3	20.0	21.6	20.6	18.7	16.4	15.6	15.5
THE ASIAN NICS												
Hong Kong	n.a.	n.a.	n.a.	n.a.	n.a.	n.a.	n.a.	n.a.	6.4	6.9	7.2	7.7
Singapore	21.2	20.8	22.7	20.7	22.0	26.3	27.3	28.8	34.3	22.7	22.4	21.9
South Korea	18.7	17.9	16.9	18.6	16.7	16.4	16.5	16.0	15.6	15.2	16.6	16.8
Taiwan	16.7	16.6	16.2	16.7	16.1	15.7	15.9	14.8	14.3	14.6	15.1	16.2

Source: IMF, *Governmental Statistics*. Washington, DC, various issues; Republic of China, (1993) *National Income in Taiwan Area of the Republic of China*, Taipei.

The period 1979–81 was characterised by the second oil price rise, the collapse of non-oil commodity prices, the rise in real international interest rates and the sharp reduction in the developed world market for imported manufactured goods – a reflection of recession and increased levels of protection. These factors triggered reductions in growth rates for all the less-developed Pacific Asian economies (Table 11.1), which was most serious for the region's major oil importers, the Philippines, South Korea and Thailand.

The impact of the external shocks was most striking in the case of South Korea, where the 1979–81 recession brought an abrupt halt to the 'Korean miracle'. Between 1963 and 1979, GDP and export earnings had grown at 10.5 per cent and 37.5 per cent respectively. In 1979 export earnings contracted by 0.1 per cent[4] and in 1980 GDP declined by 6.7 per cent. Between 1973 and 1979, South Korea had managed to maintain a high rate of growth by offsetting the deteri-

4. In 1978 export earnings had expanded by 15.1 per cent.

oration in the terms of trade by a massive increase in the volume of exports and overseas borrowing.

In contrast, the Pacific Asian oil exporters – Singapore, Malaysia and Indonesia – were again largely cushioned from the external shocks of the early 1980s. However, the fall in oil prices after 1983, together with the continuing low level of other commodity prices and the further contraction of developed world markets, brought serious problems to these economies by the middle of the decade.

Indonesia was particularly severely affected by the fall in oil prices.[5] By the early 1980s, oil and gas exports accounted for over 60 per cent of total export earnings and government revenue. In addition, the exploitation of the oil and gas reserves had become a major focus for foreign investment and transnational activity. During the 1970s, Indonesian development strategy had become heavily dependent on the earnings from the oil 'boom'. This was particularly the case for the heavily protected import-substituting manufacturing sector.

The collapse of oil prices reduced Indonesian export earnings by nearly 54 per cent between 1982 and 1986. This, reinforced by the contracting markets for other staple exports, resulted in a sharp increase in the balance of payments deficit and an escalation of overseas debt. The rate of growth of GDP contracted sharply during 1985, remaining at a low level until 1988 (Table 11.1).

While the fall in oil prices provided some relief for the region's net importers, they all experienced a measure of slower growth during 1985 and 1986. However, with the exception of Hong Kong, they remained more insulated from the international economy and had already begun to adjust to changing internal and external conditions.

Hong Kong experienced a sharp reduction in growth to only 0.1 per cent during 1985. This reflected the very open nature of the Hong Kong economy and, like Singapore, the continued importance of the entrepôt function. However, the almost static level of GDP was not reflected in other indicators. For example, real wages rose by 3 per cent during 1985–6. Thus, while the slowing of growth in Hong Kong was abrupt, it probably had the least impact on the domestic economy as a whole of any of the Pacific Asian countries.

Between 1980 and 1985 all the less-developed pro-capitalist Pacific Asian economies experienced serious economic problems. The Economic and Social Commission for Asia and the Pacific (ESCAP) (1990) identified three areas of particular concern that had emerged in the region by the early 1980s:

1. Heavy, expensive foreign loans had been taken out to maintain government expenditure;
2. Growing debt burdens were eroding the funds available for development;

5. Indonesia also adhered closely to the OPEC export quotas which served to reduce export earnings in advance of the price fall.

and
3. Countries were slow to adjust their exchange rates and relied on borrowing and foreign assistance to meet balance of payments deficits.

In general, governments initially responded to these and other consequences of the external shocks as they had done to previous crises by attempting to implement a variety of often short-term, *ad hoc* domestic stabilisation measures. However, the severity of the various crises necessitated fundamental reviews of long-term development policies and, in a number of cases, appeals to, and intervention by, the IMF and World Bank.

The Pattern of Adjustment in Pacific Asia

The international agencies considered that the way in which individual countries responded to the external shocks reflected their internal structures as well as past and present development policies. Changed external circumstances had brought to the fore deep-seated contradictions of the development process. Further, they revealed the nature of Pacific Asian growth, most significantly the extent to which the state had become deeply involved in the whole development process. The crises of the early 1980s effectively exposed and destroyed the myth of the *laissez-faire* Pacific Asian states under which rapid growth and economic transformation had been fostered (White, 1988; Dixon and Drakakis-Smith, 1993).

The external shocks exposed two contrasting patterns of development in the Pacific Asian region. For the NICs the gradual loss of comparative advantage in labour-intensive manufactured goods was exacerbated. This process, which was posing problems for all the NICs by the late 1970s, was, particularly in the case of Singapore, accelerated by state policies aimed at moving industrial production towards more skill- and capital-intensive activities. In Singapore, the 'wage correction' policy introduced during 1979 raised labour costs by 40 per cent. The intention was to stimulate a 'second industrial revolution' by squeezing out labour-intensive manufacturing processes. As the Director of the Economic Development Board stressed: 'We decided ... that making transistor radios was not a job for us. Nor do we want workers in the rag trade. We wanted technical services' (cited in Smith *et al.*, 1985, p. 87).

In the less-developed economies of the ASEAN Four, the external shocks exposed the continued emphasis given to ISI (import-substituting industrialisation). Indeed, in many instances, the partial adoption of EOI (export-oriented industrialisation) strategies by these states had resulted in conflicting, expensive and often highly ineffective policies. In addition, both internal and external changes were making ISI an increasingly untenable strategy. Indeed, since the early 1970s, EOI had become the development orthodoxy advocated by the international agencies (Robison *et al.*, 1987, p. 7). This view also became a basic tenet of structural adjustment (see Chapter 1). However, the availability of cheap international loans and high oil prices had made it possible for some of the region's countries to continue with ISI during the 1970s and early 1980s (Dixon, 1991a, p. 153).

For both the NICs and the ASEAN Four development strategies had come to involve high levels of state involvement in the economy, resulting in what the IMF termed distortions of the market (IMF, 1990, p. 192). This involved high levels of state expenditure (Table 11.10), direct government involvement in production and, with the exception of Hong Kong and Singapore, high levels of tariff protection. It was these aspects of economic policy that were targeted by structural adjustment and related liberalisation programmes. For the ASEAN Four, in addition, the proposed reforms also highlighted the ending of ISI and the emphasising of EOI.

During the 1980s, with the exception of Hong Kong, all the less-developed Pacific Asian countries accepted the need for reforms along the lines suggested by the international agencies. Agency-based SAPs were implemented in the Philippines, South Korea and Thailand as early as 1981. In Indonesia a programme of 'home grown' structural adjustment was implemented during 1983 and used to support substantial funding by the IMF and World Bank. In Malaysia, Taiwan and Singapore a variety of liberalising measures was implemented, principally from 1985 onwards.

The agency-based structural adjustment and related funding[6] were in operation in South Korea between 1980 and 1985, in Thailand between 1981 and 1986 and in the Philippines between 1980 and 1992. In each case, liberalisation measures were incorporated into national plans, and in Thailand and South Korea extended well beyond the periods covered by the funding arrangements. However, measures were introduced extremely slowly. Only austerity measures and currency devaluations were implemented with any rapidity.[7] Despite this in South Korea and, to a lesser extent, Thailand, the pattern of rapid economic growth was rapidly re-established (Table 11.1). Only in the Philippines was the slowdown protracted. While the agencies tended to blame the very slow progress made in implementing adjustments (World Bank, 1987), it is apparent that the external shocks had exposed serious long-term weaknesses in the Philippines economy, the resolution of which was inhibited by the prevailing socio-economic structure and political instability. Under prevailing conditions, reforms were politically very difficult to implement and, in isolation, apparently incapable of initiating any rapid rehabilitation of the economy.

The Taiwanese economy 'bounced back' rapidly after the slowdown of the early 1980s. This reflected both the less-exposed nature of the economy, the increased competitiveness of exports as a result of the floating of the currency during 1985 (which, by 1989, had resulted in an effective devaluation of 37.5 per cent) and the spectacular outflow of domestic capital which followed the

6. These include standby credit arrangements and SALs.
7. Currency adjustments were initiated in South Korea during 1980 and in the Philippines and Thailand during 1981.

liberalisation of foreign exchange controls during 1986. The rapid economic recovery was followed during the period 1987 to 1990 by a substantial reduction in the level of industrial tariff protection. This later element of liberalisation was principally a reaction to pressure from the US and the threat of the imposition of retaliatory 'equalisation tariffs' on Taiwanese imports (Economist Intelligence Unit, 1992–3, p. 11). Overall, during the late 1980s, there was a marked retreat from the 'siege mentality' which had characterised Taiwanese economic policy since the 1950s and provided a shield against external shocks.

In Malaysia the government initially attempted to counter the economic slowdown of the early 1980s by sharply increasing government expenditure (Table 11.10). This resulted in an escalation of the budget deficit and the level of overseas debt (Table 11.8). The latter was exacerbated by the fall in oil prices and the general deterioration of international trading conditions. In 1983 the government reversed the policy, freezing expenditure until 1988. This measure reduced the rate of growth of public sector debt from 35 per cent in 1982 to 10 per cent in 1985. In 1985 the currency was floated, effectively devaluing it by 10 per cent, and a programme of privatisation initiated. During 1986 the industrial master plan was announced. Under this, the emphasis was placed on EOI. The level of tariff protection was to be reduced, incentives given for exports, restrictions on foreign ownership limited and costs lowered by reductions in utility prices. In total these measures increased the attractiveness of Malaysia for foreign investment and transnational activity. However, they also compromised the new economic policy, which, since 1969, had imposed controls over ownership and investment with the objective of redistributing economic power into the hands of the Malaysian majority of the population.

In Indonesia a similar programme of public expenditure cuts was initiated from 1983, when the currency was devalued by 50 per cent, and by a further 50 per cent in 1986. A programme of budgetary austerity was implemented during 1986–7 and 1987–8; this included the freezing of all public sector salaries until 1989. During 1986 a trade deregulation programme was implemented and the procedures for approving foreign investments simplified. As in Malaysia, these measures ran counter to the long-term government policy of controlling foreign investment and channelling it into particular locations and sectors.

For Singapore the 1985 recession resulted in a major reconsideration of development policy, particularly with respect to the forcing of the transition to more skill- and capital-intensive activities. A programme of cost-cutting measures was implemented, including a reduction in labour costs by wage cuts, reduction of employers' contributions to the Central Provident Fund and a relaxation of the controls on the inflow of cheaper foreign labour. However, it was apparent that Singapore could not 'turn the clock back' and recoup the lost advantage in labour-intensive manufacture. Indeed, the re-establishment of high levels of growth, as in the other NICs, rested heavily on 'high tech' production, the service sector and the exporting of more labour-intensive activities.

Thus, during the 1980s and early 1990s, structural adjustment and related policies became the norm amongst the less-developed economies of Pacific Asia. This was least apparent in Hong Kong where, from 1982 onwards, measures were introduced to reduce the level of state expenditure. These included substantial cuts in the public infrastructure programmes. Similarly, during 1986 and 1987, government policy was mildly deflationary. However, these policies have to be set against increased state involvement in the economy. This has been most noticeable with respect to research and development. The limited implementation of liberalisation in Hong Kong reflects both the fact that it was by far the least managed economy in the region as well as the very limited impact that the external shocks had on its domestic economy.

By the early 1990s, other than in Hong Kong, there had been an appreciable measure of reform along the lines advocated by the international agencies. In addition, with the exception of the Philippines, all the Pacific Asian economies have re-established a pattern of high levels of economic growth, and rapid structural change since the mid-1980s (Tables 11.1 and 11.2). While this is taken as a vindication of structural adjustment and related policies, there have been few attempts to examine in detail the relationship between policy reforms and renewed growth. The next section provides such a detailed study for Thailand, the economy which has frequently been depicted as the most successful case of structural adjustment in Pacific Asia (World Bank, 1990).

Structural Adjustment in Thailand

Between 1986 and 1991 Thailand became one of the fastest-growing economies in the world, with the value of manufactured exports rising 40 per cent per annum, total exports by 30 per cent and GDP by 9.2 per cent. This growth was accompanied by a surge in foreign direct investment, particularly from Japan and the Asian NICs. Overall, from 1986, Thailand experienced a period of accelerated integration into the global economy. This spurt of growth has been directly attributed to the application of the 'correct' government policy. For such international agencies as the World Bank, ADB and the IMF these 'correct' policies were part of a programme of structural adjustment which, from the early 1980s, transformed the kingdom's development environment. Indeed, Thailand is now being presented as the new neo-liberal model of development:

> economists, development agencies and international development specialists are already starting to forsake their hallowed Japanese, South Korean and Taiwanese models of development for a new one: the Thai model. To them, Thailand's four years of double-digit growth represents the success of a decade of deregulation and the honing of investment codes to produce one of the most user-friendly investment environments among developing countries. (Handley, 1991, pp. 34–5)

The Crisis of the Early 1980s

The 1979–80 oil price rise and the subsequent collapse of non-oil commodity prices precipitated a major economic crisis for Thailand. The terms of trade declined by 22 per cent, the current account deficit widened to 6 per cent of GDP and the debt service ratio rose to 20 per cent. The deteriorating economic situation was exacerbated by question marks over the kingdom's long-term political stability. There had been violent changes of government in 1973, 1976 and 1978; after 1976 these were followed by increased rural insurgency and state repression. Thai officials were making extremely pessimistic pronouncements, predicting escalating economic and political turmoil culminating in violent revolutionary change within two or three years (Dixon, 1979, p. 1072). During 1979 a survey of 65 Japanese corporations concluded that the Thai investment situation was 'hopeless' (cited in Tasker, 1990, p. 49).

During 1979–80 the Thai government initiated an austerity programme aimed at curtailing inflation, the balance-of-payments deficit and the growth of overseas debt. In addition, moves towards longer-term structural change were incorporated into the draft Fifth National Plan (1982–6). However, these measures and proposals were insufficient to change the pessimistic views of investors or the international agencies.

Late in 1980 the World Bank produced an economic review of Thailand (World Bank, 1980b). This advocated a five-year programme of structural adjustment. Five areas were identified where adjustments were necessary:

- resource mobilisation, particularly in the public sector;
- monetary policy, including measures to maintain high rates of private saving and to manage external debt and the capital account;
- energy policy and conservation, with particular attention to pricing;
- industrial policy and measures to promote industrial exports; and
- agricultural policy and measures to maintain high rates of growth of agricultural production and exports.

Specific recommendations included:

- the raising of domestic energy prices to the international level (they were 20 per cent below and were a key element in the subsidised industrial sector);
- the ending of other fuel and transport subsidies;
- reducing government expenditure;
- ending the import-substitution policy for industry;
- placing emphasis on export-oriented industry;
- reducing import taxes;
- removing all export restrictions and taxes;
- substantially reducing foreign exchange controls;

- imposing strong deflationary monetary and fiscal policies;
- privatising state concerns; and
- reform of the taxation system to increase efficiency of collection and yields.

Overall, these recommendations involved the opening of the economy to international capital and substantially reducing the role of the state. This involved what the ADB (1990, p. 26) called 'finding a non-inflationary role for the state', reducing the government's developmental role to matters of policy. Further, structural adjustment reflected the

> need to shift the pattern of growth from one based on the extension of land under cultivation and on import substitution to one based on increasingly intensive use of land and industries producing for domestic and export markets under competitive conditions. (World Bank, 1980b, p. 19)

The Thai government accepted the World Bank's analysis that the kingdom's economic problems were long-term, structural ones and stemmed from what the World Bank (1980b, p. 20) termed 'past governments' mismanagement'. The impact of external shocks – oil price rise, fall in commodity prices, contraction of tourism and markets for manufactured exports – had merely exposed underlying contradictions in the country's economically, socially and geographically uneven development process.

Following the acceptance of the World Bank recommendations, they became an integral part of the fifth national plan (1982–6). More significantly, the implementation of the recommendations became a formal pre-condition for the granting of two Structural Adjustment Loans (SALs) with a combined value of US$250 million. These were initiated in 1982 and 1983 respectively.

In addition to the SALs, there were discussions with the IMF on 'appropriate policy responses' (Panayotou and Sussangkarn, 1991, p. 6). The most significant result was a standby credit arrangement of Special Drawing Rights (SDR) 814.5 million for the period 1981 to 1983. This arrangement was granted with the general objectives of restructuring demand, reducing the public savings–investment gap and limiting the growth of foreign debt.

The Implementation of Structural Adjustment

The World Bank accepted the moves towards structural adjustment during 1979-80 'as a down-payment' for the SALs (Sahansakul, 1992, pp. 13–15). The view appears to have been that, while the progress was very limited, the various studies and proposals, particularly those in the draft outline for the Fifth National Plan (1982–6), indicated that the government was thinking along the approved lines and was serious about structural adjustment. However, Thai administrations encountered serious problems in implementing the World Bank recommendations. Attempts to reduce fuel and transport subsidies, coming on top of the recession and government austerity measures, sparked a series of mass public protests. In addition, both domestic and foreign ISI interests would have been adversely affected by such measures as the raising of energy and utility prices and the reduction of tariff barriers. Given the very close and complex interrelations between the bureaucracy, military and domestic capital, there was considerable pressure to hold back on the reforms. Indeed Thailand, like a number of Pacific Asian economies, was 'caught in a bind and could engage in only a very limited degree of restructuring' (Robison *et al.*, 1987, pp. 11–12). In consequence, between 1981 and 1985 a variety of reforms were introduced which gave the impression of great activity in implementing structural adjustment, but few were of real significance.

The World Bank's (1984) review of the progress of the SAP was extremely critical of the limited progress.[8] In 1985 plans for further SALs were abandoned, Thailand turning instead to the IMF for a two-year funding package of US$586.6 million. In December 1986 an IMF review was also extremely critical of the lack of progress with structural adjustment. Subsequent negotiations broke down and Thailand abandoned further World Bank and IMF funding. In both cases the 'sticking point' was the size of the budget deficit, which had expanded to 5 per cent of GDP instead of contracting to 3.5 per cent. The growth in the budget deficit reflected both the failure to reduce government expenditure and shortfalls in government revenue, the latter being a product of slower growth and associated lower tax yields.[9]

By 1985 very limited progress had been made towards implementing the main World Bank and IMF recommendations. Sahansakul (1992) reviewed the programmes and concluded that, in general, they had a very slight, but beneficial impact on the economy. Panayotou and Sussangkarn (1991, p. 9) concluded that while it is extremely difficult to quantify the impact of the adjustment programmes:

> Nevertheless, it can probably be said that with the serious attention of the government on the structural imbalance problems, supported by the World Bank and the IMF, and the adoption of generally prudent monetary and fiscal policies, the Thai economy avoided getting into serious difficulties during the structural adjustment period. When the world economy recovered, and beneficial changes occurred in the world economic environment, Thailand did not have a serious overhang from the structural adjustment period, and was in a position to take advantage of the changes that occurred.

8. For a detailed review of the implementation of each of the proposed structural adjustment measures see World Bank (1986).
9. Tax yields had in recent years repeatedly fallen below target. This was a reflection of the cumbersome and inefficient revenue system, an area that the World Bank had targeted for reform.

Despite the economic problems of the early 1980s, the Thai economy maintained growth rates that were, by international standards, extremely respectable (Table 11.1). However, many of the structural adjustment-related targets for the Fifth Plan (1982–6) were not achieved, notably the debt service ratio and government expenditure. Indeed, these only began to show significant decline in 1988. The abandonment of the IMF and World Bank programmes in 1985 and 1986 was accompanied by signs of economic recovery. To a degree, the improved global trading situation, falling oil prices and the expansion of export earnings gave the Thai government the confidence to forgo funding from the international agencies. However, the commitment to structural adjustment was not abandoned with the programmes. The Sixth Plan (1987–91) reiterated the commitment to structural adjustment-like reforms, though not directly by name. Since 1986 and more especially 1988 a significant number of the original recommendations have been implemented.[10] The fuel and public transport subsidies were progressively removed between 1986 and 1988.

In addition, price controls and import controls on a wide range of minor items, such as certain drugs, cosmetics and toothpaste, were removed during this period. For the industrial sector a key element was the reform of the protective structure. Despite some reduction and simplification of tariffs the average level of protection continued to rise until 1988. Indeed, tariff levels only began to decline from October 1990 when the duty on imported machinery was reduced from 35 per cent to 5 per cent. In the following July, duty on computers fell from a range of 20 to 40 per cent to 5 per cent, and for components from 40 per cent to 1 per cent. Other reductions still provide a considerable measure of protection, notably for motor cars, where the duty on vehicles of over 3,000cc has been reduced from 300 per cent to 112.[11]

There was a similar long delay in reducing the foreign exchange regulations. While some simplification of procedures took place, there was no effective relaxation until May 1990, when the Board of Trade announced a three-stage programme which effectively removed all restrictions by early 1992.

During 1991–2 the financial markets were deregulated, oil prices floated and the tax structure revamped. The level of personal income tax was reduced from 35 to 30 per cent and an across-the-board 7 per cent value added tax imposed. Exports were exempted from VAT and foreign investors became subject to the same tax laws as local companies. Since 1990 there have been moves towards the privatisation of the 60 state enterprises. This was marked by the sale of 15 per cent of the holdings in Thai International early in 1991. However, despite the importance that the World Bank attached to privatisation, the Thai state sector

10. For a tabulated comparison with the situation described by the World Bank see Sahansakul (1992, pp. 20–7).
11. The delay in reducing the level of tariffs also reflected their importance as a source of government revenue. Earlier cuts would have exacerbated the already problematic budget deficit.

is by no means a drain on public expenditure. In 1990 the state concerns employed 260,000 people, had a turnover of US$11.7 billion and returned pre-tax profits of US$1.8 billion, a return of 14.7 per cent. Only five concerns made losses – the largest of which was the Bangkok Metropolitan Transport Administration, followed by the State Railways. The pressure for privatisation has come from the inability of the concerns (and unwillingness/inability of the government) to finance the much-needed expansion of the kingdom's infra-structure.

Thus a range of 'home-grown' structural adjustment measures was implemented well after the boom was under way. Indeed, only with renewed economic growth, political stability and the reduction of the political influence of the ISI sector was it possible to implement some of these policies at all. It is extremely difficult to make a case for structural adjustment *causing* the acceleration of economic growth and structural change. At most the reforms may be viewed as sustaining the processes of rapid change rather than initiating them.

The Causes of Rapid Economic Growth

If the SAPs did not give rise to the acceleration of growth, what did? Were there, for example, policies outside of structural adjustment that stimulated growth? Akrasanee *et al.* (1991, p. 17) reviewed Thai commercial policies in general and concluded that:

> Thailand's recent economic success appears to have been attained *despite*, rather than because of, the evolution of trade and commercial policies. Commercial policies have been of the classical import-substitution and anti-export nature and have become increasingly so in the second half of the 1980s.

While various simplifying and streamlining of export and investment procedures took place before the relaxations of protection and exchange controls, it is difficult to attribute any significant role to such measures in isolation. However, like other measures aimed at attracting foreign investment, it is often the 'message' that their implementation sends that is of greatest significance (ESCAP, 1983).

The acceleration of economic growth was based on the export of labour-intensive manufactured goods. Thailand was able to expand markets for such products during a period of relatively rapid growth in the global economy when the Asian NICs were beginning to vacate such areas of production. Two questions have to be answered: first, what was the mechanism by which Thailand was able to expand the production of manufactured goods, and second, what gave Thailand a competitive 'edge' for the production of labour-intensive man-ufactured goods?

An attractive explanation of Thailand's success is that, from 1987, it became a major destination for East Asian investment in labour-intensive manufactur-ing operations. As the Asian NICs lost their competitive position in these activities they sought alternative, stable, low-cost locations within the Pacific Asian region. The flow of Taiwanese investment into Thailand and later other parts of South East Asia after 1987 is particularly striking. Overall, this relocation is giving rise to a regional division of labour between the Asian NICs and the ASEAN four, of which Thailand is a key element.

While there is no doubt that foreign investment has come to play a major role in the Thai manufacturing sector, the rapid growth of exports appears to predate the influx of investment. The growth of exports was under way in 1986, while the influx of investment only started in 1987. Further, as Akrasanee *et al.* (1991, pp. 22–3) have argued, given the normal start-up time for factories, the 1987 investment could not have been making any significant contribution to exports before 1988. These authors have further demonstrated that, given the expansion of domestic investment from 1987 and the ratio of foreign to domestic investment[12] 'at least through 1989, the export and investment boom were over-whelmingly Thai supplied and financed' (1991, p. 23).

However, the acceleration of the rate of growth of exports also appears to predate the upswing in domestic investment. Thus the initial stages of the export expansion reflected the ability of the Thai manufacturing sector to expand production with little additional investment. There is, indeed, considerable evidence of overcapacity in manufacturing during the early 1980s, particularly in textiles, the lead sector during the early stages of the expansion of exports (Dixon, 1991b, p. 1035). In general, excess capacity had resulted from the over-expansion of heavily protected and privileged sectors exacerbated by the recession. This excess capacity was utilised by a dynamic export marketing sector in the initial stages of the boom.

In the mid-1980s Thailand had one of the lowest levels of industrial labour cost in ASEAN[13] and the devaluation and realignment of the baht[14] had sub-

12. Foreign direct investment's share of private domestic capital formation rose rapidly:

Period	Per cent
1980–5	3–4
1986–7	5
1988–9	9–10
1990–1	c. 25

Source: Akrasanee *et al.*, 1991, p. 23; Bank of Thailand, *Quarterly Review*, various issues.

13. Hourly wage rates in the electronics sector during 1985 (US = 100):

Hong Kong	16	Indonesia	4
Malaysia	10	Philippines	8
South Korea	14	Singapore	19
Taiwan	16	Thailand	5

Source: Scott, 1987.

14. The baht was devalued by 8 per cent in 1981 and by 14.8 per cent in 1984. More significantly, the 1984 devaluation introduced a managed fixed exchange system which tied the baht to a 'basket' of the currencies of the kingdom's major trading partners. This made Thai exports more competitive and allowed greater flexibility in responding to changes in trade and exchange rates (Jitsuchion, 1989, p. 41).

stantially improved the competitiveness of exports. The receding of the economic crises and the appearance of relative political stability[15] gave the kingdom an advantage over the rest of the ASEAN four. Economic and political crises in the Philippines, question marks over economic and political stability in Malaysia and the persistence of high levels of control over investment in Indonesia all contributed to the attractiveness of Thailand for foreign investors. There is, in all this, a clustering of favourable global and regional circumstances of which Thailand was able to take advantage, rather than any particular policies or strategies that could be isolated and applied elsewhere. It is certainly extremely difficult to conclude that the Thai economic 'boom' is a direct result of the imposition of SAPs and related policies. More importantly, it is difficult to endorse the World Bank (1990) view that Thailand is one of the two most 'successful' cases of structural adjustment (the other is Chile) and thereby to hold it up to the SSA economies as an example of what they could achieve if only they adopted the 'correct' policies.

Conclusion: Lessons of Structural Adjustment and Economic Recovery Growth in Pacific Asia

The detailed examination of the Thai experience of structural adjustment and economic liberalisation casts serious doubt over their role as determinants of economic recovery. However, the critical question is whether Thailand was an exception, while elsewhere in Pacific Asia structural adjustment played the critical role that the international agencies have asserted.

In the absence of detailed studies, any conclusions must be treated with caution. However, circumstantial evidence does not point to structural adjustment and economic liberalisation having played key roles in any of the region's economies. The dramatic slowing of growth that most of the Pacific Asian economies experienced during the early 1980s was, with the exception of the Philippines, of short duration (Table 11.1). It is difficult to reconcile the very rapid nature of the economic recoveries with the much more gradual introduction of liberalisation measures.

Perhaps the most telling case is the Philippines. Here the external shocks impinged on the weakest and least stable economy of the Pacific Asian group, resulting in a protracted period of recession and crisis. Despite an almost continuous series of SAPs since 1980, there has been little sign of economic recovery. The continued economic and political instability have largely precluded the Philippines from benefiting from the changed global and regional circum-

15. Despite an attempted *coup d'état* in 1981, there was only one Prime Minister between 1980 and 1988. This contrasted markedly with the instability that prevailed during the 1970s.

stances which, since the mid-1980s, had been instrumental in re-establishing the pattern of rapid economic growth and structural change elsewhere in the region.

In total, since the early 1980s, there has been a considerable degree of liberalisation of trade and investment regimes within the Pacific Asian region. However, as in Thailand, the implementation of measures appears either to have accompanied or followed the beginnings of recovery; there is little evidence of effective liberalisation preceding recovery. Further, even by the early 1990s, there has been only limited *effective* implementation of such key structural adjustment policies as the reduction in government expenditure, removal of tariffs and privatisation of state enterprises. While many of the region's economies have reduced tariff barriers substantially, the effective levels of protection still remain high.

It can, however, be argued that the liberalisation of trade and investment regimes in Pacific Asia has *supported* development and structural change. Policy changes, and the 'messages' that they sent to international capital, undoubtedly influenced the timing, degree and location of foreign investment in Pacific Asia, particularly that originating in the NICs and Japan. The relaxation of exchange controls in Taiwan in 1987, for example, was followed by a massive outflow of funds. Initially, Thailand was the main recipient, a reflection of low costs and perceived relative political and economic stability. Subsequent flows of Taiwanese capital into Malaysia stemmed from reappraisal of the country's long-term political stability, and the decanting of more skill-intensive processes from Taiwan. These were prepared to pay higher wage rates in order to utilise Malaysia's more abundant skilled labour force. In Indonesia, despite lower labour costs, investment lagged because of the continuation of tighter controls over investment and trade. Similarly, investment in the Philippines was discouraged by the country's continued lack of economic and political stability. However, while relaxation of control over foreign investment in Malaysia and more especially Indonesia may be related to increased inflows of capital, as in Thailand, economic recovery predated these developments. Overall, liberalisation has facilitated regional integration and the emergence of regional divisions of labour, most strikingly between Japan, the NICs and the ASEAN Four.

Recovery in the Pacific Asian economies strongly reflected changed international circumstances, notably the fall in oil prices, the decline in international interest rates, the appreciation of the yen and the growth of export markets for manufactured goods. These factors were enhanced by internal economic restructuring within the NICs which increasingly 'exported' labour-intensive manufacturing activities to lower-cost locations elsewhere within the region. Liberalisation policies may be regarded as easing the export and receipt of capital- and labour-intensive manufacturing processes but not as initiating any return to high and consistent levels of growth. This is further borne out by the slowdown of growth experienced by a number of economies during the early 1990s. The slowdown strongly reflects the growth of protectionism, particularly on the part of the US, rising labour costs and, in a number of instances, an increased incidence of industrial disputes and signs of political unrest. Indeed, liberalisation has, in many instances, increased the exposure of the Pacific Asian economies to external shocks.

Within Pacific Asia structural adjustment and associated liberal economic policies must be viewed as, at most, making a contribution to longer-term and more far-reaching processes of structural change and regional integration. The contributions of policy changes during the 1980s must be seen in the context of adjustments to changing regional and global trading conditions on the part of economies that had experienced some 20 years of comparatively high and consistent rates of growth. It is important not to treat the changes of the 1980s as sudden and unexpected developments. The rapid structural change that Thailand, for example, experienced after 1985 has to be placed in a long period of development that had laid the basis of a manufacturing sector by the early 1970s.

In conclusion, the exceptional nature of Pacific Asia's long-term pattern of development must be stressed. This has been the product of highly distinctive national, regional and international circumstances. These include Japanese colonialism in Taiwan and South Korea, American colonialism following the Spanish in the Philippines, colonial entrepôt development in Singapore and Hong Kong, non-colonial development in Thailand and the exploitation of an exceptionally rich and broad range of resources in Indonesia and Malaysia. The long-term significance of Pacific Asia's colonial experience *vis-à-vis* those of the SSA countries is worthy of detailed investigation. In addition, since the 1940s, Pacific Asia has occupied a critical geopolitical position, particularly with respect to American international policy. There is little doubt that this has been of critical importance in directing and supporting economic development. Finally, Japan, and more recently the NICs, have not only served as important role models for the region's other economies but, through the internationalisation of production and finance at the regional level, they play a crucial role in the spreading of large-scale, export-oriented manufacturing production. The significance of Japan's leading and 'linchpin' functions within Pacific Asia, and the absence of any similar situation in SSA, has attracted considerable attention. This has given rise to speculation that, in the long term, South Africa's development and relations with other African states may be critical to the region's development.

The differences between the 'success' of Pacific Asia and the 'failure' of SSA do not lie in the nature or degree of policy reforms undertaken since the early 1980s. The divergence between the two regions is the product of long-term, deep-seated national, regional and international changes. However, despite the evidence from Pacific Asia, the international agencies and their apologists continue to insist that the crucial difference remains one of national development policy (see particularly World Bank, 1993b).

References

Akrasanee, N., Daprice, D. and Flatters, F. (1991) *Thailand's Export-led Growth: Retrospect and Prospects*. Thailand Development Research Institute Foundation, Bangkok.

Asian Development Bank (1990) *Annual Report 1990*. Manila.

Bello, W. and Rosenfield, S. (1992) *Dragons in Distress*. Penguin, London.

Booth, A. (1993) Progress and poverty in South East Asia. Paper presented to the British Pacific Rim Research Group, Liverpool John Moores University.

Burnett, A. (1992) *The Western Pacific: Challenge of Sustainable Growth*. Earthscan, London.

Caldwell, J.A. (1974) *American Economic Aid to Thailand*. Lexington Books, Lexington, Mass.

Canlas, M., Mirand, M. and Putzel, J. (1988) *Land, Poverty and Politics in the Philippines*. Catholic Institute for International Relations, London.

Cummings, B. (1987) 'The origin and development of the Northeast Asian political economy: industrial sector, product cycles, and political consequences'. In F.C. Deyo (ed.) *The Political Economy of the New Asian Industrialisation*. Cornell University Press, Ithaca, NY.

Dixon, C.J. (1979) 'Thailand: economic survey'. In *The Far East and Australia*. Europa, London, pp. 1067–72.

Dixon, C.J. (1991a) *South East Asia in the World-Economy*. Cambridge University Press, Cambridge.

Dixon, C.J. (1991b) 'Thailand: economic survey'. In *The Far East and Australia*. Europa, London, pp. 1030–8.

Dixon, C. and Drakakis-Smith, D. (1993) 'The Pacific Asian region'. In C. Dixon and D. Drakakis-Smith (eds) *Economic and Social Development in Pacific Asia*. Routledge, London.

Economist Intelligence Unit (1992–3) *Country Report: Korea*. London.

Economic and Social Commission for Asia and the Pacific (1983) *Foreign Investment Incentives Schemes*. United Nations, Bangkok.

Economic and Social Commission for Asia and the Pacific (1990) *Restructuring the Developing Economies of Asia and the Pacific in the 1990s*. United Nations, New York.

Far Eastern Economic Review (1993), 18 February.

Fornader, K. (1991) 'Taiwan: the grimy side of the boom'. *Tomorrow*, 1, 2, pp. 66–72.

Forbes, D. (1993) 'What's in it for us? Images of Pacific Asian development'. In C. Dixon and D. Drakakis-Smith (eds) *Economic and Social Development in Pacific Asia*. Routledge, London.

Handley, P. (1991) 'Growth without tears'. *Far Eastern Economic Review*, 18 July, pp. 34–5.

Henderson, J. (1993) 'The role of the state in the economic transformation of East Asia'. In C. Dixon and D. Drakakis-Smith (eds) *Economic and Social Development in Pacific Asia*. Routledge, London.

Hsiao, M. (1992) 'The Taiwanese experience'. In *Development and Democracy*, 2, pp. 17–32.

International Monetary Fund (1990) *Strategies for Structural Adjustment: The Experience of Southeast Asia*. Washington, DC.

Jitsuchion, S. (1989) *Alleviation of Rural Poverty*. Thailand Development Research Institute Foundation, Bangkok.

McDowell, M.A. (1989) 'The development of the environment in ASEAN'. *Pacific Affairs*, 62, pp. 307–29.

Montemayor, B.T. (1993) 'Banking on the poor'. *Far Eastern Economic Review*, 11 March, p. 29.

Panayotou, T. and Sussangkarn, C. (1991) *The Debt Crisis, Structural Adjustment and the Environment: The Case of Thailand*. Thailand Development Research Institute Foundation, Bangkok.

Population Crisis Commission (1992) *The International Human Suffering Index*. Washington, DC.

Robison, R., Higgott, R. and Hewison, K. (1987) 'Crisis in economic strategy in the 1980s: the factors at work'. In R. Robison, R. Higgott and K. Hewison (eds) *South East Asia in the 1980s: The Politics of Economic Crisis*. Unwin, Sydney.

Sahansakul, C. (1992) *Lessons from the World Bank: Experience of Structural Adjustment Loans: The Case of Thailand*. Thailand Development Research Institute Foundation, Bangkok.

Scott, A.J. (1987) 'The semi-conductor industry in South East Asia: organisation, location and international division of labour'. *Regional Studies*, 21, 2, pp. 143–60.

Smith, M., McLoughlin, J., Large, P. and Chapman, R. (1985) *Asia's New Industrial World*. Methuen, London.

Tasker, R. (1990) 'Bangkok on the brink'. *Far Eastern Economic Review*, 29 November, pp. 52–3.

United Nations Development Programme (1991) *Human Development Report 1990*. Oxford University Press, New York.

White, G. (1988) 'Developmental states in East Asia: an introduction'. In G. White (ed.) *The Developmental State in East Asia*. Macmillan, London.

World Bank (1980a) *Aspects of Poverty in the Philippines: A Review and Assessment*. Washington, DC.

World Bank (1980b) Thailand: Coping with Structural Adjustment. Report no. 3067a, Washington, DC.

World Bank (1984) *Thailand: Managing Public Resources for Structural Adjustment: A World Bank Country Study*. Washington, DC.

World Bank (1986) *Program Performance Report Thailand: First and Second Structural Adjustment Loans*. Report no. 6085, Washington, DC.

World Bank (1987) *The Philippines: A Framework for Economic Recovery*. Washington, DC.

World Bank (1988) *The Philippine Poor: What is to be done?* Washington, DC.

World Bank (1990) *World Development Report 1990*. Oxford University Press, New York.

World Bank (1993a) *The East Asian Miracle Economies*. Washington, DC.

World Bank (1993b) *Sustainable Rapid Development*. Washington, DC.

CHAPTER 12

Conclusions: On the Contextuality
of Structural Adjustment
in a Not So New World Order

Wim van Spengen

Structural adjustment (SA) as a development catchword is rapidly losing its monolithic image. If one thing has become clear it is that SA is not a uniform or uniformly applicable policy instrument which will solve all problems of economic development across a set of widely disparate Third World countries. As a geographer, and moreover one with a historical bent, I have always felt surprised at the ease with which the success stories of quite a restricted number of East Asian countries have been put forward by protagonists of liberal economic policies as a proof of their validity as models of development. For a start, they have been quoted for the wrong reason: the relative absence or withdrawal of the state in Taiwan, Hong Kong, South Korea and Thailand is a myth. Much of their success in terms of economic growth on closer inspection has been brought about by governments which, over a much longer period than the past 15 years of structural adjustment programmes (SAPs), showed all the characteristics of a developmental state with a certain autonomy and capacity for statecraft. Second, their specific geopolitical situation *vis-à-vis* a continental East Asia 'gone red' netted substantial external support (mainly from the US) in times of political and economic hardship from the early 1950s onwards (see Dixon, Chapter 11). Finally, there are questions of scale and region-specific history which, together with the reasons already cited, make it extremely difficult to compare the experience of rapid economic growth in a few selected Pacific Rim countries with stagnation in many other Third World countries, let alone to prescribe the same SA medicine to states that differ like the moon from the sun as Hong Kong differs from Chad. Indeed, it has been one of the main objectives of this book to show that the development contexts of individual countries are highly diverse and that the impact of SAPs needs to be examined at different geographical scales as well.

If we accept the argument that measures of SA, which *at most* have *supported* a complicated growth context, as in the case of the ASEAN Four, cannot just be transplanted to other parts of the world in the hope of comparable development effects, the discussion on SA becomes one of an inquiry into the desired policy differentiation in view of the many geographic, economic and political differences between countries. To be fair, SA policy makers have recently shown an increased awareness of the widely different contexts in which they are working. This is not so much because their belief in liberal economic adjustment has diminished, but because the effects of SA in some countries have proved so disastrous that substantial sections of the population are impoverished beyond a threshold for future recovery. As this may jeopardise the whole SA enterprise, attention – some would say lip-service – is now being paid to 'adjustment with a human face' although, strictly speaking, the World Bank's recent plea for greater investment in social sectors like education and health produces something of a contradiction with regard to one of the main objectives of SA, namely an overall reduction in government spending (see Wahab, Chapter 10).

Preceding the *political* conditionality drive of the 1990s, the praxis of neo-liberal adjustment during the 1980s was basically characterised by an increasing *economic* conditionality. Donors, whether institutional or governmental, were keen to point out what economic reforms should be carried through and how aid money was to be used. The granting of financial support and project aid was made dependent on the capacity or willingness of governments to bring about economic policy reforms. On the whole we might say that this kind of tied aid was never very effective. Only the World Bank and especially the IMF seemed capable of enforcing SA measures. However, a direct connection between donor conditionality and economic reform is far from easy to prove. On closer inspection it appears that quite a few countries had already committed themselves to the neo-liberal philosophy of the Bretton Woods institutions, even before any stringent conditionalities were proffered. Therefore a case can be made for self-selective measures by the would-be recipient countries, as their chance of obtaining the much-needed financial support without at least a token policy of economic liberalisation was remote. The exceptions to this rule proved to be those countries which in one way or another were considered of geopolitical importance.

Despite the bitter adjustment pills to be swallowed, many countries accepted the stringent terms of the financial donor institutions in the course of the 1980s. Obtaining a loan from the IMF under the new conditionalities was thought to symbolise a country's turn for the better, which might act as a positive sign for other donor agencies. Macro-economic indicators acquired holy grail status, while falling standards of living for particular groups were seen as dragons to be slain along the road to economic salvation. As explained in Chapter 1, it was claimed that improved economic efficiency leading to greater competitiveness would generate the necessary export earnings against the background of a withdrawing state.

Initially, SA measures had a blueprint quality, but as the international development machine is not a set of isolated actors dealing with fixed societal structures, policies tended to change and diversify *in interaction* with the many different governments in their respective geographic and politico-economic environments. But even if this differential interaction has, in some cases, produced

SAP measures to fit a particular country, macro-economic targets, perhaps only softened by a special sectoral or human support programme, remained the ultimate touchstone of intrinsic performance. Evaluation of SAPs therefore tended to concentrate on macro-economic indicators on the one hand and impact studies for particular sections of the population on the other. This being the case, an overall view of a decade and a half of SAP experiences stressing a more comparative and holistic perspective has been lacking so far. The present book has tried to remedy this shortcoming, in particular with reference to sub-Saharan Africa (SSA), and it is surprising and at the same time staggering to see the disastrous outcome of SAPs at the local level in countries like Tanzania and Zimbabwe. The collapse of local government in intermediate towns (Holm, Chapter 6), the devastating blow to agriculture because of fivefold price increases (Mbonile, Chapter 8) and the socio-politically induced deprivation and marginalisation among pastoralists in Tanzania (Mung'ong'o and Loiske, Chapter 9), as well as declining school attendance and a growing number of street children in Harare (Tevera, Chapter 5) all testify to these developments. However, a macro-level sectoral view, like the one on Tanzania's sugar industry presented by Sterkenburg and Van der Wiel in Chapter 7, produces a slightly brighter picture. Thus, at the level of macro-economic indicators, there is 'some evidence of progress, but the overall picture to emerge gives cause for grave concern' (Simon, Chapter 2).

From an analyst's point of view, the problem with SA is the difficulty of measuring its effects separately from other factors such as drought, political disruption and general economic plight. In many parts of semi-arid Africa, for example, the variability of rainfall is such that economic gains in the world market as a result of more efficient production can always be nullified by intermittent or persistent drought, as has been referred to in the case of Zimbabwe. Add to this the fluidity and contingency of much of the African political scene, and it will be clear that measuring the relative impact of SA is an extremely elusive exercise. This elusiveness is enhanced by considerable flows of illegal trade across boundaries that separate political entities while often compromising official economic policies. Chapter 4, on regional food trade in West Africa by De Haan *et al.*, illustrates this point nicely. Then there is the overriding question regarding the extent to which the economic plight of a country can be explained from its particular setting in the capitalist world system. If its position is structurally adverse to whatever measures of SA might be taken, are the negative effects for some sections of the population then the result of these very measures or rather of its disadvantageous structural place in the international economy? And what about the influence of world economic recession?

All these are complicated questions and we may well wonder whether structural adjustment policies are really so crucial to the overall development process as some macro-economists would have us believe. For one thing, structural adjustment policies were to a large extent made possible by a relaxation of the international political situation. The end of the Cold War, consequent upon the collapse of state communism in eastern Europe and above all the Soviet Union, made it opportune to impose stringent conditions on recipient countries. For another, strategically located countries in terms of the East-West encounter that formerly received much money without too much questioning as to how it was used (as long as regimes showed the desired stability and political orientation) lost support overnight and found themselves confronted with economic and, increasingly also, political conditionalities.

As has already been pointed out by David Simon in Chapter 2, the idea of *political* conditionality, which links aid to demands concerning human rights and democracy in recipient countries, has surfaced since the beginning of the 1990s. The international development discourse made 'good governance' an integral part of its aid philosophy. Sound economic policies, competent public admin-istration, open and accountable government and respect for the rule of law and human rights were made the hallmark of a new political conditionality bent upon introducing and fostering particular forms of democracy in Third World countries. As an observer of things African over the past 20 years, as well as a former resident in one of its countries, I cannot help feeling baffled at such simplistic ideas and blueprint prescriptions for introducing democracy in Africa from the outside, if this is a real option at all. To my mind, democratisation is an ongoing process of internal development, allowing societal groups to gain gradually in popular participation and empowerment. This applies especially to SSA, where post-inde-pendence regimes were more often than not of an authoritarian nature, as well as characterised by patronage politics of ethnic and regional elites around a strongman exercising unquestioned personal power (Sorensen, 1993a, p. 15ff). Even though many of these authoritarian regimes have now gone (with or without political conditionalities), the resulting multiparty states have a long way to go to genuine participatory democracy. Perhaps political conditionalities were helpful in the early stages of the democratic process in a number of African countries, but they now seem to have been superseded by the need for positive measures aiming at strengthening specific groups within the civil society of these frail democracies. As it stands, it seems that further pressure from the outside will contribute little to an ongoing process of democratisation and may even prove counterproductive (Uvin, 1993, p. 76).

Notwithstanding the above, SA on the basis of political conditionalities seems to be the wisdom of the day. The problem with today's wisdom is that it may not be tomorrow's. These fad- and fashion-like changes in the developmental discourse may perhaps be partly explained by the inability or the unwilling-ness of analysts to take a more comprehensive and long-term view of development. Too often a geohistorical perspective is lacking, in other words an analytical awareness of the structural characteristics of underdevelopment as conditioned by a particular regional setting or developmental history. The inappropriateness and hence frequent failure of development policy prescriptions is also often attrib-utable, at least in part, to such ahistoricity.

Take SSA in relation to the much sought-after democracy: by now it has become clear that, as some leaders and observers had warned from the outset, the introduction of multiparty systems in Africa has opened a Pandora's Box of political parties, frequently separated along lines of ethnicity. Their leaders generally lack a clear ideological vision and, consequently, the way ahead seems one of further competition for electoral spoils around the vacant strongman's seat in the hope of becoming strongmen themselves. Ethnicity, unfortunately, too often remains a symbolic and organising principle behind these conflicts. And this is nothing new: Biafra, Angola, Sudan and Uganda have recently been supplemented by the carnages in Liberia and Rwanda. The last-mentioned case, in particular, is a typical example, not so much of age-old 'tribal' animosities, as of political crime perpetrated by extremists seeking to monopolise power by literally exterminating the political opposition. The ethnic factor comes in only where former Belgian colonial rule destroyed the former reciprocity in Hutu–Tutsi relations and antagonised both groups to produce a calamitous historical result (De Waal, 1994).

Though ethnicity is clearly not a peculiarly African phenomenon, in an African historical setting it has had less chance of expressing itself into formative statehood over the past 200 years – due to colonial rule – than many ethnic groups elsewhere in the world, including Europe. This is not to say that each and every ethnic group, however defined, should build its own ethnic state, but that there should be an openness to the idea that current African states might shift away from their presently centralised forms towards more loosely defined political federations of ethnic groups. Perhaps with a growing measure of commonly perceived ethnic–territorial histories, the foundations can be laid for more stable forms of statehood.

The above reasoning is far removed from the present donor call for blueprint western-style democracy. The conditionality of greater political freedom, combined with the now-or-never realisation of macro-economic targets, tends to a situation in which SA-induced poverty may lead to increased political and perhaps ethnic strife within existing states. As societal upheaval cannot be the objective of political conditionality, it brings back the question of the role of the state. In what ways can state power in SSA be fruitfully conditioned to produce its own decentralisation, even if only partially? Under the present circumstances, the answer is none. As long as current national elites are bolstered by externally induced policy measures basically leading to the preservation of the political–economic status quo, namely one of the continued bid for power fed by unrestrained greed and corruption, there can be no hope for genuine change (Robinson, 1993, pp. 86–7). Perhaps funding agencies and donor countries could pressurise governments to reflect more upon their own legitimacy and autonomy. The latter concepts refer to the degree to which state policy can be formulated and implemented as independent from economic and political class interests, assuming the latter is possible at all. In an African application, we might add ethnic interests as well. Thus, if a state with a high degree of autonomy can be created, a first step on the road towards politico–territorial decentralisation can be made, because the political symbolisation and manipulation of ethnicity stands a lesser chance.

The conflicts that are currently plaguing much of SSA are closely intertwined with and exacerbated by widespread resource scarcity. Had we still been living in the 1970s, we might have been tempted to write an elaborate treatise on 'unequal exchange', demonstrating the nefarious effects of a capitalist world system geared towards the brutal exploitation of dependent economies. However, even without the normative jargon of two decades ago we still find an interdependent world, perhaps more so than ever. And, true enough, prices paid for export products in the First World still bear no relation to the prices paid for products exported to the Third World. As asked by Anders Närman in Chapter 3, 'What is it in the international economic structure that prevents the Africans from negotiating a deal that will close the gap of paying the true cost of productive work instead of widening it?' Unable to answer such a complicated question on the spot, we must nevertheless admit that the delinking of individual countries in order to escape external dependency has not produced the expected redistribution with growth either. What remains is the sad conclusion that the world economy is a rat race in which everybody has to compete with everybody else. Some countries are better placed in this capitalist world system than others, which really is a function of their position with regard to the international division of labour. However, there are no inherent determinants which account for the relative success or failure of individual countries. There is an element of historical contingency which escapes formal analysis, which in effect means that there is no single policy, no panacea, that can guarantee success. Recently this feeling was even more strongly expressed in an interview by André Gunder Frank (1994), who for once found himself in agreement with his old teacher, Milton Friedman, who stated that policy makers usually make things worse.

The above observations shed an additional light on structural adjustment policies. As was pointed out earlier, tied aid, whether by economic or political conditionalities, has never been very effective and may have a far more limited role to play in the near future than the current state of the adjustment debate suggests. Moreover, as it is the rich donors who are formulating demands on poor recipients, it is understandable that only voices from the periphery speak of the true nature of SA measures: do they really aim at introducing democracy in Third World countries, or are they to be seen as the *nth* conspiracy to ensure the continued benefits of an existing world order for the West? One does not have to be a firm believer in conspiracy theories to see that there is something in this argument. Such reasoning leads, as one committed observer recently pointed out, to the question 'whether donor countries practise political conditionality with one hand while upholding an unequal economic system with the other, which in turn undermines the prospects for sustained progress in human rights' (Sorensen, 1993b, p. 5).

If we finally come to evaluate structural adjustment policies and the connected idea of political conditionality, we have to conclude that the record of their effectiveness remains unproven. Given the wider contextuality of SAPs, their interwovenness with other than economic factors alone and their application in countries that remain anchored in a not so new world order, it remains to be seen whether their long-term impact will be as positive as some macro-economists want us to believe. We hope that this book has given some food for thought in that respect.

References

De Waal, A. (1994) 'Genocide in Rwanda'. *Anthropology Today*, 10, 3, pp. 4–5.

Frank, A.G. (1994) Interview. *NRC Handelsblad*, 11 June.

Robinson, M. (1993) 'Aid, democracy and political conditionality in sub-Saharan Africa'. *European Journal of Development Research*, 5, 1, pp. 85–99.

Sorensen, G. (1993a) 'Democracy, authoritarianism and state strength'. *European Journal of Development Research*, 5, 1, pp. 6–34.

Sorensen, G. (1993b) 'Introduction' to the Special Issue on Political Conditionality, *European Journal of Development Research*, 5, 1, pp. 1–5.

Uvin, P. (1993) '"Do as I say, not as I do": the limits of political conditionality'. *European Journal of Development Research*, 5, 1, pp. 63–84.

Index

Adjustment (*see* ERMs, Liberalisation and SAPs)

African Development Bank (AfDB) 2
  mirroring of World Bank policies 3

Africanisation
  in Tanzania 110

African socialism (*see also* Socialist policies) 94

Aid (*see* ODA)

AIDS 152

Arusha Declaration 94, 110

Asian Development Bank (ADB) 2
  mirroring of World Bank policies 3

Bretton Woods
  institutions 1, 18
  suspension of 2

Budget deficit 194
  in Thailand 219
  in Zimbabwe 82

Central African franc (CFA) zone 19, 69

Chile
  as a successful case of structural adjustment 8, 9, 223

Civil society 35, 208–9

Commodity import support (CIS) 112
  for Tanzanian sugar 129–30
  politics of 11

Commodity price falls (*see also* Trade) 195–6
  contribution of dematerialisation 196

Community based organisations (CBOs) (*see also* Empowerment, Grassroots political action, Indigenous peoples organisations, NGOs and Resistance) 36, 39

Comparative advantage 18
  in the Sahel 63, 64

Conditionalities *see also* ERMs, ODA and SAPs) 230
  and development aid in Tanzania 95–7
  and local government in Tanzania 98–9
  political 35, 36, 230, 232, 233

Conservative revolution 3

Currency adjustment (*see* Exchange rates)

Current account balances
  in Pacific Asia 210, 211 (Table 11.9)

Debt crisis (*see also* Foreign debt)
  association with Latin America 10, 17
  origins of 18

Decentralisation in Tanzania 93–5, 137, 151

Demography and development 37–8

Deregulation of markets (*see also* Liberalisation)
  in west Africa 59

Devaluation (*see also* Foreign exchange rates) 79–80, 222

237

Published by Pluto Press

WORLD ORDERS, OLD AND NEW

Noam Chomsky

In this new, ambitious and expansive study of global politics, Noam Chomsky challenges conventional definitions of the 'New World Order', examining the acts of imperialism and economic manipulation which have produced the unbalanced world order of the 1990s. Chomsky begins with a reconsideration of the Cold War, revealing how it became a pretext for the USA to expand politically, economically and militarily under the guise of self-defence.

In the post-Cold War era, he argues, the break-up of the Soviet Union has clouded a convenient distinction between 'good' free market westerners and 'evil' communists. The book also offers a startling new commentary on the Gulf War, and the relationship between America and Britain and the 'enemy' before, during and after hostilities. In a detailed analysis of the strategic manoeuvres between the West and the Third World, Chomsky concludes that George Bush's New World Order has become a domestic and international propaganda tool in the hands of the powerful.

Noam Chomsky is Professor of Linguistics at the Massachusetts Institute of Technology and an internationally acclaimed scholar and political activist.

ISBN hardback: 0 7453 0920 8 softback: 0 7453 0919 4

Order from your local bookseller or contact the publisher on 0181 348 2724.

Pluto Press
345 Archway Road, London N6 5AA

Published by Pluto Press with the
Transnational Institute

SHORT CHANGED
Africa and World Trade

Michael Barratt Brown and Pauline Tiffen

'Strikes at the very heart of the World Bank's free market
integrationist ideology' *Commodity Week*

'A goldmine of useful data and specific case studies'
Peter Bosshard, Berne Declaration

Short Changed is a detailed and devastating critique of the
economic strategies which the International Monetary Fund
and the World Bank have imposed on African countries. In
return for some limited rescheduling of debts, African countries
have been forced to remove controls over trade and foreign
exchange, thus increasing exports and draining primary
commodities at home. The damaging effects on African social
programmes and economies are examined through studies of
the markets for 22 major African exports.

Despite all the talk of 'level playing fields' and the 'international community', some participants in the world economy
are more equal than others. *Short Changed* supplies over-
whelming evidence that the World Bank's export-led strategy
cannot open the way to greater prosperity for Africa and that
new approaches are long overdue.

ISBN hardback: 0 7453 0694 2   softback: 0 7453 0699 3

Order from your local bookseller or contact the publisher on
0181 348 2724.

Pluto Press
345 Archway Road, London N6 5AA
5500 Central Avenue, Boulder, Colorado 80301, USA